Transforming Everything?

Transforming Everything?

Evaluating Broadband's Impacts
Across Policy Areas

EDITED BY KAREN MOSSBERGER,

ERIC W. WELCH, AND YONGHONG WU

Oxford University Press is a department of the University of Oxford. It furthers
the University's objective of excellence in research, scholarship, and education
by publishing worldwide. Oxford is a registered trade mark of Oxford University
Press in the UK and certain other countries.

Published in the United States of America by Oxford University Press
198 Madison Avenue, New York, NY 10016, United States of America.

Library of Congress Cataloging-in-Publication Data
Names: Mossberger, Karen, editor. | Welch, Eric W., editor. | Wu, Yonghong
(Professor of public administration), editor.
Title: Transforming everything? : evaluating broadband's impacts across policy
areas / Karen Mossberger, Eric W. Welch, and Yonghong Wu.
Description: New York, NY : Oxford University Press, [2022] |
Includes bibliographical references and index.
Identifiers: LCCN 2021029418 (print) | LCCN 2021029419 (ebook) |
ISBN 9780190082871 (hardcover) | ISBN 9780190082888 (paperback) |
ISBN 9780190082901 (epub)
Subjects: LCSH: Telecommunication policy—United States. | Broadband communication
systems—Social aspects—United States. | Broadband communication systems—Law and
legislation—United States.
Classification: LCC HE7781 .T75 2022 (print) | LCC HE7781 (ebook) | DDC 384.0973—dc23
LC record available at https://lccn.loc.gov/2021029418
LC ebook record available at https://lccn.loc.gov/2021029419

DOI: 10.1093/oso/9780190082871.001.0001

1 3 5 7 9 8 6 4 2

Paperback printed by Marquis, Canada
Hardback printed by Bridgeport National Bindery, Inc., United States of America

ACKNOWLEDGMENTS

This volume has its origins in a 2012 Chicago workshop on broadband evaluation sponsored by the John D. and Catherine T. MacArthur Foundation. The editors, who were organizers of that workshop, thank the foundation for their support and thank the scholars who attended as presenters and discussants, as well as others who contribute here as chapter authors. Broadband policy has evolved since that initial meeting and will continue to change. What remains constant is the need for good evidence for policymaking.

Karen Mossberger is the Frank and June Sackton Professor in the School of Public Affairs at Arizona State University and the director of the Center on Technology, Data and Society. Her research interests include local governance, urban policy, digital inequality, evaluation of broadband programs, and digital government. Her most recent book is *Choosing the Future: Technology and Opportunity in Communities* (Oxford University Press, 2021, with C. Tolbert and S. LaCombe). Previous books on technology include *Digital Cities: The Internet and the Geography of Opportunity*, *Digital Citizenship: The Internet, Society and Participation*, and *Virtual Inequality: Beyond the Digital Divide*. Her coauthored research on "Race, Place, and Information Technology" won the best paper award for the Public Policy Section of the American Political Science Association in 2005, and "The Effects of E-Government on Trust and Confidence in Government" was named one of the seventy-five most influential articles in the first seventy-five years of *Public Administration Review*. Her research has included the evaluation of Chicago's Smart Communities Program, and she has received support from the National Science Foundation, the Smith Richardson Foundation, the U.S. Department of Housing and Urban Development, and the John D. and Catherine T. MacArthur Foundation, among others. She has served as president of the Information Technology and Politics section and Urban Politics section of the American Political Science Association, chair of RC-10 Electronic Democracy in the

International Political Science Association, and is an elected fellow of the National Academy of Public Administration.

Eric W. Welch earned his PhD in public administration at Syracuse University's Maxwell School of Citizenship and Public Affairs (1997) and is currently a professor in the School of Public Affairs at Arizona State University where he also directs the Center for Science, Technology and Environmental Policy Studies (CSTEPS), a unit that promotes collaborative research among faculty, graduate students, scientists, and practitioners on interdisciplinary problems related to science, technology, information, and environment. Dr. Welch's research interests include information technology and electronic government, science and technology policy, environment policy, and public management. He has received external funding in the areas of electronic government including several grants on the use of information and communication technologies in city and state governments for civic engagement, and CSTEPS undertakes a biannual survey on local government use of information technology for management and governance in the United States. Dr. Welch has been awarded several NSF, NIFA, and US DOT grants to conduct national and international studies at the intersection of science, technology, and environment. Dr. Welch is author of over one hundred articles and book chapters. He has published in journals such as *Journal of Public Administration Research and Theory*, *Administration and Society*, *Political Communication*, *Government Information Quarterly*, *Public Administration Review*, *Research Policy*, *Science and Public Policy*, *Ecological Economics*, *Leadership Quarterly*, *Entrepreneurship Theory and Practice*, *Urban Studies*, and *Journal of Policy Analysis and Management*.

Yonghong Wu is a professor in the Department of Public Administration at the University of Illinois at Chicago. He received his PhD degree in Public Administration from the Maxwell School of Syracuse University. His fields of specialization include state and local public finance, and science and technology policy. Wu's research agenda is composed of two components: one component explores public finance issues in science and technology policy arenas; the other addresses state and local tax policymaking. Wu has published a number of articles in premier journals in public policy and administration. His article in the *Journal of Policy Analysis and Management* (2005) examines the effects of state R & D tax credits on private R & D expenditure in the US states. Another cross-state empirical research paper published in the *Journal of Policy Analysis and Management* (2009) analyzes a federal subsidy program—NSF's Experimental Program to Stimulate Competitive Research (EPSCoR)—and discloses a disturbing crowd-out effect of the program on state government funding of academic research. His article in *Research Policy* (2011) evaluates the effects of EPSCoR on the distribution of federal obligations for academic science and engineering research. Dr. Wu's policy research provides important evidence to assist and improve policymaking in science and technology policy arenas. Wu coauthored with Karen Mossberger the report *Civic Engagement and Local E-Government: Social Networking Comes of Age*, which received a great deal of media attention in the United States. He also coauthored a book chapter "Municipal Government and the Interactive Web: Trends and Issues for Civic Engagement" in *E-Governance and Civic Engagement: Factors and Determinants of E-Democracy* published by IGI Global in 2011.

Mattia Caldarulo is a PhD student in the School of Public Affairs at Arizona State University. His research interests include innovation in local governments, technology policy, and nonprofit organizations. He has a Master's in International Management from a dual degree program at Fudan University in Shanghai and Bocconi University in Milan. His undergraduate degree is from Bocconi, and he has attended programs at Rotterdam School of Management and London School of Economics.

Jessica Crowell is an assistant professor in the Department of Digital Media and Journalism at SUNY New Paltz. She holds a PhD in Media Studies from Rutgers University. Her ethnographic research addresses the intersection of media and social justice issues, including digital inequality and the impact of digital technology on work. Jessica's most recent project tracks the economic lives of the digitally connected urban poor in Philadelphia. Her work has appeared in *Communication, Culture & Critique*, the *Journal of Media Literacy Education*, and *Digital Journalism*. Jessica has also authored policy papers on broadband access in low-income urban communities for state and federal governments. She is currently an affiliated scholar with the Media, Inequality, and Change Center and is a former fellow at the Eagleton Institute of Politics.

Robert Fairlie is a professor of Economics at the University of California, Santa Cruz, and a research associate at the National Bureau of Economics Research. He has held visiting positions at Stanford University, Yale

University, UC Berkeley, and Australian National University. His research interests include entrepreneurship, technology, racial and gender inequality, labor economics, education, and immigration. He has written several articles on the causes and consequences of the Digital Divide, and the effects of technology on educational outcomes. He has received funding for his research from numerous government agencies and foundations, including the National Science Foundation, the William T. Grant Foundation, U.S. Small Business Administration, U.S. Department of Commerce, U.S. Department of Labor, Kauffman Foundation, Russell Sage Foundation, and Spencer Foundation. He has testified to the U.S. Congress, U.S. Department of Treasury, and the California State Assembly regarding the findings from his research. Fairlie holds a PhD and MA from Northwestern University and BA with honors from Stanford University.

Natasha Gaydos graduated with an M.A. in Political Science from the University of Iowa in 2019. She received her BA in Political Science from the University of Illinois-Urbana Champaign in 2014. Her research interests include race and ethnic politics, inequalities, public policy, and political behavior. She is a senior consultant in PBM and Clinical Product Analytics at CVS Health.

Alfred T. Ho is a professor and department head of Public Policy at City University of Hong Kong. From 2010 to 2020, he was a faculty member at the School of Public Affairs and Administration at the University of Kansas in the U.S. His research focuses primarily on budgeting and financial management, performance management and governance, and e-government. In addition to academic journal articles and book chapters, he has done contracted research on e-government and local management issues for various organizations, including the Asian Development Bank, the Alfred P. Sloan Foundation, the National Science Foundation (US), the IBM Center for the Business of Government, the William T. Kemper Foundation, and local governments in various US states.

John B. Horrigan is a senior fellow at the Benton Institute for Broadband and Society, with a focus on technology adoption, digital inclusion, and evaluating the outcomes and impacts of programs designed to promote communications technology adoption and use. Horrigan is also currently a consultant to the Urban Libraries Coalition. Additionally, he has served as an associate director for research at the Pew Research Center, where he focused on libraries and their impact on communities, as well as technology adoption patterns and open government data. Horrigan is a nationally recognized leader on home broadband adoption patterns, the impact of connectivity on individuals, and strategies for closing adoption gaps. Horrigan was part the leadership team at the Federal Communications Commission for the development of the National Broadband Plan (NBP). For the NBP, Horrigan was responsible for the plan's recommendations on broadband adoption. As a consultant, Horrigan is author of landmark reports on Comcast's Internet Essentials program. The reports, "The Essentials of Connectivity" and "Deepening Ties," demonstrate the impact of online access for low-income families with children and make recommendations on how to accelerate broadband adoption and usage. Horrigan has also written reports for the Aspen Institute, including "Skirting Bottlenecks" on the impact of evolving network technology on the broadband market and digital inclusion. Horrigan has a PhD in public policy from the University of Texas at Austin and his undergraduate degree is from the University of Virginia.

William Lehr is an Internet and telecommunications industry economist and research scientist in the Computer Science and Artificial Intelligence Laboratory (CSAIL) at the Massachusetts Institute of Technology (MIT), where he is part of the Advanced Network Architectures group. Dr. Lehr's research focuses on the economic implications of ICT technologies for public policy, industry structure, and the evolving Internet ecosystem. He is engaged in multiple multidisciplinary research projects focusing on issues such as broadband Internet access, cybersecurity, next generation network architectures, and spectrum management. In addition to his academic work, Dr. Lehr advises public and private sector clients in the US and abroad on ICT strategy and policy matters. Dr. Lehr holds a PhD in Economics from Stanford and an MBA in Finance from the Wharton School, and MSE, BA, and BS degrees from the University of Pennsylvania. For more information, see http://people.csail.mit.edu/wlehr/.

Sharon Strover is the Philip G. Warner Regents Professor in Communication and former chair of the Radio-TV-Film Department at the University of Texas, where she directs the Moody College's Technology and Information Policy Institute. Her research projects examine policy responses to digital inclusion issues internationally and domestically; the economic outcomes associated with broadband, particularly in rural areas; the role of libraries in local information environments; and the social impacts of technologies and infrastructure systems, including AI, machine learning, and various digital media devices and platforms. She has directed an international Digital Media program as part of a broader collaboration effort between the University of Texas at Austin and the government of Portugal, and she has worked with several international, national, and regional government agencies and nonprofits including the U.S. Department of Agriculture, the Institute of Museum and Library Services, Facebook, the Center for Rural Strategies, the Benton Foundation, the Center for Rural Strategies, the European Union, the Ford Foundation, the State of Texas, and the European Union, among others. She has chaired both the Law and Policy and the Mass Communication Divisions for the International Communication Association, sits on the editorial boards of *The Information Society* and *Government Information Quarterly*, and has served as a visiting faculty member at Stockholm University, Aarhus University (Denmark), Westminster University (UK), and the New University of Lisbon (Portugal). She received her BA with Honors from the University of Wisconsin-Madison and her PhD from Stanford University.

Caroline J. Tolbert is the Lowell C. Battershell University Distinguished Professor of Political Science at the University of Iowa. Her work is driven by a theoretical and normative interest in strengthening American democracy and fostering inclusive economic growth. Her research and teaching weave together a concern with diversity and inequality, elections and representation, technology policy and local economic development, subnational politics and policy, and data science. She is the coauthor of *Accessible Elections: How the States can Help Americans*

Vote (Oxford, 2020) on absentee/mail voting, early voting and same-day registration. She has coauthored four books on the Internet and politics/policy, the most recent of which is *Choosing the Future: Technology and Opportunity in Communities* (with K. Mossberger and S. LaCombe, Oxford, 2021). Others include *Digital Cities: The Internet and the Geography of Opportunity*, *Digital Citizenship: The Internet, Society, and Participation*, and *Virtual Inequality: Beyond the Digital Divide*. Her research has been funded by the National Science Foundation, and numerous private foundations. She was honored by the Carnegie Foundation as a 2021 Andrew Carnegie Fellow.

Michael A. Xenos is a professor in the Department of Life Sciences Communication at the University of Wisconsin. Xenos conducts research and teaches courses on the effects of digital media on political engagement and public deliberation. His primary focus is on the extent to which the Internet and social media may help individuals learn about political issues, form opinions, and participate in politics. He is also interested in the ways that political candidates, journalists, and other political actors adapt to changes in information and communication technologies, and how these adaptations affect broader dynamic political communication and public deliberations.

Introduction

Broadband as Experimentation and Policy Learning

**KAREN MOSSBERGER, ERIC W. WELCH,
AND YONGHONG WU**

INTRODUCTION

How we address broadband development has been called *the* most important infrastructure challenge of this century by the federal government's National Broadband Plan (FCC 2010). High-speed internet can connect remote communities, help coordinate and streamline healthcare services, enable our children with unparalleled access to learning opportunities, and spark and support innovation in numerous fields.

The critical need for broadband connectivity throughout society, if ever it was in doubt, became painfully apparent during the Covid-19 pandemic. The internet became the lifeline for remote learning and work, food deliveries, telemedicine, and social contact with friends and family. This crisis exposed, however, persistent inequalities in broadband access and capabilities across the US, not just in sparsely populated rural areas without high-speed networks but in low-income urban and suburban neighborhoods as well (Fishbane and Tomer 2020). Nationally, nearly one in five elementary and secondary school students lacked broadband

Karen Mossberger, Eric W. Welch, and Yonghong Wu, *Introduction* In: *Transforming Everything?*. Edited by: Karen Mossberger, Eric W. Welch, and Yonghong Wu, Oxford University Press. © Oxford University Press 2022. DOI: 10.1093/oso/9780190082871.003.0001 at home (Romm 2020; Associated Press 2020), though in Philadelphia less than half the students had computers and broadband connections at home, according to surveys the district had conducted in 2019 (Kopp 2020). Schools and local governments struggled to find and distribute emergency tablets and to provide hotspots on school buses, in parking lots, in homeless shelters, and outside shuttered libraries (Stewart 2020; Romm 2020; Associated Press 2020). The internet was the backbone for the millions of newly unemployed workers filing claims as well as the "touchless" economy that emerged (Wu 2020). Older individuals, who were especially vulnerable in the health crisis, were among the most digitally isolated (Conger and Griffith 2020).

The Federal Communications Commission (FCC) estimated prior to the pandemic that 21.3 million Americans lacked broadband, defined as having advertised speeds of at least 25 Mbps download/3 Mbps upload (2019, 2). Microsoft, however, places that figure at 162.8 million if use at actual broadband speeds is considered (Wu 2020). While bandwidth is critical for applications such as remote learning and telehealth, factors such as the cost of connections and devices are a barrier for many low-income households (Goldberg 2019). At the onset of the coronavirus crisis, FCC Commissioner Rosenworcel described the pandemic as a "reckoning" (Romm 2020), and it has reshaped the policy environment for broadband, from the local to the federal level.

Broadband interventions in the wake of this reckoning have been varied in their approach and scale, addressing the availability and capacity of networks, affordability and adoption, and specific uses for telehealth and remote learning. Between the March 2020 and December 2020 Covid relief bills, Congress allocated just under $450 million for telehealth, $90 million to the US Department of Agriculture for rural telehealth and education, $285 million for broadband in historically Black, Hispanic-serving, and Tribal colleges, $50 million for libraries, $1 billion for Tribal broadband networks, and $400 million added to prior US Department of Agriculture funding for rural broadband infrastructure (Taglang 2020, 2021a). The $81.8 billion for the Governors' Emergency Education Relief Fund allowed use to support school and student internet use as well

(Taglang 2021a). The March 2020 CARES Act provided $150 billion to state, local, and Tribal governments for Covid-related expenses, and many state and local governments used the funds for devices and connections for students, public Wi-Fi, telehealth, and improved broadband infrastructure (DeWit 2020). In the American Rescue Act of March 2021, schools and libraries were authorized to spend over $7 billion in E-rate funds on broadband infrastructure, connectivity, and devices, including for home use by students and patrons (Taglang 2021c). Previously these funds only supported broadband service in schools or libraries.

What will these new uses of the E-rate funds and the other investments in devices and connections for students mean for educational practices in the future, especially in newly connected school districts? After the pandemic, the expansion of broadband may lead to the shrinking of the "homework gap" for low-income students previously unable to study online outside the classroom (Horrigan 2020). While some of the interventions were clearly stopgap or crisis-driven, such as Wi-Fi hotspots in parking lots, others may have more long-lasting effects. With systematic evaluation, new programs can shed light on fundamental questions about how to address persistent disparities.

Debates over what constitutes affordability can be informed by evaluation of the $3.2 billion Emergency Broadband Benefit administered by the Federal Communications Commission (FCC). The FCC increased previous subsidies for broadband subscriptions by more than 500 percent and extended benefits to a broader group of recipients than ever before. The pre-pandemic Lifeline program offered $9.25 per month for a mobile or fixed broadband subscription to low-income social service recipients. The emergency benefit expanded this to a maximum of $50 per month or $75 per month in Tribal communities, along with subsidies for computers, laptops, or tablets that are Wi-Fi enabled and capable of videoconferencing. Criteria for eligibility included receipt of many different social services, incomes up to 135 percent of the poverty threshold, and layoff or furlough during the prior year (Taglang 2021b). While the benefit is temporary and designated for termination within six months of the end of the Covid emergency, it provides an unprecedented opportunity to learn how a robust level of support affects broadband adoption, uses, and recipient outcomes.

Pandemic-related initiatives have accompanied other measures to expand broadband connectivity and use. The FCC's $20 billion Rural Digital Opportunity Fund for broadband deployment was announced in January 2020, representing the commission's largest investment for closing connectivity gaps.[1] In February of 2020, the commission opened the Rural Tribal Window, allowing federally recognized Tribes to apply for priority in use of the 2.5 GHz spectrum in rural Tribal lands. The 2.5 GHz band had been used for educational services and is appropriate for both mobile and point-to-point coverage.[2] Since 2017, the FCC had sponsored a variety of telehealth initiatives, and in March 2020 the commission allocated up to $100 million from the Universal Service Fund for telehealth broadband connectivity through the Connected Care Pilot Programs.[3]

In addition to these multi-billion-dollar investments undertaken by government, the private sector also affected the broadband landscape, building infrastructure and promoting its use. Microsoft has implemented projects experimenting with TV white space to deliver high-speed internet in rural communities (Microsoft 2018). Elon Musk's Starlink is exploring the use of satellite beaming technologies in Alaska for use in remote Tribal communities (Kunze 2021). As the much-heralded 5G, or 5th generation, broadband is deployed nationwide, evaluation will be needed on the extent to which it promotes innovation and economic recovery.

Beyond the infrastructure investments are efforts encouraging new uses and widespread use by organizations and individuals. Nonprofit organizations like US Ignite promote research and innovation for the use of gigabit speeds. The "smart city" movement, supported by technology companies and local governments, advocates digital solutions for many needs, including energy, public safety, waste management, traffic control, health programs, and aging in place, just to name a few (Smart Cities Council n.d.). Libraries, local governments, and nonprofit organizations around the country mobilized to provide devices, connectivity, training, and skills support during the pandemic, devising new approaches that bear evaluation going forward.

Broadband expansion and experimentation are occurring across communities and policy domains and are likely to accelerate in the future. Yet, there is limited research on the near-term or long-term impacts of past and current projects. Crisis has demonstrated the extent to which daily life has already been transformed by broadband, though not equally for all. As new broadband-enabled technologies proliferate, from autonomous vehicles and drones to sensors and big data, there is an unprecedented opportunity for learning how to best fulfill technology's promise of further transformation.

EVALUATION AND POLICY LEARNING

Given broadband's transformative potential, the first question should be, can we afford *not* to learn from experience? This volume argues that there is a critical need to understand whether or how public and private investments in broadband make a difference, and the best way to do that is to invest in high-quality program evaluation to assess the full range of crucial outcomes and impacts. This book focuses on two challenges: (1) offering guidance and methods for evaluation based on social science standards, for policymakers as well as researchers; and (2) raising the potential for broadband evaluation research that can be compared across diverse contexts.

Policymakers sometimes view evaluation as a cost that competes for resources needed for carrying out the program. But it is precisely because budgets are tight and resources are scarce that evaluation is needed to maximize the return on broadband investment. Evaluations often track results for demonstration or pilot projects that could inform broader change. In the Digital Promise education initiative, for example, a commitment to rapid and rigorous evaluation included randomized experiments on the effects of Khan Academy classes and other innovations such as flipped classrooms in school districts (White House 2011). This approach can help policymakers and others to understand whether classes or other learner-centered strategies are effective, and whether they are promising alternatives to current educational programs.

Program evaluation is needed to understand both impacts and processes, to guide policy decisions, and to inform good practice. Without evaluation built into projects from the beginning, resources may be wasted, new problems may be created, and opportunities for improved practice may be lost.

Recognizing this, the National Science Foundation developed recommendations for a broadband research agenda (National Telecommunications and Information Administration and National Science Foundation 2017), supporting program evaluation as a national research priority.

How that research is carried out is essential for policy learning. Program evaluation must be undertaken in a systematic and rigorous manner using social science methods, and this is not always the case in the evaluation industry. Social scientific methods—both quantitative and qualitative—are needed to ensure the validity and reliability of findings regarding these substantial public and private investments. This is particularly true for facilitating comparisons and drawing lessons across different policy areas, varied applications, and diverse communities. The potential value is the ability to look across evaluation studies to identify models and outcomes of higher impact that can be adapted locally. Yet exploiting that advantage requires thinking about the strategies needed for evaluating a general-purpose technology with many different possible uses and effects.

Broadband was already a rapidly growing area of public policy before the 2020 crisis, but there has been little discussion within the research community about the distinctive demands of broadband evaluation. Many books and other resources offer evaluation strategies for health, education, human services, and other policy domains. With countless uses and major potential impacts, broadband evaluation warrants serious consideration. We aim to engage both researchers and decision makers in the issues we present in the following pages.

Although this volume focuses on the US experience, we believe that the need for evaluating broadband's impacts resonates internationally as well. Many countries have implemented large-scale broadband initiatives, expecting the investment to foster positive social and economic outcomes. The pandemic has only accelerated these investments and focused additional policy attention on unmet needs. The British government has announced goals for universal broadband, reaching every part of the UK (UK Department for Digital, Culture, Media, and Sport 2017). In February 2021, the mayor of London committed £1.5 million to tackle digital exclusion in the city (Mayor of London 2021). The French government sponsors a Digital Society Program[4] promoting digital inclusion as well as the Very High-Speed Broadband Plan to extend such service to all homes, businesses, and government offices by 2022 (Agence Nationale de la Cohésion des Territoires 2020). Australia's National Broadband Network has struggled to fulfill its ambitious goals (McMillen 2017), but in summer of 2020 the government established the Australian Broadband Advisory Council to develop strategies for broadband and economic development, including recovery from the pandemic (Australian Government 2020). These investments are not limited to industrially advanced countries. The Chinese government has focused on increasing investment in telecommunication infrastructure, deepening broadband price cuts, encouraging innovation of broadband applications, and optimizing increased connection speeds, setting explicit goals in its five-year plan.[5] In African nations, many of which are emerging economies, satellite-enabled broadband has the potential to increase incomes and raise living standards for some of the world's economically poorest populations.[6] The context differs substantially across these countries in terms of population size, terrain, social inequality, industrial advancement, and regulation, yet there is a common drive toward modernization of infrastructure and broadband adoption.

Broadband expansion and adoption are also important goals of international bodies, such as the European Union, the Organisation for Economic Co-operation and Development (OECD 2008), and the United Nations. For example, the Broadband Commission for Sustainable Development considers broadband access to be critical for accelerating progress toward accomplishment of the Millennium Development Goals.[7]

Program evaluation has been an explicit part of broadband policy in the UK[8] and for the OECD, which has called for improved policy assessment and evaluation for broadband policy (OECD 2008). The World Bank has conducted some assessment of the impact of satellite broadband on economic growth and development.[9] More generally, the idea of more frequent and more rigorous evaluation of broadband initiatives fits well with international movements toward more evidence-based policymaking, supported by the European Commission, OECD,[10] and United Nations. One academic review of evaluations for broadband infrastructure and adoption initiatives in OECD member nations found that there is currently a lack of evidence on many important questions, along with a lack of high-quality impact studies (What Works Centre for Local Economic Growth 2015). The capacity to conduct such evaluations differs across countries, with some places lacking expertise, data resources, or funding. This is where international organizations, NGOs, and international collaboration can play an important role for examining impacts, in developing nations, for example. Overall, there is a need to promote evaluation and to advance the quality of broadband evaluation studies.

In this introduction, we first discuss policy relevance and goals for broadband, the policy concerns that evaluations can address, and special challenges for broadband evaluation. We summarize the plan of the book, introducing contributions that represent a range of disciplines, including public policy, public administration, economics, communications, political science, and anthropology, reflecting the need for interdisciplinary knowledge and collaboration in broadband evaluation.

WHY BROADBAND IS AN ISSUE FOR PUBLIC POLICY

Broadband, or high-speed internet, is defined by the Federal Communications Commission (FCC) as internet service that provides download speeds of at least 25 Mbps (megabits per second) and upload speeds of 3 Mbps. Broadband is a public policy issue rather than just another consumer product because its use can generate extensive "externalities" beyond individual users, with benefits as well as costs for the larger society. The many anticipated benefits touch a wide range of policy areas and evolve continually with the development of new technologies. Possible costs, however, are consequential as well, including vulnerability to hacking and cybersecurity failures. The challenge is to harness the potential of broadband, maximizing its benefits and minimizing social costs. For these reasons and more, we need to know how best to employ these powerful new technologies, discovering the policies and practices that are most effective.

For purposes of evaluation, there are several types of broadband interventions, emphasizing availability of high-speed networks, organizational innovation, and individual adoption. When the FCC redefined the standards for broadband in 2015, it estimated that 20 percent of the country lacked access to networks meeting the new requirements (Singleton 2015), and so providing greater availability of high-bandwidth networks is one policy goal. Beyond speed, realizing the potential social benefits of broadband also depends on how it is used by organizations and individuals. Do businesses and public institutions innovate through its use? Do individuals have adequate skills to employ technology effectively? Introducing infrastructure does not assure that this resource will be well-employed in classrooms, public institutions, and workplaces. Digital inclusion, or widespread individual adoption, is also needed for social benefit—network externalities increase with the number of users. At the same time that broadband-enabled advances are occurring in areas such as the use of big data and artificial intelligence, the 2019 American Community Survey of the US Census estimates that nearly 14 percent of households lack any type of broadband, and 12 percent more have only mobile broadband connections.

Availability as a Goal

Programs addressing availability provide infrastructure, and these projects have been particularly prevalent in rural areas where the market offers limited options for internet access (this includes many of the federal stimulus projects and Tribal efforts). In urban areas, infrastructure programs have developed to experiment with faster speeds. These include Google Fiber in Kansas City, and public, university, and nonprofit-led initiatives in cities including Chattanooga, Urbana-Champaign, and the One Community area surrounding Cleveland, among others. Public infrastructure projects, which may fill gaps in availability or speed, often serve what federal agencies have called "community anchor institutions" such as schools, hospitals, libraries, and governments, as well as businesses and residents. This is what Hauge and Prieger (2015) have called the "supply side" of broadband policy.

Organizational Use and Innovation as a Goal

It is possible to evaluate how organizations implement broadband-enabled technologies for a variety of purposes. This could include the examination of changes in local elementary schools once broadband is available in classrooms, and barriers to pedagogical use. Organizational evaluation includes the study of emerging, innovative uses as well. Examples of such applications include the use of predictive analytics and case management software to reduce recidivism in homelessness[11], drone streaming for disaster response[12], energy management in residential communities[13], tracking the resilience of water resources,[14] and use of virtual reality for education[15] or job training.[16]

Adoption and Digital Skills as Goals

Many broadband programs aim to promote the "demand side" (Hauge and Prieger 2015), or the adoption of high-speed networks by residents, and the skills to use technologies effectively. As Chapter 6 by Tolbert and colleagues demonstrates, adoption varies widely across communities in the US, even where high-speed networks are available. This reflects other social inequalities. While mobile phones substitute for home broadband for some low-income and minority households, reliance on such access has limitations for some uses, such as filling out forms, writing, or doing homework, and mobile users do less online (Horrigan and Duggan 2015 Mossberger, Tolbert, and Anderson 2017). Broadband adoption remains a concern even for those who have some internet access through mobile. Adoption and skill initiatives often include some combination of outreach, training, public access, technical support, and sometimes discounted or subsidized internet access or devices. Whitacre, Gallardo, and Strover (2014) compared the outcomes for both availability/supply and adoption/demand in their study of rural counties and found significant results for both, but stronger effects for adoption. This supports the need for other studies of adoption and use, as well as availability. With such differences in treatments and populations, there are significant opportunities to learn what works for various approaches, demographic groups, and communities.

Evaluation of specific interventions can lead to a better understanding of how broadband use is connected to both desired and unintended outcomes and what practices are most effective. Prior research on the geographic spread of broadband infrastructure has provided some evidence that broadband affects regional employment and educational outcomes, although the lessons for policy are often unclear (Gillett et al. 2006; Crandall et al. 2007; Kolko 2010; Vigdor and Ladd 2010; Fairlie and London 2011). Much of the prior research is based on data on broadband *availability* rather than information about specific interventions. Researchers often lack data on how broadband actually was used by organizations or individuals in these communities, leading to questions about why outcomes occur or why they differ. For example, some studies show that localities with broadband availability have more favorable economic outcomes (Gillett et al. 2006; Crandall et al. 2007), while others, applying similar econometric approaches, demonstrate fewer effects at the community level (Kolko 2010). Simply introducing broadband networks may not be sufficient to generate more jobs in areas with few employers or low levels of skill. But we don't know whether there were certain conditions or programs in some communities that led to more success. Research has sometimes revealed negative effects as well. Vigdor and Ladd (2010) found that the introduction of high-speed internet in rural North Carolina was associated with slightly decreased proficiency scores for low-income students in affected communities. The authors speculated that broadband created new distractions that harmed educational achievement, though to a modest degree. We do not know whether this was the case, or whether other influences weakened proficiency scores. But, in all these studies tracking the effects of broadband availability in communities, the "black box" processes underlying differing results remained unknown. Studying interventions and use rather than infrastructure availability alone offers better guidance for public policy.

WHAT DOES PROGRAM EVALUATION CONTRIBUTE?

To answer whether the promise of broadband is being fulfilled, we need more systematic examination of interventions across different contexts, asking questions such as:

- Under what conditions, and for whom does broadband have demonstrable impacts?
- How do we understand what works and why across different policy domains?
- How do we best connect individuals, institutions, and communities to promote opportunity?
- How can we maximize positive social and economic impacts, and avoid unintended consequences?

Program evaluation can measure impacts and shed light on processes of change, especially if it is built into new programs and policies from the start. It is often most appropriate to gather baseline data prior to or at the inception of programs, comparing conditions at the beginning and end of the program. When evaluation is undertaken as an afterthought, it may be too late to collect data to provide meaningful measures of change.

Another reason to address evaluation early is to examine program implementation as one aspect of the evaluation. As new programs are being carried out, *formative evaluations* can help to diagnose problems and inform modifications. They can also highlight best practices for how such innovations can be implemented. Formative evaluations can provide early feedback so that midstream corrections can be made cost effectively. Such formative evaluations also provide information on effective practices and can lead to more efficient programs.

In addition to formative evaluations, *outcome evaluations* provide information on whether the program achieved its goals, what should be done in the future, or whether the outcomes were worth the resources invested. Outcomes may be measured at different levels—for example, for individual patients, for health organizations, or for health trends in the communities in which broadband interventions are located. Programs may aim to affect one or all these outcomes. And results can be measured over different time spans. For example, initial outcome evaluations of technology training programs can address short-term results such as increases in internet adoption and use. Intermediate outcomes might include the different activities that new users pursue online and the skills they acquire. Do new internet users look for jobs more readily than individuals who are not online? Do parents who receive training communicate through email or social media with their children's teachers and become more involved in their children's education than before? Long-term impacts may include later improvements in wages or proficiency scores for those who are digitally engaged.

And, while it is important to consider evaluation even before programs begin, many of the effects of broadband use develop over time and require *longitudinal evaluations*. There may be initial lags in outcomes, as individuals and organizations acquire the skills and knowledge to apply broadband internet in new ways. And ultimately, it is the long-term effects that we care about—increases in graduation rates, incomes, employment, reduction of emergency room visits, or improvements in health from telemedicine, for example. Without long-term analysis, we run the risk of concluding prematurely that technology has had little impact or only a short-term impact. The effects of computers and information technology on productivity were not apparent for many years for this reason (Brynjolfsson and Hitt 1996), and we can expect lagged effects in other areas as well. Chapter 5 provides an example of a longitudinal evaluation of neighborhood-level change over nine years. Without longitudinal studies, we are unlikely to know whether investments in broadband have led to real change in employment, health, or education.

Consider how these different types of evaluations can be applied to interventions focused on broadband availability, organizational use, and individual adoption. Evaluation of infrastructure projects might examine community-level changes in the near term for broadband adoption at home, and community-level outcomes over time in areas such as employment, economic development, education, or health. Formative evaluations of implementation are especially valuable at the organizational level, with an emphasis on understanding processes of innovation and barriers. Quasi-experimental methods or randomized trials can be used to examine outcomes for clients (such as students or patients) resulting from changes in organizational practices, or for digital inclusion initiatives. Ethnographic methods can inform our understanding of adoption decisions and skill acquisition for different populations. Experiments, quasi-experimental designs, surveys, and many other evaluation methods can also be utilized to study adoption and skills for participants in digital inclusion programs. Panel studies might also track the development of skills and impacts over the long term.

We need evaluation research at different stages and at individual, organizational, and community levels. There is not really a single intervention here—broadband deployment—but an integrated chain of interventions that occurs over time—broadband deployment leading to intended and unintended uses and activities (short-term and intermediate-term outcomes) that may in turn influence longer-term health- or education-related outcomes.

SPECIAL CHALLENGES FOR BROADBAND EVALUATION: DIVERSE USES AND COMPLEX PROCESSES

Evaluation research aims to provide answers about whether program objectives were realized or not and why. It aims to disentangle the effects of the program from other influences, that is, to determine whether changes can be attributed to the intervention. While often a dilemma in evaluation research, the problem of complex and multiple causes is especially prominent in broadband evaluation. In part this is because broadband is an enabling technology with many uses. Broadband uptake and use also occurs within a complex social environment. Studies correlating the introduction of broadband with regional employment outcomes are suggestive, for example, but can't address issues of cause and effect. Was it broadband that was responsible for apparent changes, or something else about the economic development potential of such areas? Identifying causation can be difficult because there are many variables other than technology that can influence outcomes, technology use is typically conditioned by other factors, and the effect of technology on social outcomes is often moderated by other institutional and behavioral variables. For example, organizations and individuals that adopt broadband may simply be more motivated or more prepared to accomplish employment, health, or educational goals than those who fail to adopt new technologies. Evaluation research seeks to understand these interactions and behavioral processes as well as to measure impacts. Separating out and attributing effects requires well-developed research designs, based on social science research methods.

Insights are needed, too, from a variety of disciplines to evaluate varied broadband applications and goals. Because broadband is a general-purpose technology that can be used differently across many policy areas, there is often a need for expertise in the policy domain of interest, such as health or education. At the same time, knowledge of technology is needed, including an understanding of how or why technology use would make a difference for health or education, as well as knowledge of processes of technology adoption.

The authors in this edited volume provide guidance for evaluating these complex programs, which have goals that reach across different policy areas and populations.

PLAN OF THE BOOK

To address diverse uses and complex processes, this collection brings together expertise on program evaluation, broadband and information technology, and substantive policy areas such as health, education, civic engagement, and community development. Authors include prominent researchers who have examined the impact of broadband from a variety of perspectives and disciplines—computer science, economics, communications, political science, public administration, and anthropology. Contributors include scholars known for their pioneering work in this field as well as those who have conducted recent evaluations of major broadband initiatives. Together, these authors are scholars and evaluators who are providing leadership in this area.

This book was inspired by a roundtable sponsored by the John D. and Catherine T. MacArthur Foundation in Chicago in October 2012, where the authors had a chance to compare experiences and engage with each other and with other experts on broadband and program evaluation.[17] Since the roundtable, more experience has been gained through evaluations of the Broadband Technology Opportunities Program and other efforts, and insights from these studies are incorporated here. These chapters represent the state of the field and raise important questions for improving both research and the use of evaluation, with implications for future practice across many policy areas.

In Chapter 1, William Lehr, an economist who participated in some of the earliest studies of broadband, discusses the goals for broadband in the evolving Internet of Things, and challenges for evaluation, such as the need for more data. The next four chapters introduce methods that have been used in evaluation research, comparing the opportunities and challenges they present. John Horrigan has worked for the Pew Internet and American Life Project, on the national broadband plan for the Federal Communications Commission, and on an evaluation of Comcast Internet Essentials using panel surveys. In his discussion of data sources in Chapter 2, he examines the use of survey research, including panel data, and the strengths and weaknesses of different types of government data from the Federal Communications Commission Form 477 and the Bureau of the Census American Community Survey. The American Community Survey data on broadband subscriptions only became available for all census tracts in December 2018 but could provide a baseline for interventions going forward. One of the challenges for place-based evaluation of broadband initiatives has been the lack of precision in the FCC data on both deployment and subscriptions. Robert Fairlie has conducted randomized control trials to evaluate the impact of free laptops for low-income community college students. In Chapter 3 he discusses the strengths and weaknesses of experimental methods for evaluating educational initiatives and other broadband programs. Jessica Crowell evaluated one of the broadband stimulus programs, Let Freedom Ring in Philadelphia, through ethnographic study of program participants, and Chapter 4 discusses her two-year study and the value of qualitative work for opening the black box. In Chapter 5, Tolbert and her colleagues discuss the evaluation of another broadband stimulus program, Chicago's Smart Communities, to measure neighborhood-level change and long-term impacts of the program. The chapter also examines longitudinal designs and other forms of quasi-experimental evaluation.

Subsequent chapters present needs for understanding the policy context of broadband applications, asking the right questions, and understanding complex interactions. They present questions and strategies for evaluation in the context of several policy areas: rural healthcare, digital government, and civic engagement. Sharon Strover, an expert on broadband in rural communities, focuses on evaluation of telemedicine and other health-care strategies enabled by broadband connectivity in Chapter 6, which requires an understanding of both health policies and rural issues. This is a particularly promising application for rural communities, where much of the early 21st-century infrastructure efforts have been focused. Alfred Tat-Kei Ho has written extensively on digital government use by cities, and in Chapter 7 he demonstrates how to construct a stakeholder logic model for evaluating e-government. His recommendations can be useful for many other policy areas where the perspectives of multiple stakeholders are relevant for evaluation. Michael Xenos is studying civic engagement of youth in a cross-national project. In Chapter 8, he considers the issues involved in evaluating the impacts of broadband for civic engagement, demonstrating how theory can be useful for deriving relevant metrics and informing practice.

The final chapter summarizes the arguments made across authors and policy areas, recommending directions for evaluation research. Handling complexity—the likelihood that there are many different causes for results—means employing a range of methods, which may be chosen based on the types of questions the evaluation addresses. Because broadband use is a social process that involves individuals, organizations, and communities, evaluation research must collectively address impacts and processes at all these levels. Without common concepts and data, however, comparison across policy areas, programs, and scales will be difficult. Longitudinal research will also be needed to assess the long-term consequences of broadband investments and use, as organizations and individuals adapt and possibly innovate.

No single study can answer all the questions that are relevant for broadband policy. There is a need for consistent commitment and support of evaluations, large and small, across different policy contexts and in various types of communities. There is a need to build a research community—to share tools for implementation and evaluation, including logic models, metrics, approaches, and methods. There is also a critical need to share information across researchers, practitioners, and decision makers. Though learning through evaluation of broadband is demanding, the payoff can be substantial as well, for public policy and social science across so many areas of human endeavor.

NOTES

1. https://www.fcc.gov/document/fcc-launches-20-billion-rural-digital-opportunity-fund
2. https://www.fcc.gov/25-ghz-rural-tribal-window
3. https://www.fcc.gov/wireline-competition/telecommunications-access-policy-division/connected-care-pilot-program
4. https://www.linkedin.com/company/agence-du-num%C3%A9rique/about/
5. https://www.bbc.com/news/technology-32736199
6. http://interactive.satellitetoday.com/via/may-2016/broadband-in-africa-untamed-opportunities/
7. http://www.broadbandcommission.org/about/Pages/default.aspx
8. https://www.gov.uk/government/publications/national-broadband-scheme-evaluation-plan
9. http://pubdocs.worldbank.org/en/391452529895999/WDR16-BP-Exploring-the-Relationship-between-Broadband-and-Economic-Growth-Minges.pdf
10. http://www.oecd.org/gov/evidence-informed-policy-making.htm
11. http://na.smartcitiescouncil.com/article/more-street-strategies-its-not-data-its-what-you-do-it
12. https://www.us-ignite.org/announcing-the-demos-selected-for-the-2019-us-ignite-application-summit/
13. https://www.us-ignite.org/announcing-the-demos-selected-for-the-2019-us-ignite-application-summit/
14. https://www.us-ignite.org/apps/LGTrguXLfUHPwfU2ai7AZj/
15. https://www.us-ignite.org/announcing-the-demos-selected-for-the-2019-us-ignite-application-summit/
16. https://www.us-ignite.org/apps/AR-training-first-responders/
17. Expert participants in the roundtable, in addition to the authors here, included Stuart Bretschneider of Syracuse University (now Arizona State University), Dan Bugler of WestEd, Jane Fountain of the University of Massachusetts-Amherst, Jon Gant of the University of Illinois at Urbana-Champaign (now North Carolina Central University), Timothy Johnson of the University of Illinois at Chicago, Craig LeFebvre of socialShift, Stephen Rhody of ASR Analytics, and Scott Wallsten of the Technology Policy Institute.

REFERENCES

Agence Nationale de la Cohésion des Territoires. Ensuring Very High-Speed Broadband for All by 2020. https://www.amenagement-numerique.gouv.fr/fr/garantir-du-tres-haut-debit-tous-2022

Associated Press. 2020. "School Shutdowns Raise Stakes of Digital Divide for Students."
    PBS Newshour, March 30, 2020. https://www.pbs.org/newshour/education/
    school-shutdowns-raise-stakes-of-digital-divide-for-students

Australian Government, Department of Infrastructure, Transport, Regional Development,
    and Communications. 2020. Broadband Advisory Council Established. https://www.
    communications.gov.au/departmental-news/broadband-advisory-council-established

Brynjolfsson, E., and L. Hitt. 1996. "Paradox Lost? Firm-Level Evidence on the Returns
    to Information Systems Spending." *Management Science* 42 (4): 541–558.

Conger, K., and E. Griffith. 2020. "As Life Moves Online, an Older Generation Faces
    a Digital Divide." *The New York Times*, March 27, 2020. https://www.nytimes.com/
    2020/03/27/technology/virus-older-generation-digital-divide.html

Crandall, R. W., W. H. Lehr, and R. Litan. 2007. *The Effects of Broadband Deployment
    on Output and Employment: A Cross-Sectional Analysis of U.S. Data.* Issues
    in Economic Policy. Washington, DC: The Brookings Institution. https://
    www.brookings.edu/research/the-effects-of-broadband-deployment-on-output-
    and-employment-a-cross-sectional-analysis-of-u-s-data/

deWit, K. 2020. "States Tap Federal CARES Act to Expand Broadband." Pew Charitable
    Trusts.   https://www.pewtrusts.org/en/research-and-analysis/issue-briefs/2020/11/
    states-tap-federal-cares-act-to-expand-broadband

Fairlie, R., and R. London. 2011. "The Effects of Home Computers on Educational
    Outcomes: Evidence from a Field Experiment with Community College Students."
    The Economic Journal 122: 727–753.

Federal Communications Commission. 2010. *National Broadband Plan.* https://
    www.fcc.gov/general/national-broadband-plan

Federal Communications Commission. 2019. *2019 Broadband Deployment Report.* FCC
    19–144. https://docs.fcc.gov/public/attachments/FCC-19-44A1.pdf

Fishbane, L., and A. Tomer. 2020. "Neighborhood Broadband Data Makes It
    Clear: We Need an Agenda to Fight Digital Poverty." The Brookings Institution. https://
    www.brookings.edu/blog/the-avenue/2020/02/05/neighborhood-broadband-data-
    makes-it-clear-we-need-an-agenda-to-fight-digital-poverty/

Gillett, S. E., W. H. Lehr, C. A. Osorio, and M. A. Sirbu. 2006. *Measuring Broadband's
    Economic Impact.* Boston, MA: Massachusetts Institute of Technology. http://
    cfp.mit.edu/publications/CFP_Papers/Measuring_bb_econ_impact-final.pdf

Goldberg, R. 2019. "Unplugged: NTIA Survey Finds Some Americans Still
    Avoid Home Internet Use." National Telecommunications and Information
    Administration, U.S. Department of Commerce. https://www.ntia.doc.gov/blog/
    2019/unplugged-ntia-survey-finds-some-americans-still-avoid-home-internet-use

Hauge, J. A., and J. E. Prieger. 2015. "Evaluating the Impact of the American Recovery
    and Reinvestment Act's BTOP on Broadband Adoption." *Applied Economics* 47
    (60): 6553–6579.

Horrigan, J. B. 2020. "Students of Color Caught in the Homework Gap." https://
    futureready.org/wp-content/uploads/2020/08/HomeworkGap_FINAL8.06.2020.pdf

Horrigan, J. B., and M. Duggan. 2015. *Home Broadband 2015.* http://www.pewinternet.org/
    2015/12/21/home-broadband-2015/

Kolko, J. 2010. *Does Broadband Boost Local Economic Development?* Public Policy Institute of California. http://www.ppic.org/content/pubs/report/R_110JKR.pdf

Kopp, J. 2020. "Philly School Year Could End with an 'Asterisk' if Coronavirus Pandemic Persists, Superintendent Hite Says." *Philly Voice*, March 24, 2020. https://www.phillyvoice.com/philly-school-district-distribute-chromebooks-coronavirus-pandemic-keeps-return-doubt/

Kunze, J. 2021. "Rural Alaska Natives Hope Elon Musk's Starlink Internet Service Can Level Playing Field." *Native News Online*, February 4, 2021. https://nativenewsonline.net/business/rural-alaska-natives-hope-elon-musk-s-starlink-internet-service-can-level-playing-field

Mayor of London. 2021. "Mayor of London and London Councils Work to Help Close the Digital Divide." https://www.london.gov.uk/press-releases/mayoral/mayor-and-london-councils-tackle-digital-divide

McMillen, A. 2017. "How Australia Bungled Its $36 Billion High-Speed Internet Rollout." *The New York Times*, May 11, 2017. https://www.nytimes.com/2017/05/11/world/australia/australia-slow-internet-broadband.html?mcubz=0&_r=0

Microsoft. 2018. "An Update on Connecting Rural America: The 2018 Microsoft Airband Initiative." https://blogs.microsoft.com/uploads/prod/sites/5/2018/12/MSFT-Airband_InteractivePDF_Final_12.3.18.pdf

Mossberger, K., C. J. Tolbert, and C. Anderson. 2017. "The Mobile Internet and Digital Citizenship in African-American and Latino Communities." *Information, Communication & Society* 20 (10): 1587–1606.

National Telecommunications and Information Administration and National Science Foundation. 2017. *The National Broadband Research Agenda: Key Priorities for Broadband Research and Data.* https://www.ntia.doc.gov/files/ntia/publications/nationalbroadbandresearchagenda-jan2017.pdf

Organisation for Economic Co-operation and Development. 2008. *Broadband Growth and Policies in OECD Countries.* https://www.oecd.org/sti/broadband/40629067.pdf

Romm, T. 2020. "'It Shouldn't Take a Pandemic': Coronavirus Exposes Internet Inequality among US Students as Schools Close Their Doors." *The Washington Post*, March 16, 2020. https://www.washingtonpost.com/technology/2020/03/16/schools-internet-inequality-coronavirus/

Singleton, M. 2015. "The FCC Has Changed the Definition of Broadband." *The Verge.* http://www.theverge.com/2015/1/29/7932653/fcc-changed-definition-broadband-25mbps

Smart Cities Council. N.d. Smart Cities Solutions. http://smartcitiescouncil.com/article-category/smart-cities-solutions

Stewart, N. 2020. "She's 10, Homeless and Eager to Learn. But She Has No Internet." *The New York Times*, March 26, 2020. https://www.nytimes.com/2020/03/26/nyregion/new-york-homeless-students-coronavirus.html

Taglang, K. 2020. "How Does the CARES Act Connect Us?" Benton Institute for Broadband and Society. https://www.benton.org/blog/how-does-cares-act-connect-us

Taglang, K. 2021a. "The Last Broadband Gifts from the 116th Congress." Benton Institute for Broadband and Society. https://www.benton.org/blog/last-broadband-gifts-116th-congress

Taglang, K. 2021b. "Introducing the Emergency Broadband Benefit Program." Benton Institute for Broadband and Society. https://www.benton.org/blog/ introducing-emergency-broadband-benefit-program

Taglang, K. 2021c. "American Rescue Plan: Broadband and the Social Safety Net." Benton Institute for Broadband and Society. https://www.benton.org/blog/american-rescue-plan-broadband-and-social-safety-net

UK Department for Digital, Culture, Media, and Sport. 2017. "Universal Broadband to Reach Every Part of the UK." https://www.gov.uk/government/news/universal-broadband-to-reach-every-part-of-the-uk

Vigdor, J. L., and H. F. Ladd. 2010. *Scaling the Digital Divide: Home Computer Technology and Student Achievement*. National Bureau of Economic Research, NBER Working Paper Series, No. 16078. http://www.nber.org/papers/w16078.pdf

What Works Centre for Local Economic Growth. 2015. *Evidence Review 6: Broadband*. London: What Works Centre for Local Economic Growth. http://www.whatworks growth.org/policy-reviews/broadband/

Whitacre, B., R. Gallardo, and S. Strover. 2014. "Broadband's Contribution to Economic Growth in Rural Areas: Moving Towards a Causal Relationship." *Telecommunications Policy* 38: 1011–1023.

White House. 2011. "Fact Sheet: Digital Promise Initiative." https://obamawhitehouse. archives.gov/the-press-office/2011/09/15/fact-sheet-digital-promise-initiative

Wu, T. 2020. "We Need to Protect the 'Touchless Economy.'" *The New York Times*, March 25, 2020. https://www.nytimes.com/2020/03/25/opinion/coronavirus-economy-delivery.html

PART I

Evaluation In the Context of Broadband

The Changing Context for Broadband Evaluation

WILLIAM LEHR

INTRODUCTION

We are living in an information society. Access to electronic communications and computing and the always-/everywhere-connected services they enable are increasingly taken for granted as essential for our everyday work and social lives. The Internet is becoming *the* principal platform for electronic communications internationally. Full realization of the Internet's capabilities requires broadband access. Consequently, broadband is now widely recognized as basic infrastructure, like roads, water, and electricity.[1] And, like the need to ensure universal access to safe roads, clean water, and reliable electricity, policymakers recognize the need to ensure universal access to adequate broadband. However, figuring out and agreeing on what comprises adequate broadband and how best to ensure its provision is difficult.

In order to figure out what constitutes an appropriate level of broadband service, how to use broadband most effectively, and how best to achieve our broadband goals, we need further research to evaluate the social and economic impacts of broadband and our broadband policies. Addressing

William Lehr, *The Changing Context for Broadband Evaluation* In: *Transforming Everything?*. Edited by: Karen Mossberger, Eric W. Welch, and Yonghong Wu, Oxford University Press. © Oxford University Press 2022.
DOI: 10.1093/oso/9780190082871.003.0002

this research challenge requires that we appreciate the changing context for broadband evaluation.

CHANGING FACE OF BROADBAND

In the United States, broadband only began to become widely available after 1995,[2] and by 2000 broadband household adoption was still below 5 percent.[3] However, 81 percent of US households reported having broadband connections by 2016, and 76 percent had smartphones (Ryan 2018). Considering that roads, electricity, and water have been basic infrastructures for more than one hundred years, it is important to note how recently the Internet and broadband have emerged as essential infrastructure.

Furthermore, the quality and capabilities of the Internet and broadband have improved substantially over time. In the early days, most users accessed the Internet via dial-up connections.[4] It was not until 2005 that always-on broadband became the dominant mode of access in the United States, and by 2015, only 3 percent were still relying on dial-up access.[5] Over time, broadband speeds have increased significantly.[6] The FCC (Federal Communications Commission) reported that the median speed for fixed broadband was 72 Mbps down and 14 Mbps up for the ISPs tested by September 2017 (FCC 2018). These speeds can support interactive rich multimedia communications, enabling resource-intensive applications like multiparty videoconferencing, high-definition video streaming, and highly interactive gaming.

But how much speed is enough? This remains an interesting question. What past experience has taught us is that faster and more capable services encourage the development and use of more resource-intensive applications. As broadband has become faster, the quality and capabilities of Internet-available content and services and the capabilities of home computers, displays, and other end-user devices have improved also. A growing number of households have multiple computers or other Internet-connected devices and larger displays (e.g., big-screen TVs) that can consume and generate much larger volumes of data traffic.[7] This growth is symbiotic. With faster connections more common, content sites like YouTube and Netflix can increase picture quality and usage grows accordingly.

A potentially even more profound development is the growth of mobile broadband services that first became available in the United States beginning in 2002 but grew rapidly thereafter, especially after the introduction of the iPhone in 2007 demonstrated the potential for a mass-market, hand-held, Internet-enabled "smartphone" device.[8] By 2010, mobile broadband exceeded fixed broadband connections worldwide (West 2011). Moreover, Ookla reported mean mobile broadband speeds of 27 Mbps down and 9 Mbps up by 2018.[9] The expansion of wireless Internet access via both 4G LTE cellular providers and via unlicensed Wi-Fi (which is often end-user deployed) means users can take the broadband Internet with them, expanding the scope for always-on/everywhere-connected services and computing/data accessibility. In addition to driving increased demand for smartphones,[10] this has helped support and spawn new classes of end-user devices ranging from e-readers like the Nook or Kindle to tablet devices like the iPad and Android Nexus.

As we look to the future, further important developments are in the offing. With the proliferation of mobile networking, embedded processors, and wireless sensors, we are in the beginning stages of realizing the vision of the Internet of Things (IoT): everywhere/all-the-time access to electronic computing and communications services for everybody and *everything*.[11] This creates the potential for integrating the real and virtual worlds much more extensively. With such integration comes the potential to further embed the Internet into our daily social and economic lives, automating a growing range of functions. We can make our technology "smarter"— more capable of sensing and interacting with our environment and dynamically customizing its behavior to account for real-time information. These computing/sensing/communications-enabled "smarts" facilitate just-in-time production,[12] market-of-one customization,[13] and better green and energy-efficient resource management. Smart technology can help integrate renewable (but more irregular) sources of power like solar and wind into our electricity grids,[14] help smooth the flow of traffic on "smart" highways,[15] and revamp the way we monitor patients and deliver healthcare through the introduction of new "smart" healthcare.[16]

Strictly speaking, neither the Internet nor the IoT vision of connected devices *requires* broadband access, or at least, much higher-speed broadband access services than we have in 2021. However, all of the growth in mobile broadband and home multimedia traffic (e.g., streaming video from services like Netflix, YouTube, and Amazon Prime[17]) does require substantial upgrades in Internet capacity in backbone and local distribution networks, motivating providers to expand investments in fiber optic capacity throughout their networks. And, while IoT "smarts" may not *require* broadband, it seems likely that more real-time decision-making and sensing capabilities at the network edge will motivate a demand for more data-hungry communication services that will put pressure on last-mile access capacity unless it expands to keep pace. The growth in surveillance and monitoring video are an obvious example (with the potential for both good and bad social implications). For example, wirelessly connected cameras can facilitate remote monitoring of infrastructure or of crime areas; when coupled with Artificial Intelligence (AI) tools to facilitate automated analysis of the video feeds, they may improve our ability to identify and respond to problems faster. At the same time, the proliferation of such capabilities may threaten privacy and pose a risk of realizing Orwell's dystopian future.

Moreover, the pace of innovation is not slowing as the next generation of wireless networking infrastructure, 5G, is already beginning to be deployed. 5G is the vision of the next generation of networking infrastructure that is needed to support the transition to a digital economy (ITU 2015; Lehr 2019). It calls for an order-of-magnitude improvement in wireless networking performance along multiple dimensions (data rates, connected devices, latency, reliability, etc.).

Whether and when we might need to realize the full capabilities of 5G or even to achieve home broadband service levels of 1 Gbps or more depends on a number of factors that leave lots of room for dispute, given how little we currently know about broadband usage.

Furthermore, speed is not the only dimension of broadband service that matters. Different services have different service quality requirements. For example, we might tolerate relatively high latency (delays) when downloading big files but find such delays unacceptable if we are trying to support real-time voice or video telephony, or real-time control (e.g., gaming). As the services become more embedded in our lives and we become more dependent on them, and as the user population extends to the entire population (and not just the techno-savvy elite), expectations about customer service and reliability are also expected to change (Lehr et al. 2011). For example, the quality of video demanded may depend on the context (e.g., is it entertainment or a tele-health application? Is the video cacheable or being displayed on a small screen? etc.). Additionally, in a mobile broadband world, coverage and accessibility to predictable performance over wide areas is important. The inherent challenges of supporting predictable performance in wireless networks operating in different frequencies makes it even more challenging to evaluate broadband performance in wireless or mobile environments than wired (Bauer and Lehr 2018).

While speed is not the only dimension that matters, it has often been used as a proxy for identifying the generation of broadband technology that is available, which in turn served as a reasonable proxy for the range of services that could be supported and were in use. For example, if we know a household is served by broadband with only a few Mbps, then we know that household cannot be doing much high-definition video streaming (either up or down) and is likely served with a lower-quality Digital Subscriber Line (DSL) or wireless service; whereas if the household is getting 100–1,000 Mbps then we know the household's broadband connection is unlikely to be the bottleneck for whatever the users might want to do, and the household is likely served either by fiber-to-the-home or a network with dense fiber in the neighborhood. At the speeds currently available to most households in the United States, it is increasingly less likely that their fixed broadband service is the bottleneck (Bauer and Lehr 2018).

Moreover, with the increasing usage of smartphones, tablets, and other Internet-enabled devices (increasingly replacing laptop and desktop

computers as the dominant mode of access for many subscribers), mobile broadband is becoming the dominant modality for broadband access. Mobile and fixed broadband are both complements and substitutes.
Most of the mobile broadband usage, especially for resource-intensive
applications like entertainment video or videoconferencing, is used no-
madically,[18] and most of the smartphone and other mobile device traffic is
carried via Wi-Fi rather than cellular networks (Adobe 2017; Cisco 2017).

Keeping track of all these developments and their implications for
network costs (e.g., investment requirements to keep pace with traffic
growth), consumer tastes and expenditures for services and devices/
equipment, and broadband usage poses a significant challenge for broadband policymakers as broadband remains a moving target.

Changing Face of Broadband Impact Research

As broadband has evolved, the focus of broadband research has shifted
also. Initially, the focus was appropriately on the availability and adoption
of broadband access. The focus was on fixed rather than mobile services
because mobile services only became available later. With the expansion
in service coverage, we have significantly addressed the availability challenge for at least second-generation broadband for both fixed and mobile services.[19] Understandably, adoption has lagged availability: whereas
availability is above 92 percent, only 66 percent of Americans have
adopted fixed broadband (FCC 2018, Table 1 and Table 11). There are many
reasons for this discrepancy, including cost, lack of perceived need, lack of
complementary skills and equipment, and lack of knowledge of available
options (NTIA 2011).[20] There are also significant differences in adoption
rates by location, income, skill level (education), age, and ethnic classification that need to be addressed to realize the public policy goal of universal
accessibility to essential infrastructures.[21]

Moreover, with the continuous evolution in broadband services, the
availability and adoption of broadband of different technologies is also
quite heterogeneous. Even if we progress toward ensuring a minimal level

of adequate broadband for everyone, we may see increased heterogeneity in the services available and adopted because of cost and taste differences. Not everyone who needs broadband needs or wants ultrafast broadband, or at least, at the price at which it may be available. Furthermore, the costs of deploying broadband infrastructure vary by geography and density. It is natural that 1 Gbps broadband is likely to become available first in denser urban markets where the costs of deployment are typically lower.

While this discussion makes clear that availability and adoption questions will remain important as broadband continues to evolve, research needs to shift increasingly toward focusing on broadband usage. To understand the social and economic impacts of broadband, we need to understand how broadband is being used. This is also necessary if we want to enhance the potential that optimal use will be made of the broadband resources we have available.

In 2001, in the early days of broadband market growth, a *New Yorker* cartoon[22] highlighted the problem: a little girl, newly arrived on her doorstep with a broadband cable in hand exclaims "Look, Mom! A broadband digital subscriber line followed me home. Can we keep it?" In those days, it was unclear what broadband might be used for and whether its use would contribute to economic growth or other socially desirable outcomes. Since then, academic researchers have compiled a convincing body of evidence demonstrating that broadband can contribute to economic growth and job creation (see Sharafat and Lehr 2017; World Bank 2016). However, realizing the economic benefits of broadband and the Information and Communications Technology (ICT) capabilities broadband enables depends on more than just ensuring that broadband is available.

ICTs are amplifiers and accelerators of socioeconomic trends, and not all of those trends need be beneficial. For example, the rise of the sharing economy and the gig economy it helped spawn has created new flexible job options (e.g., Uber, TaskRabbit, AirBnB, etc.) that many find appealing, but which typically lack the job security and regulatory protections associated with the more traditional fulltime employment that gig jobs displace. Or, the promise of Big Data analytics and artificial intelligence to enhance economic productivity and efficiency by enabling better real-time, computer-aided decision-making may result in human workers being replaced by robots, may further threaten privacy, or may automate algorithmic discrimination. Figuring out how to realize the benefits of broadband will require further research on understanding how broadband may contribute to both desirable *and* undesirable outcomes.

Currently, and in the near term, the two principal drivers for broadband traffic and usage seem to be the growth in multimedia streaming traffic and mobile broadband services. While these services represent significant value to our economy, it seems unlikely that folks watching more movies over the Internet or expanding mobile broadband usage (which has mostly meant just watching more movies over the Internet or interacting even more on social media sites like Facebook from more locations) will contribute significantly to net job or economic growth. In the case of entertainment media services—the single biggest component for Internet traffic—the move from traditional distribution channels to Internet-based channels, whether via fixed or mobile Internet, is likely to be partially if not largely offset by a loss of economic activity associated with legacy channels. We see these effects in the problems confronting traditional media industries like publishing, music, and, with the growth in over-the-top streaming media (i.e., entertainment video services that are accessed via a broadband Internet access service), traditional cable and satellite television services.

The promise of broadband for producing significant economic growth and other social benefits seems more likely to lie in the promise of our information society to transform the ways we work and play. The promise is for the benefits that will be delivered by the realization of Smart-X, where X may be healthcare, education, distribution chains, transportation and energy grids, e-government, or green technologies. The potential is that the Internet will evolve into a general platform or *cloud* of ubiquitously available and scalable computing and communication resources. This Internet cloud will provide the scaffolding with which to support Smart-X. Broadband is a key component of that scaffolding. While not strictly essential for the realization of Smart-X functionality, and also obviously not sufficient in itself to support adoption of Smart-X functionality, broadband is generally necessary and will significantly aid progress toward the realization of Smart-X functionality.[23]

The vision for Smart-X to transform the US economy was articulated in the American Recovery and Reinvestment Act of 2009 (ARRA)[24] and the US National Broadband Plan (NBP).[25] Of the almost $1 trillion included in the ARRA, almost $100 billion was focused on Smart-X-related technologies, including $7 billion for investment in expanding broadband infrastructure.[26] After assessing the current status of broadband in the United States and considering policy reforms to better promote broadband, the NBP highlighted the potential positive benefits of broadband in separate chapters devoted to healthcare, education, energy and the environment, economic opportunity (where broadband can assist in lowering business costs and facilitating skills upgrading), government operations and civic engagement, and public safety. By highlighting these area-specific potentials, the NBP signaled both (1) that the potential for broadband to deliver significant benefits is large; and (2) that realizing these benefits will take much more than simply ensuring that broadband is available and adopted. Stimulus dollars spent on broadband ought to be viewed as an investment in our future, rather than as a quick way to directly create jobs. The benefits in job creation are likely to be indirect and associated with growth in all of the businesses that believe in the promise of our economy's future and are more willing to invest when they believe we are collectively on track to realize that future.

Although it may not be appropriate to evaluate broadband investments on their short-term job impacts, we do need to monitor such investments to make sure they are on track. This is just good project management practice. While it is reasonable to make the decision to invest in broadband based on our conclusion that broadband is necessary for the future we want, and to inform that discussion by considering the potential costs and benefits to be realized in that Smart-X future, realizing the outcomes of those decisions will take time. Having decided that universal broadband is necessary basic infrastructure, we may need to supplement private-sector investment with public investments, as in the ARRA. Evaluation of such investments (as with all investments) is important to make sure costs are being appropriately minimized and, over time, to ensure that we still believe that our projections of the future are reasonable.

Moreover, the $7 billion invested in broadband as part of the one-time effort of the ARRA is dwarfed over time by accumulated investments in universal service subsidy programs. Collectively, those programs constitute almost $9 billion per year.[27] Ensuring that these funds are best directed to achieve good broadband outcomes over time represents an enduring research challenge. With $3.2 billion in Emergency Broadband Benefits, $20 billion from the FCC for rural broadband,[28] and additional efforts for adoption and infrastructure funded through Covid-19 relief to states, local governments, and anchor institutions, there is an urgent need to evaluate outcomes and derive lessons for policy.

Furthermore, realizing the Smart-X future will require changes in business practices, organizational and market structures, and public policies. Like the personal computer, the broadband Internet may be viewed as a General Purpose Technology (GPT) that is used in productive activities by businesses, government, and social institutions in diverse ways to produce many different types of intermediate and final goods and services (Bresnahan and Trajtenberg 1995). By itself a GPT does nothing. It needs to be combined with other resources and applied to specific purposes to be productive. The additional resources will increasingly include mobile and IoT devices, AI, and Big Data analytics. And, the economic and social impacts of broadband, and potentially the best uses for broadband, are likely to be different whether one is looking at healthcare, education, energy management, or finance. This suggests that significant vertical domain expertise may be needed to evaluate the impacts.

Another complicating factor arises by virtue of broadband becoming an essential basic infrastructure. An important feature of basic infrastructures is that they are used ubiquitously in our social and economic lives. Businesses and households increasingly need broadband to fully participate in today's Information Society. From an evaluation and measurement perspective, what that means is that the effects of broadband—both good and bad—are multiple and widely distributed. Consider the challenges of measuring the economic impacts of roads on a community. We rely on roads to move about our daily lives and to trans-port goods and services, but roads also enable traffic accidents, noise, and pollution. Broadband may allow better access to consumer information and education opportunities, but it also facilitates access to child pornography or collaboration among terrorists. Broadband, and especially mobile broadband, changes the way we interact and work.

To understand these myriad impacts and to craft and evaluate policies to promote beneficial impacts from broadband, we need more granular data and more micro-studies. We need research that analyzes individual user, firm, and context-specific behaviors. Collecting such data poses numerous problems, including threats to individual privacy, and sharing the data publicly may pose security risks.[29] It is unlikely and undesirable that such granular data become generally available. That means that we will confront the challenge of generalizing and extrapolating results from one micro-study to infer estimates for other markets/situations. For example, it may be very difficult to trace a causal relationship between improved healthcare outcomes and broadband without conducting a detailed sector-specific study. Doing such a study for a single country or market would be challenging enough, so we will need to leverage the detailed studies that are done for what they can help us infer in other markets. The ability to make such inferences will benefit from data management and study design practices that anticipate this need. That could be as simple as making sure that geocoding is done on a consistent basis so that results from one market might be more readily adapted for another. Or it could involve greater attention to robustness tests to distinguish those factors that are not context-specific from those that are. For example, a study of mobile usage by youths in Finland is not obviously transferrable to understand the behavior of youths in Boston—but it is unlikely to be wholly uninformative either. Figuring out which inferences reasonably transfer across markets and which do not is a topic worthy of research in its own right.

Understanding that broadband evaluation will require consideration of multiple effects and usage contexts implies that it will require diverse and new types of data sets. Even if one focuses solely on assessments of broadband service quality, it is clear that measuring and characterizing broadband quality is a complex challenge. Even measuring and assessing something as seemingly simple as the speeds of broadband services proves both technically and analytically difficult (Bauer et al. 2010, 2016, 2018). The challenge is worse if one considers other aspects of broadband quality, like reliability (Lehr 2015). Policy analysts and economists will need to collaborate with engineers or otherwise gain the multidisciplinary expertise required to work with the new data.

Furthermore, the expansion of 5G, IoT, AI, and Big Data analytics are enabling new tools for collecting and analyzing data. Machine-learning algorithms based on neural nets are capable of extracting new insights from massive data stores that, in principle at least, may be made available from networked sensors and video feeds. The availability of new large data sets from sources like click-stream data, social networking, fit-bits, and other active and passive data collection sources creates new opportunities for empirical economic analysis. Econometrics in a world of Big Data is very different, opening up more scope for non-parametric analyses and opportunities to test economic theories that previously were beyond the reach of empirical testing (Varian 2014).

Finally, because of the rapid pace of change in broadband technology and markets, and the shift toward real-time decision-making that it helps enable and propel, policymakers need research results in a timelier fashion to inform dynamic policies. Although economists might prefer to wait ten years until they can get sufficiently accurate measurements of inputs and outputs to determine what the economic effects were, policymakers do not have that luxury. Broadband evaluators who want to inform such dynamic policies will need to take advantage of novel data sets. They cannot wait until the Census Bureau revises job classification data to track broadband or Internet jobs better, but will need new approaches.[30] And, government policymakers and data managers will need to recognize that in a world of Big Data where everything is potentially measurable, lots of folks will have access to data. Aspirations for government statistical agencies to be *the* authoritative source of data-of-record will need to give way to a more curatorial approach (Lehr 2012). Policymakers will need to opportunistically integrate data and analysis from multiple sources, and more of the analysis and data management will depend on private-public partnerships. Additionally, the new capabilities for collecting and analyzing data and the changing issue-space in which policies will need to be framed will have obvious implications for disclosure and transparency policies.

SUMMING UP AND THE EVALUATION CHALLENGE FOR POLICY

Taking seriously the perspective that broadband is now basic infrastructure means there is an enduring public interest in ensuring that it be generally available under reasonable terms (whether subsidized or not) to everyone. Furthermore, recognizing it as basic infrastructure implies that we recognize that its effects are pervasive and multiple and have large multiplier effects for the economy. For both of these reasons, we need a robust broadband evaluation research program. We need to be able to identify gaps between where we want to be and where we are, and to target investment and other policies to address those gaps. Spending resources on broadband means we are not spending those resources on something else, so we must always consider the economic tradeoffs of alternative strategies (i.e., investing more/less in broadband or investing in broadband differently).

While the need for evaluation is obvious, the challenge is difficult. First, because broadband is a moving target. While availability and adoption of the next generation of broadband will continue to concern us, we need to focus more on developing a better understanding of how broadband is used. This is necessary if we are to trace the effects of broadband through to things we really care about like improved healthcare outcomes, educational performance, green/energy efficiency, and improving the quality of life for all of society.

We need more sector-specific and micro-studies of usage, and we need to tap into the different perspectives of the multiple academic disciplines. We need economists and management experts, but we also need sociologists, psychologists, community development, and other expertise to inform the research. The research will require novel and more dynamic and heterogeneous data sets. Good broadband evaluation research will need to be informed by knowledge of the technology, so help from engineers will be necessary to interpret the data in many cases.

In short, we will need richer, multidisciplinary, dynamic data sets and repositories. And we will need to build multidisciplinary capacity in collaborations and research programs that blend the requisite skill sets. The benefit of this, hopefully, will be a better broadband Internet for all.

NOTES

1. As of 2010, policymakers in many countries had identified broadband services as critical components of their digital agendas (see OECD 2011a; Domingo and Lehr 2013). Moreover, as of 2016, the UN has identified internet access as a basic human right (see Howell and West 2016).
2. Internet adoption was 14 percent of American adults (aged eighteen and over) in 1995, had reached 52 percent by 2000, and was 89 percent by 2018 (Pew 2018a).
3. Household broadband access in the United States rose from close to 4 percent in 2000 to 68 percent by 2010 and to 81 percent by 2016 (Figure 1 in NTIA 2011).
4. In addition to offering much lower speeds (56 Kbps or less), the burden of having to dial and wait for an internet connection to be established severely limited the usability and user-experience of dial-up internet access.
5. In March 2005, 33 percent of American adults who accessed the internet from home did so via broadband, compared to 28 percent who used dial-up access; by July 2015, 67 percent accessed via broadband and only 3 percent via dial-up (see Pew 2018b).
6. When the FCC first began tracking the progress of broadband, it classified broadband as services offering a data rate of 200 Kbps or higher. Today, fixed services offering that low a data rate would no longer be even considered as broadband. The FCC first raised the standard to 4/1 Mbps (down/up) in 2010, and then to 25/3 Mbps (down/up) in 2015. The FCC reaffirmed that standard as appropriate in its review of 2018 (see FCC 2018, 2015, 2010).
7. In 1984, only 8 percent of US households reported having a computer, and none had tablets or smartphones. By 2016, 76 percent had smartphones, 58 percent had tablets, and 77 percent had a laptop or desktop computer (Ryan 2018).
8. In 2016, the average smartphone used 1.6 GB of traffic, up 38 percent from the year before. The typical smartphone generated an order of magnitude more mobile data traffic than the typical basic-feature cell phone, and the average tablet generated two to three times the traffic of the average smartphone (see Cisco 2017).

9. Ookla reported mean speed test results of 27.33/8.63 Mbps down/up in the first two quarters of 2018 for mobile speed tests conducted using their suite (Ookla 2018a), and 96.25/32.88 Mbps down/up in the last two quarters of 2018 for fixed broadband speed tests (Ookla 2018b). Because the sampling methodologies are different, these results should be compared with each other and with the FCC test results with care.

10. As of 2018, in advanced countries (including the United States), 94 percent of adults own a mobile phone and 76 percent own a smartphone, compared with 83 percent and 45 percent for emerging countries (see Taylor and Silver 2019).

11. For example, see http://www.internet-of-things-research.eu/ (accessed February 17, 2019), DoC (2017), or European Commission (2009).

12. Rai et al. (2006) show how internet-powered supply chain management that facilitates just-in-time production contributes to sustainable firm-level performance gains.

13. Dewan et al. (1999) show how use of internet-enabled customization can allow firms to earn higher revenues.

14. See Kabalci (2016) and Noam et al. (2012).

15. See Calderone (2014) and Wenger et al. (2008).

16. See Kulkarni and Sathe (2014) and Laplante and Laplante (2016).

17. In 2018, streaming video comprised 58 percent of the downstream traffic on the global internet from services like Netflix (15 percent), Google's YouTube (11 percent), Amazon Prime (4 percent), and others (see Sandvine 2018).

18. That is, users are quasi-stationary when using the application, rather than moving among access points at highway speeds. While some folks are watching television in cars, most are watching in their homes.

19. According to the FCC (2018), 92.3 percent of the US population had access to fixed broadband offering 25/3 Mbp (down/up), and 99.6 percent had access to 4G LTE mobile broadband offering 5/1 Mbps (down/up).

20. See NTIA (2011).

21. Adoption rates are lower for rural (than urban), for poorer, less well educated, older, and non-white consumers.

22. See *New Yorker Magazine*, May 28, 2001, p. 90.

23. For example, control system traffic does not typically require high data rate services. However, when we embed sensors in everything and make everything potentially measurable and real-time responsive, we will create Big Data problems and generate demand for more high-bandwidth services. For example, the sensor tells me that the window in my vacation home is open so I then want to download the video from my monitoring cameras to diagnose the cause. Furthermore, even if broadband provides higher data rates than are typically necessary, those excess data rates can enable the relaxation of other design constraints in the same way that having a bigger disk drive may simply render data management practices designed to conserve disk space less important because capacity constraints are relaxed. The excess bandwidth can support future growth or multiple separate virtual networks (and hence competition).

24. The American Recovery and Reinvestment Act (2009) was passed on February 13, 2009, as a government spending and stimulus package to revitalize the US economy following the financial market collapse in 2008 (see https://www.congress.gov/111/

plaws/publ5/PLAW-111publ5.pdf). The original Act proposed spending $787 billion across a range of programs. Of that, $30 billion was for "smart" power grid technology, $20 billion for renewable energy, $15 billion for basic research and education, $19 billion for healthcare records, $8 billion for high-speed rail, and $7 billion for broadband.

25. See FCC (2010).

26. The $7 billion spending program was not expected to be sufficient to address the challenge of providing universal access to broadband services. To put this in perspective, the universal service subsidy program for telephone service is about $8 billion per year, with about $4 billion devoted to subsidizing services in high-cost (mostly rural) markets.

27. In 2017, universal service subsides totaled $8.9 billion, spread over four programs: high-cost support ($4.5 billion), low-income support ($1.5 billion), schools and libraries "e-Rate" support ($2.4 billion), and rural health care support ($0.3 billion) (see Table 1.9 in FCC 2017).

28. https://www.fcc.gov/document/fcc-launches-20-billion-rural-digital-opportunity-fund

29. For example, detailed data on the location of critical broadband infrastructure may facilitate terrorist targeting.

30. For example, Mandel (2012) looked at want-ad data for new jobs to infer the growth in internet job creation. Looking at legacy data on software jobs created does not allow one to infer what are legacy technology jobs and what are internet/broadband-related jobs.

REFERENCES

Adobe. 2017. "Mobile Metric Refresh." Adobe Digital Insights Q2 2017. https://www.slideshare.net/adobe/adobe-mobile-trends-refresh-q2-2017

Bauer, S., D. D. Clark, and W. Lehr. 2010. "Understanding Broadband Speed Measurements." *TPRC38: The 38th Research Conference on Communications, Information, and Internet Policy, 2010.* http://ssrn.com/abstract=1988332

Bauer, S., and W. Lehr. 2018. "Measuring Mobile Broadband Performance." *TPRC46: The 46th Research Conference on Communication, Information, and Internet Policy 2018.* https://ssrn.com/abstract=3138610

Bauer, S., W. Lehr, and M. Mou. 2016. "Improving the Measurement and Analysis of Gigabit Broadband Networks." *TPRC44: The 44th Research Conference on Communication, Information, and Internet Policy.* https://ssrn.com/abstract=2757050

Bresnahan, T., and M. Trajtenberg. 1995. "General Purpose Technologies: Engines of Growth." *Journal of Econometrics* 65: 83–108.

Calderone, L. 2014. "Are Intelligent Highways in the Near Future?" *Robotics Tomorrow.* September 25, 2014. https://www.roboticstomorrow.com/article/2014/09/are-intelligent-highways-in-the-near-future/4774/

Chamberlain, K. 2018. "Smart Grids: Why They Matter for American Infrastructure Initiatives." BroadbandNow. https://broadbandnow.com/report/smart-grids-american-infrastructure-initiatives/

Cisco. 2017. "Visual Networking Index: Global Mobile Data Traffic Forecast Update; 2016–2021." https://www.cisco.com/c/en/us/solutions/collateral/service-provider/visual-networking-index-vni/mobile-white-paper-c11-520862.pdf

Cisco. 2018. "Cisco Visual Networking Index: Forecast and Trends, 2017–2022." https://www.cisco.com/c/en/us/solutions/collateral/service-provider/visual-networking-index-vni/white-paper-c11-741490.pdf

Dewan, R., B. Jing, and A. Seidmann. 1999. "One-to-One Marketing on the Internet." In *Proceedings of the 20th International Conference on Information Systems (ICIS) 8 (1999)* 93–102.

DoC. 2017. *Fostering the Advancement of the Internet of Things.* US Department of Commerce (DoC), Washington, DC. https://www.ntia.doc.gov/files/ntia/publications/iot_green_paper_01122017.pdf

Domingo, A., and W. Lehr. 2013. "Will Broadband Pricing Support 1Gbps Services?" Paper presented at the 24th European Regional Conference of the International Telecommunication Society (ITS). October 20–23, 2013. http://www.econstor.eu/handle/10419/88482

European Commission. 2009. *Internet of Things: An Action Plan for Europe.* COM(2009) 278. Commission of the European Communities, Brussels. http://eur-lex.europa.eu/LexUriServ/LexUriServ.do?uri=COM:2009:0278:FIN:EN:PDF

FCC. 2010. *National Broadband Plan: Connecting America.* Washington, DC: Federal Communications Commission. http://www.broadband.gov/download-plan/

FCC. 2015. *2015 Broadband Progress Report and Notice of Inquiry on Immediate Action to Accelerate Deployment: In the Matter of Inquiry Concerning Deployment of Advanced Telecommunications Capability to All Americans in a Reasonable and Timely Fashion; Before the Federal Communications Commission; GN Docket No. 14-126; Released February 4, 2015, Federal Communications Commission (FCC), Washington, DC.* https://apps.fcc.gov/edocs_public/attachmatch/FCC-15-10A1.docx

FCC. 2017. *Universal Service Monitoring Report.* Washington, DC: Federal Communications Commission. https://www.fcc.gov/sites/default/files/2017_universal_service_monitoring_report.pdf

FCC. 2018. *2018 Broadband Deployment Report: In the Matter of Inquiry Concerning Deployment of Advanced Telecommunications Capability to All Americans in a Reasonable and Timely Fashion, Before the Federal Communications Commission, GN Docket No. 17-199; Released February 2, 2018, Federal Communications Commission (FCC), Washington, DC.* https://docs.fcc.gov/public/attachments/FCC-18-10A1.pdf

Howell, C., and D. West. 2016. "The Internet as a Human Right." Brookings Institution. https://www.brookings.edu/blog/techtank/2016/11/07/the-internet-as-a-human-right/

ITU. 2015. *Recommendation ITU-R M.2083-0: IMT Vision; Framework and Overall Objectives of the Future Development of IMT for 2020 and Beyond.* International Telecommunications Union, Geneva. https://www.itu.int/dms_pubrec/itu-r/rec/m/R-REC-M.2083-0-201509-I!!PDF-E.pdf

Kabalci, Y. 2016. "A Survey on Smart Metering and Smart Grid Communication." *Renewable and Sustainable Energy Reviews* 57: 302–318.

Kulkarni, A., and S. Sathe. 2014. "Healthcare Applications of the Internet of Things: A Review." *International Journal of Computer Science and Information Technologies* 5 (5): 6229–6232.

Laplante, P., and A. Laplante. 2016. "The Internet of Things in Healthcare: Potential Applications and Challenges." *IT Professional* 3 (May/June 2016), 2–4.

Lehr, W. 2012. *Measuring the Internet: The Data Challenge.* OECD Digital Economy Papers 184, Paris. http://www.oecd-ilibrary.org/science-and-technology/measuring-the-internet_5k9bhk5fzvzx-en

Lehr, W. 2015. "Reliability and the Internet Cloud." In *Regulating the Cloud: Policy for Computing Infrastructure.* Edited by C. Yoo and J.-F. Blanchette, 87–113. Cambridge, MA: MIT Press.

Lehr, W. 2019. "5G and the Future of Broadband." In *The Future of the Internet: Innovation, Integration, and Sustainability.* Edited by G. Kneips and V. Stocker, 109–141. Baden-Baden, Germany: Nomos.

Lehr, W., M. Heikkinen, D. Clark, and S. Bauer. 2011. "Assessing Broadband Reliability: Measurement and Policy Challenges," *39th Research Conference on Communication, Information and Internet Policy (TPRC39), 2011.* Available at SSRN: http://ssrn.com/abstract=1979746)

Mandel, M. 2012. "Where the Jobs Are: The APP Economy." Paper prepared for TecNet. https://www.slideshare.net/judyscherer21/app-economy-38574329

Noam E., L. Pupillo, and J. Kranz, eds. 2012. *Broadband Networks, Smart Grids and Climate Change.* New York: Springer Science & Business Media.

NTIA. 2011. *Digital Nation: Expanding Internet Usage.* Washington, DC: National Telecommunications and Information Administration. http://www.ntia.doc.gov/files/ntia/publications/ntia_internet_use_report_february_2011.pdf

OECD. 2011a. "National Broadband Plans." *OECD Digital Economy Papers* 181, Organisation for Economic Cooperation and Development (OECD), Paris. http://dx.doi.org/10.1787/5kg9sr5fmqwd-en

OECD. 2011b. "Economic Impact of Internet/Broadband Technologies." DSTI/ICCP/IE(2011)1/REV1. Organisation for Economic Cooperation and Development (OECD), Paris.

Ookla. 2018a. Mobile SpeedTest: United States. https://www.speedtest.net/reports/united-states/2018/mobile/

Ookla. 2018b. Fixed Broadband SpeedTest: United States. https://www.speedtest.net/reports/united-states/2018/fixed/

Pew. 2018a. "Internet/Broadband Fact Sheet." Pew Research Center. http://www.pewinternet.org/fact-sheet/internet-broadband/

Pew. 2018b. "Broadband vs. Dial-up Adoption over Time." https://www.pewresearch.org/internet/chart/broadband-vs-dial-up-adoption-over-time/

Rai, A., R. Patnayakuni, and N. Seth. 2006. "Firm Performance Impacts of Digitally Enabled Supply Chain Integration Capabilities." *MIS Quarterly* 30 (2): 225–246.

Ryan, C. 2018. "Computer and Internet Use in the United States: 2016." American Community Survey Reports (ACS-39). U.S. Census Bureau. Washington, DC. https://www.census.gov/content/dam/Census/library/publications/2018/acs/ACS-39.pdf

Wenger, J., J. Opiola, and T. Ioannidis. 2008. "The Intelligent Highway: A Smart Idea?" Strategy+Business. February 26, 2008. https://www.strategy-business.com/article/li00064

Sandvine. 2018. *The Global Internet Phenomena Report.* https://www.sandvine.com/hubfs/downloads/phenomena/2018-phenomena-report.pdf

Sharafat, A., and W. Lehr, eds. 2017. *ICT-Centric Economic Growth, Innovation and Job Creation.* Geneva: International Telecommunications Union. http://www.itu.int/pub/D-GEN-ICT_SDGS.01-2017

Taylor, K., and L. Silver. 2019. "Smartphone Ownership Is Growing Rapidly around the World, but Not Always Equally." Pew Research Center. http://www.pewglobal.org/wp-content/uploads/sites/2/2019/02/Pew-Research-Center_Global-Technology-Use-2018_2019-02-05.pdf

Varian, H. 2014. "Big Data: New Tricks for Econometrics." *Journal of Economic Perspectives* 28 (2): 3–27.

West, D. 2011. "Ten Facts about Mobile Broadband." Center for Technology Innovation at Brookings. https://www.brookings.edu/wp-content/uploads/2016/06/1208_mobile_broadband_west.pdf

World Bank. 2016. *World Development Report 2016: Digital Dividends.* Washington, DC: World Bank. http://www.worldbank.org/en/publication/wdr2016

PART II

Diverse Methods

Measuring Broadband and Its Impacts

JOHN B. HORRIGAN

INTRODUCTION

In the early 2000s, measurement of broadband began to take on importance for US policymakers, and this was initially due to trends in international broadband data that did not shine a good light on the United States. The Organisation for Economic Co-operation and Development (OECD) periodically published data on the number of broadband subscriptions per one hundred people in OECD countries. By 2008, the United States ranked 15th in broadband subscriptions per one hundred people among OECD countries, but that was below its ranking of 4th in 2001 (TR 2008, 2005).

The other important context for interest in broadband measurement was the economy. As the decade wore on and US economic performance started to slow, broadband became seen as part of the toolkit that might reverse economic decline as well as improve other metrics of quality of life. By 2010, when the Federal Communications Commission (FCC) released the National Broadband Plan (NBP), it was common to frame broadband as the NBP did, as "a foundation for economic growth, job creation, global competitiveness, and a better way of life" (*Connecting America* 2010, xi).

John B. Horrigan, *Measuring Broadband and Its Impacts* In: *Transforming Everything?* Edited by: Karen Mossberger, Eric W. Welch, and Yonghong Wu, Oxford University Press. © Oxford University Press 2022. DOI: 10.1093/oso/9780190082871.003.0003

All this contributed to the demand for understanding how many Americans had a broadband internet connection at home. Parties in the government and the private sector had a track record in exploring the share of Americans with broadband at home, often through telephone surveys. The US Commerce Department in 2001 published a figure on the share of Americans using "wired" high-speed internet service at home— 9.1 percent in September of 2001 (NTIA 2011, 7). At the Pew Internet & American Life Project—now part of the Pew Research Center—the share of Americans with broadband at home was 8 percent in November 2001 (Pew Research Center 2019).

MEASURING BROADBAND AND IMPACT OVER TIME

By the end of the 2000s, however, measuring broadband took on new urgency. As part of the NBP, the FCC conducted a survey (pursuant to authority under the Broadband Data Improvement Act of 2008) of consumers on the type of technology they use to access the internet as well as the kinds of online applications they use. That survey, which was a random digit dial telephone survey, found in 2009 that 65 percent of Americans had broadband at home (Horrigan 2010). The survey also had a particular focus on why non-broadband users did not have service at home. Those findings have formed the three pillars in policy discourse about why people do not have broadband: cost (36 percent of non-broadband users said it was the main reason they lacked service), digital literacy (22 percent said insufficient digital skills was the main reason they did not have service), and relevance (19 percent said the internet just was not relevant to them).

The Obama Administration also marked the continuation and expansion of federal government programs to measure broadband adoption. NTIA's "Digital Nation" surveys continued that agency's survey of internet use that dates to the 1990s and continued throughout the 2000s. In those surveys, NTIA collaborated with the U.S. Census Bureau for a Computer and Internet Use Supplement to the Current Population Survey (CPS). The CPS is conducted by telephone and has a sample size of about sixty thousand households, which permits analysis of results on a state-by-state basis. The Census has been asking about people's computer use since 1984 and about internet use since 1997. Response rates are high for CPS supplements, with about 85 percent of households contacted completing CPS surveys (CPS 2019). NTIA has created its Digital Nation Data Explorer to allow users to query the survey data from pulldown menus.

The Broadband Data Improvement Act also required the Census Bureau to ask questions about home internet use in the American Community Survey (ACS). For the ACS, households receive notices through the mail that they have been selected for the survey, and they can respond through the mail, using the internet, or by telephone. If contacted households do not respond, ACS follows up with phone calls to ask that the survey be completed. In 2017, 93.7 percent of contacted households completed the ACS. The ACS started asking the question about home internet use and type of connection in 2013 (ACS 2019).

The large sample size of the ACS allows analysis of fairly disaggregated geographic units. Since the ACS is an ongoing survey, Census aggregates the data in different ways. For analysis of census tracts (roughly akin to a neighborhood, though census tracts can be geographically large in rural areas), the ACS aggregates data over five years, meaning some 17.5 million households are available for analysis. The 2013–2017 five-year ACS estimates were released at the end of 2018. The ACS also releases one-year estimates, which have a sample size of 3.5 million; these so-called "one-year ACS estimates" are appropriate for places with populations of sixty-five thousand or more (United States Census Bureau 2019a).

The trade-off in using the one-year estimates versus five-year has to do with geographic granularity and phenomena of interest to the analyst. The five-year estimate allows investigation of a certain variable—say broadband subscriptions at home—in a specific neighborhood. To do that requires combining data over five years. However, broadband adoption may change over five years—and in fact did from 2013 to 2017. To understand change, the one-year estimate is the tool to use, but, as noted, it can only paint a geographic picture for places whose population is sixty-five thousand or more. In 2013, ACS shows that 73.4 percent of Americans had broadband at home, a figure that rose to 83.5 percent in 2017. The entire 2013–2017 five-year estimate, however, shows 78.3 percent of Americans with broadband at home.

It is also worth noting that ACS and CPS surveys of broadband adoption at home yield roughly similar results in the aggregate. While ACS 2017 data found 83.5 percent of Americans with broadband at home, NTIA's CPS found that 85.9 percent of Americans had broadband. Given the sample sizes in each survey, the 2.4 percentage point difference is statistically significant. Though it is hard to know precisely the source of the difference, it may be due to question-wording and the nature of the survey instrument. ACS and CPS use broadly similar questions, but there is a difference. The ACS asks "Do you or any member of this household have access to the Internet using a . . ." and gives the following choices; the respondent can choose all that apply (ACS 2017):

a. cellular data plan for a smartphone or other mobile device?
b. broadband (high speed) Internet service such as cable, fiber optic, or DSL service installed in this household?
c. satellite Internet service installed in this household?
d. dial-up Internet service installed in this household?
e. some other service?

NTIA's November 2017 CPS supplement asks "I am going to read a list of ways that people access the Internet from their homes, other than a mobile data plan. At home, [do you/does anyone in this household] access the Internet using" and offers the following choices (and the respondent can choose all that apply):

a. High-speed Internet service installed at home, such as cable, DSL, or fiberoptic service? (If needed) This type of Internet service is often provided by a cable company or phone company.
b. Satellite Internet service?
c. Dial-up service?
d. Some other service?

The cellular data plan question precedes the broadband question in the CPS, which is why the respondent sees a shorter list of choices (CPS 2017). Separating the mobile data plan question from the overall broadband question may influence people's responses. It is also possible that the CPS supplement, which is a lengthy instrument about not just whether people have access at home but also about their online activities, yields a slightly higher incidence of broadband-at-home due to selection bias. Households with broadband may be more likely to participate in the lengthy CPS survey about the internet than the ACS survey (for which the household receives a brief survey with only a few questions about broadband).

Another part of the measurement of broadband is the FCC's 477 Form. This is a data collection exercise under which carriers are required to report to the FCC, twice a year, information on deployment of broadband networks as well as the number of subscribers. The 477 Form's data on broadband subscription receives less attention than other sources on broadband subscription due to Form 477's data collection approach. Whereas the ACS (as well as other surveys) ask individuals directly whether they subscribe to broadband at home, Form 477 reports broadband subscription rates on the basis of carrier-provider information on how many subscribers carriers have in a given area—in this case Census tracts. In the aggregate, this may yield a result similar to ACS—and the 2017 FCC Form 477 shows 84 percent of Americans with broadband compared with 83.5 percent from ACS data. For specific geographies, however, the FCC reports adoption data in quintiles, that is, whether a particular geographic unit has subscribership between 0 percent and 20 percent, 20 percent and 40 percent, and so on to 80 percent to 100 percent. This limits data analysis researchers may want to pursue (Tomer, Kneebone, and Shivaram 2017).

For network deployment data, Form 477 is much more controversial (Horrigan 2019). The FCC requires carriers to report *advertised* speeds (which can and do differ from *actual* speeds) by Census block using Form 477. That approach overstates broadband coverage, as the Government Accountability Office has told the FCC and Congress (GAO 2018). That is because an entire Census block will show coverage even if a carrier can provide service in a small portion of it (even just one address). This lack of

granularity, namely the inability to determine the nature of service availability at the household or street level, receives widespread criticism from
some policymakers and consumer advocates. Carriers generally argue
that it would be too burdensome for them to report data at that level of
specificity and that it might reveal competitively sensitive information. It
is worth noting that the current FCC practice of requiring Census block
reporting represents an improvement. Through 2008, Form 477 required
carriers to report network deployment data by zip code. After 2008,
carriers provided data by Census tract, and in 2013 the FCC changed that
to the smaller Census block.

RESEARCHING BROADBAND'S IMPACTS

Amidst all the policy activity in the early years of the Obama Administration,
there emerged a demand to address the question: "broadband, what
for?" The American Recovery and Reinvestment Act (ARRA) of 2010
appropriated $7.2 billion for broadband—most of that for broadband in-
frastructure. But ARRA did fund programs aiming to increase broadband
adoption and the availability of computers and internet access to those
without them at home. The Broadband Technology Opportunity Program
(BTOP 2012) in NTIA distributed $452 million in funds for sustainable
broadband adoption programs and public computing centers. These
grants funded a total of 110 initiatives to encourage broadband adoption or
provide places in communities to get online. These funds—both for infrastructure and adoption—rested on an assumption that broadband would
lead to positive outcomes. Finding ways to get non-broadband adopters
to subscribe would open opportunities for people to, for example, search
for or apply for jobs.

The ARRA funds prompted an understandable impulse to assess
impacts, that is, to go deeper than the question "broadband, what for?"
and explore whether, over time, broadband access made a difference to
people. Yet there was precious little research on exactly how broadband
access impacts outcomes and also little research on whether the programs

ARRA funded were successful. As to BTOP-funded outcomes, surveys conducted in the city of Chicago in 2008, 2011, and 2013 by Mossberger and Tolbert (Mossberger, Tolbert, and Anderson 2014) found that residents of neighborhoods near BTOP-funded broadband adoption projects did a wider range of online activities than similar residents in neighborhoods without broadband programs nearby. Chapter 6 discusses this study in detail.

BTOP funds helped drive the interest in exploring impacts of broadband adoption programs, but entities that often matched BTOP funds had interest as well. These stakeholders—policymakers, politicians, local government officials, and private or non-profit funders of these initiatives—wanted to know the impact broadband access had on people. From a methodological standpoint, that is challenging. The first issue is defining "impact" in the context of the research. Does it mean improvement in educational outcomes? Or higher income? Or perhaps an improvement in health? Further defining these things (e.g., what is the right metric for an educational outcome?) is a challenge, and then measuring them for individuals is an even greater one.

As if those challenges are not enough, attributing any changes to broadband access adds another layer of complexity. A researcher may, for instance, be interested in the link between broadband and education. Let's assume she can find research subjects who agree to share a measure of educational progress, such as grades or test scores. Let's assume further some have broadband at home and some do not. A single survey may reveal that students with broadband do better than students without broadband at home. That is a helpful finding, but only to a point. Even controlling for socioeconomic characteristics of the households, those with broadband may contain parents or guardians that encourage diligence in school work. Or perhaps the households with broadband pursued other resources—such as training on where to find educational resources online—that made the difference. In that case, broadband access may account for only some of the observed difference, with the training responsible for some of it.

This example shows the difficulties in drawing inferences about broadband's impact. Defining the impact of interest is one thing, and then finding research subjects who would agree to sharing information on personal phenomena such as educational test scores or healthcare conditions is another. Muddying the waters further are difficulties in determining whether broadband access is the differentiator in observed differences. And those observed differences are not the same thing as measuring impacts. For that, the research design would have to be longitudinal, that is, following research subjects through time so that the changes in impacts in question (say, test scores) can be observed, along with changes in independent variables of interest (say, broadband access).

An ideal research design, then, would be investigating defined impacts (such as educational test scores) among the same research subjects at two time intervals. Given a hypothesis that access to the internet influences educational outcomes, it would be ideal to have a set of respondents randomly assigned to a "have broadband at home" group and a similar set of respondents assigned to a "no broadband at home" group. Such a research design would also include measures of other phenomena about the household that might influence educational outcomes.

PANEL STUDIES ASSESSING BROADBAND'S IMPACTS

Needless to say, such a research design is aspirational, but the perfect need not be the enemy of the good. One way to explore the impacts of broadband is through a panel of recent broadband subscribers; discounted offers that carriers have for low-income households is a vehicle for such research. In the Minneapolis-St. Paul area, PCs for People, a non-profit that provides low-cost refurbished computers to low-income people, partnered with Mobile Beacon, a wireless service provider, to provide service for between $10 and $13 per month (depending on the contract customers choose). This program, called "Bridging the Gap," entered into a partnership with an outside researcher to study Bridging the Gap customers. That research found that participants in this discounted internet program reported positive educational impacts from having home internet access through Bridging the Gap (Schartman-Cycyk and Messier

2017). Parents said the service helps them be more engaged with their children's education and schools, while parents themselves use internet connectivity for lifelong learning. The research design does not establish a causal link between online access and educational impacts. But it shows that research partnerships with internet service providers can shed light on questions of interest to policymakers.

Among the most prominent discounted internet offerings is Comcast's Internet Essentials (IE) program. The program began in 2011 as a voluntary condition in the merger between Comcast and NBC Universal. At the time, the program offered $9.95 per month internet access to families whose children were eligible for free or reduced-price lunches at school. The program's eligibility requirements have expanded since then. Today, IE offers discounted ($9.95 per month) service, the option to purchase a subsidized internet-ready computer for less than $150, and free digital literacy training (online, in person, and in print). Those eligible to subscribe are:

- families with children who are eligible for free or reduced-price lunches at school,
- those in U.S. Housing and Urban Development (HUD) low-income housing units,
- those receiving HUD housing benefits (such as Section 8 vouchers), and
- low-income veterans.

Comcast has also initiated pilot programs for low-income seniors and community college students in select markets. The service offers download speeds of 15 megabits per second (Mbps).

One feature of the IE program has been its openness to research. In 2014, Comcast allowed the author to conduct a survey of IE customers—and then follow up nine months later with many of the same respondents in the initial survey (Horrigan 2015). Specifically, the research involved two surveys that queried Internet Essentials customers in January 2014 and September 2014. The first survey had 1,969 respondents, and the second re-interviewed 722 who had participated in the initial survey, making the research design longitudinal. Comcast provided the author a block of telephone numbers of recent IE subscribers and allowed the author to design and conduct a survey of IE households randomly selected from the phone list.

One issue that research explored was the impact of training on people's internet usage patterns. That issue is important because, at the local level, there are a number of programs that seek to encourage (usually) low-income people to obtain service, but they often do it through digital skills training programs. The longitudinal research design enabled careful analysis of the impact of training, in that it was possible to see if changes in the incidence of training over time had any connection to frequency of online activities of interest—such as job search, applying for jobs, and reported levels of comfort with computers. In focusing on, for instance, job search as the variable of interest, the longitudinal design allows the analysis to focus on the relationship between job search and training, while controlling for demographic and other characteristics (e.g., respondents' baseline level of confidence with computers and the internet). The research did, in fact, find a "training difference" in that those who had formal training on how to use computers and the internet were more likely to use the internet for job search or applications.

CONCLUSION

Policymakers and other stakeholders will continue to have strong interests in measuring broadband—both the nature of its dissemination in the population and its impact on people's lives. Even with more than 80 percent of Americans with broadband at home, there is likely to be continued interest in how that figure varies by income, demography, educational attainment, and geography. Device adoption may also attract attention. Whereas a computer and an internet connection were once enough for thinking about measuring access, people are increasingly reliant on smartphones and tablets for access. Wearable devices for certain purposes may become metrics of interest. And the "internet of things" is an emerging frontier for measuring access. Is access to internet-enabled systems to help manage, for example, home energy consumption something of interest for policymakers?

Once the notion of measuring broadband expands to include connected devices, wearable ones, and the internet of things, the question then follows quickly of what difference new digital access tools make. That presents a host of new measurement and methodological issues, especially since the interaction between access hardware and networks is at the heart of assessing impacts. To take the home energy management example: a household may have relatively few digital devices to access the internet and also live in a place where their network access speeds are below average. If equity concerns prompt an intervention to make sure this house can manage home energy consumption as easily as others, what intervention? Is it better to subsidize access devices or improve network speeds? If one is better than the other, by what increment should something (network speeds, number of devices) be increased to justify improvements (however defined) in home energy management?

However researchers address these challenges, it seems clear that the entire range of participants in the broadband landscape will have to cooperate with one another to meet them. Internet service providers have shown it is possible to cooperate with outside researchers—and this becomes only more important as digital tools increasingly pervade people's lives. The federal government will have to continually update how and what it collects from households on their technology adoption and usage patterns.

A final issue pertains to data—a classic double-edged sword in contemporary society. Data can enable applications that have the potential to help people in important ways—think healthcare management or mobility from point to point. At the same time, sharing personal data to enable these applications raises worries about the privacy of personal information and surveillance. These examples point to expectations embedded in data today; our clickstream can enable great progress but also inflict significant penalties. A point to note, though, is the power of expectations surrounding data; they seem pervasive enough to answer almost any question, even if it is a question we would rather not have asked. This can come into play for policymakers and other stakeholders when thinking about technology and its impacts. Surely, given the volume of data all around us, we can find out whether doubling network speeds in a neighborhood improves healthcare outcomes? As the preceding discussion shows, answering that question is not easy. But there is likely to be demand for such questions to be addressed, which makes it all the more important for policymakers, researchers, and other stakeholders to continue to tackle the challenges of measuring and assessing the impacts of networked information technologies.

REFERENCES

American Community Survey Questionnaire. 2017. U.S. Department of Commerce. https://www2.census.gov/programs-surveys/acs/methodology/questionnaires/2017/quest17.pdf

Broadband Data Improvement Act of 2008. https://www.govtrack.us/congress/bills/110/s1492/text

2012. *Broadband Technology Opportunities Program (BTOP) Quarterly Program Status Report: Submitted to the U.S. Congress,* March 2012. U.S. Department of Commerce, Washington, DC. https://www2.ntia.doc.gov/files/btop_report12.pdf

2010. *Connecting America: The National Broadband Plan.* U.S. Government Printing Office. https://transition.fcc.gov/national-broadband-plan/national-broadband-plan.pdf

2017. *Current Population Survey (CPS): November 2017 CPS Computer and Internet Use Supplement.* U.S. Department of Commerce, Washington, DC. https://www.ntia.doc.gov/files/ntia/publications/november_2017_cps_supplement_draft_for_public_comment.pdf

Government Accountability Office (GAO). 2018. *Tribal Broadband: FCC's Data Overstate Access, and Tribes Face Barriers Accessing Funding.* GAO-19-134T. Washington, DC: Government Accountability Office. https://www.gao.gov/products/GAO-19-134T

Horrigan, John B. 2010. "Broadband Adoption and Use in America." OBI Working Paper No. 1. Federal Communications Commission. https://transition.fcc.gov/national-broadband-plan/broadband-adoption-in-america-paper.pdf

Horrigan, John B. 2015. "The Training Difference: How Formal Training on the Internet Impacts New Users." *TPRC 43: The 43rd Research Conference on Communication, Information and Internet Policy Paper.* https://papers.ssrn.com/sol3/papers.cfm?abstract_id=2587783

Horrigan, John B. 2019. "What Does the FCC's Broadband Deployment Report Tell Us about the Digital Divide?" Benton Foundation. https://www.benton.org/blog/what-does-fcc%E2%80%99s-broadband-deployment-report-tell-us-about-digital-divide-0

Mossberger, Karen, Caroline Tolbert, and Christopher Anderson. 2014. "Measuring Change in Internet Use and Broadband Adoption: Comparing BTOP Smart Communities and Other Chicago Neighborhoods." https://copp-community.asu.edu/sites/default/files/REVChicagoSmartCommunitiesCHANGE042514-final%20%282%29.pdf

National Telecommunications and Information Administration (NTIA). 2011. "Digital Nation: Expanding Internet Usage." https://www.ntia.doc.gov/data/digital-nation-data-explorer#sel=wiredHighSpeedAtHome&disp=map

Pew Research Center. 2019. "Internet/Broadband Fact Sheet." https://www.pewinternet.org/fact-sheet/internet-broadband/

Schartman-Cycyk, Samantha, and Katherine Messier, 2017. *Bridging the Gap: What Affordable, Uncapped Internet Means for Digital Inclusion.* https://www.mobilebeacon.org/wp-content/uploads/2017/05/MB_ResearchPaper_FINAL_WEB.pdf

2005. Telecommunications Reports (TR) 71, no. 12 (June 15, 2005).

2008. Telecommunications Reports (TR) 74, no. 22 (November 15, 2008).

Tomer, Adie, Elizabeth Kneebone, and Ranjitha Shivaram. 2017. "Signs of Digital Distress: Mapping Broadband Availability and Subscription in American Neighborhoods." Washington, DC: Brookings Institution.

United States Census Bureau. 2019. "Current Population Survey: CPS 2019; Non-Response Rates." https://www.census.gov/programs-surveys/cps/technical-documentation/methodology/non-response-rates.html

United States Census Bureau. 2019a. "When to Use 1-Year, 3-Year, or 5-Year Estimates." https://www.census.gov/programs-surveys/acs/guidance/estimates.html

United States Census Bureau. 2019b. "American Community Survey Response Rates." https://www.census.gov/acs/www/methodology/sample-size-and-data-quality/response-rates/

3

Using Random Experiments to Measure the Impact of Computers, the Internet, and Other Forms of Technology on Educational Outcomes

ROBERT FAIRLIE

INTRODUCTION

As events during the pandemic so aptly demonstrated, access to computers, the Internet, and other forms of technology is not evenly distributed across the population; large disparities exist across countries and by income and race (NTIA 2016; OECD 2015; Bulman and Fairlie 2016). Do these disparities in access to computers and technology—known as the Digital Divide—contribute to educational inequality, even without the need for distance learning? Computers and the Internet are clearly useful for word processing, research, spreadsheets, and other educational software, but they are also distracting because of games, social networking, and other entertainment use and potentially crowd out other more effective forms of teaching. A better understanding of the extent to which

Robert Fairlie, *Using Random Experiments to Measure the Impact of Computers, the Internet, and Other Forms of Technology on Educational Outcomes* In: *Transforming Everything?*. Edited by: Karen Mossberger, Eric W. Welch, and Yonghong Wu, Oxford University Press. © Oxford University Press 2022. DOI: 10.1093/oso/9780190082871.003.0004 computers, the Internet, and other forms of technology have an effect on educational outcomes is critical, because it sheds light on whether and which types of technology are important inputs in the educational production process and whether disparities in access to technology will translate into educational inequality.

This chapter examines the methodological approaches used to study the question of whether computers, the Internet, and other forms of technology improve educational outcomes. The question poses a difficult empirical challenge. The bulk of research in the literature uses multivariate regression analysis to control for differences in school, teacher, student, family, and/or parental characteristics. However, if the most educationally motivated students and families are the ones who are the most likely to purchase computers, then a positive relationship between academic performance and home computers may simply capture the effect of unmeasurable motivation on academic performance. The children may have done better in school even in the absence of the home computer because of the value placed on educational achievement.[1]

Because of concerns regarding the potential for selection bias, a relatively new literature uses random experiments to examine the educational impacts of computers and the Internet. Additionally, early 21st-century studies use quasi-experimental approaches such as natural experiments and regression discontinuity designs (RDDs) to estimate educational impacts. I review the literature using these approaches and also discuss each of the methodologies along with their strengths and weaknesses. I focus on studies that examine whether home computers have educational impacts, but the methodological discussion is clearly relevant for identifying the impacts of other forms of technology.

ESTIMATING THE IMPACTS OF HOME COMPUTERS

The use of computers in US schools is now universal and has been studied extensively, but the role of computer technology at home is not well understood.[2] A small but growing literature examines the impacts of home computers and Internet access on educational outcomes. To identify the educational effects of home computers, the starting empirical approach has been to regress educational outcomes on the presence of a home computer controlling for detailed student, family, and parental characteristics. Studies using this approach generally find relatively large positive effects of home computers on educational outcomes (Attewell and Battle 1999; Fairlie 2005; Schmitt and Wadsworth 2006; Beltran, Das, and Fairlie 2010), although there is some evidence of negative effects (Fuchs and Woessmann 2004). In some cases these controls include prior educational attainment, difficult-to-find detailed characteristics of the educational environment in the household, and extracurricular activities of the student (Attewell and Battle 1999; Schmitt and Wadsworth 2006; Beltran, Das, and Fairlie 2010; Fiorini 2010). However, these estimates of the effects of home computers on educational outcomes may still be biased due to omitted variables, as already noted.

There are more advanced statistical techniques to control for these differences. A few studies have investigated this issue using instrumental variable techniques, future computer ownership, falsification tests, or individual-student fixed effects. Estimates from bivariate probits for the joint probability of an educational outcome and computer ownership reveal large positive estimates (Fairlie 2005; Beltran, Das, and Fairlie 2008). Use of computers and the Internet at work by the child's mother and father, the presence of another teenager in the household, and the metropolitan statistical area (MSA) level home computer rate are used as excluded variables. Another approach first taken by Schmidt and Wadsworth (2006) is to include future computer ownership in the educational outcome regression. A positive estimate of future computer ownership on educational attainment would raise suspicions that current ownership proxies for an unobserved factor, such as educational motivation. Future computer ownership, however, is not found to have a positive relationship with educational outcomes similar to the positive relationship found for contemporaneous computer ownership (Schmidt and Wadsworth 2006; Beltran, Das, and Fairlie 2010). Related to this approach, Beltran, Das, and Fairlie (2010) also do not find evidence of a positive relationship between educational attainment and having a dictionary at home or cable television, which also might be correlated with unobserved educational motivation.

A possible concern with these types of analyses is that there might be unobservable differences between households that have computers and those that do not (mainly due to selection). The literature has addressed these concerns using fixed effect models, RDDs, and other quasi-experimental approaches. The inclusion of individual student fixed effects controls for differences in unobservable characteristics of students that do not change over time. Vigdor and Ladd (2014) use fixed effects models with panel data from North Carolina public schools and find modestly sized negative effects of home computer access and local-area access to high-speed Internet connections on math and reading test scores. An important finding in Vigdor and Ladd (2014) is that the estimated relationship turns negative when fixed effects are included. Beltran, Das, and Fairlie (2010) also estimate specifications with fixed effects and find smaller positive estimates that lose significance.

Malamud and Pop-Eleches (2011) address the endogeneity problem (or problem with unobservable differences) with a RDD based on the effects of a government program in Romania that allocated a fixed number of vouchers for computers to low-income children in public schools. In the RDD, schoolchildren just below the income threshold for eligibility for a computer voucher are compared to schoolchildren just above the income threshold (who do not qualify for a computer voucher). The two groups of schoolchildren close to threshold have nearly identical characteristics and differ only in their eligibility for the computer voucher. Estimates from the discontinuity created by the allocation of computer vouchers by a ranking of family income indicate that Romanian children winning vouchers have lower grades, but higher cognitive ability and better computer skills. Thus, the children did worse in school, but did experience some other benefits.

Another approach taken is to create a quasi-experiment in which a matched control group is created to look similar to the treatment group. This approach was taken in the evaluation of the Texas laptop program (Texas Center for Educational Research 2009).[3] Schools included in the control group were selected that matched twenty-one treatment schools as closely as possible on several factors, including district and campus size, regional location, proportion of economically disadvantaged and minority students, and percentage and minority/nonminority student gaps in passing all Texas Assessment of Knowledge and Skills (TAKS) tests. Using the list of control schools one school was chosen as the optimal match for each treatment school in the study. The laptop program was found to have some positive effects on educational outcomes.

Random Experiments

Randomized control experiments are also used to control for differences in unobservable characteristics related to having home computers. In a randomized control experiment students are randomly assigned computers, creating a source of variation in computer ownership that is truly exogenous and uncorrelated with any student characteristic, such as motivation to go online. The treatment and control groups of students, assuming that there is a large enough sample size, will be essentially identical along all characteristics of students. Thus, differences in educational outcomes must be the result of the randomized provision of computers.

A few studies in the literature have used random experiments to study the effects of home computers on educational outcomes. The first random experiment involving the provision of free computers to students for home use was Fairlie and London (2012). The random-assignment evaluation was conducted with 286 entering students receiving financial aid at a large community college in Northern California. Half of the participating students were randomly selected to receive free computers and all students were followed for two years. The findings from the experiment indicate that the treatment group of students receiving free computers had modestly better educational outcomes than the control group along a few measures. Estimates for a summary index of educational outcomes indicate that the treatment group is 0.14 standard deviations higher than the control group mean. Students living farther from campus and students who have jobs may have benefitted more from home computers. It makes sense that these groups might benefit more because the home computers improve flexibility and total time of potential use of computers for schoolwork.

The experimental estimates are also compared to non-experimental estimates from matching the October 2007 and 2009 Computer and Internet Supplements from the Current Population Survey (CPS) to the Education and Enrollment Supplements to the CPS one year later. Estimates of the effect of home computers using the CPS are much larger than the range of estimates from the experiment. These findings justify concerns that there might be positive selection in computer ownership and that non-experimental estimates may overstate the effects of home computers on educational outcomes.

Fairlie and Robinson (2013) also conducted a randomized control experiment. The study involved 1,123 students in grades six to ten attending fifteen schools across California. It was the first experiment involving the provision of free computers to schoolchildren for home use and the largest experiment involving the provision of free home computers to students at any level. All of the schoolchildren participating in the study did not have computers at baseline. Half were randomly selected to receive free computers, while the other half served as the control group.

The results from the experiment showed that even though there was a large effect on computer ownership and total hours of computer use, there is no evidence of an effect on a host of educational outcomes, including grades, standardized test scores, credits earned, attendance, and disciplinary actions. No effects are found at the mean, important cutoffs in the distribution (e.g., passing and proficiency), or quantiles in the distribution. The estimates are precise enough to rule out even moderately sized positive or negative effects. Evidence from a detailed follow-up survey supports these findings. We find no evidence that treatment students spent more or less time on homework, and we find that the computers had no effect on turning homework in on time, software use, computer knowledge, and other intermediate inputs in education. The pattern of time usage is also consistent with a negligible effect of the computers— while treatment students did report spending more time on computers for schoolwork, they also spent more time on games, social networking, and other entertainment. Finally, we find no evidence of heterogeneous treatment effects by pretreatment academic achievement, parental supervision, propensity for non-game use, or major demographic group. Overall, these results suggest that increasing access to home computers among students who do not already have access is unlikely to greatly improve educational outcomes but is also unlikely to negatively affect outcomes. Simply providing a computer does not appear to be enough to make big changes in educational outcomes. Perhaps more integration with classwork might tip the balance to net positive effects.

Random experiments have also been used to examine the impacts of one laptop per child (OLPC) laptops on educational outcomes in developing countries.[4] Beuermann et al. (2012) examine the impacts of randomly providing approximately one thousand laptops for home use to schoolchildren in grades one through six in Peru.[5] They find that the laptops have a positive but small and insignificant effect on cognitive skills as measured by the Raven's Progressive Matrices test (though the effect is significant among children who did not already have a home computer before the experiment). Teachers reported that the effort exerted in school was significantly lower for treatment students than control students, and that treated children reported reading books, stories, or magazines less than control children. Mo et al. (2013) randomly distribute OLPC laptops to roughly half of a sample of three hundred young schoolchildren (grade three) in China.[6] They find some evidence that the laptops improved math test scores but no evidence of effects on Chinese tests. They also find that the laptops increased learning activity use of computers and decreased time spent watching television.

Strengths of Random Experiments

The use of random experiments to evaluate the educational impacts of computers, Internet access, or any other technology has several strengths and weaknesses. In conducting two random experiments on the educational impacts of home computers I have studied the question extensively

and have received substantial feedback on my experiments. I will, however, use the evaluation of the introduction of any type of home or personal technology (i.e., computer, Internet, broadband, iPad, smart phone,
etc.) as the example for the discussion. The main and obvious strength
of random experiments is that the random assignment of a technology
to students eliminates most concerns about selection of that technology.
Students and their families who receive the technology (treatment group)
or do not receive the technology (control group) will be nearly identical
in their characteristics because of the random assignment. This removes
concerns that unobservable differences, especially educational motivation, that are correlated with technology ownership bias estimates of the
effects of the technology on educational outcomes. Because of their high
level of internal validity, random experiments are sometimes referred to as
the "gold standard" in the evaluation literature.

One of the first goals of most random experiment evaluations is to
conduct a balance check to verify that the randomization created similar treatment and control groups. Usually student and family characteristics collected before randomization from administrative data or baseline
surveys are compared. Unless sample sizes are small, randomization
usually leads to very similar groups measured by mean baseline characteristics. With larger sample sizes one often finds a few characteristics
that have statistically significant mean differences, but the magnitude of
these differences is small, and we expect to find one or two significant
differences by chance given standard levels of significance. In any case,
when estimating treatment effects it is common to present results both
without covariates as well as with controls for a large set of detailed baseline characteristics.

Another major advantage of conducting a random experiment is that
the analysis of data is straightforward, essentially relying on a comparison
of differences in means or the distribution of educational outcomes between the treatment and control groups. The econometric analysis does
not require a large number of assumptions about error distributions and
functional form. Although regression analysis is commonly used to estimate adjusted differences, only standard and commonly used techniques

such as Ordinary Least Squares (OLS) or probit models and not more sophisticated techniques are typically used to estimate impacts. Because the
random assignment creates essentially identical treatment and control
groups, the inclusion of controls typically does not change the estimates
from mean differences, although in many cases the estimates are more
precise.

Although random experiments have many advantages, the approach
also has several disadvantages and concerns that need to be carefully
considered. I discuss several potential problems with conducting a random
experiment to evaluate the impacts of a technology. The list is not intended
to be exhaustive but instead is intended to point out the main concerns in
conducting an experiment to evaluate the educational impacts of a new
technology. An excellent discussion of the random experiment approach
in the broader setting is Duflo, Gennerster, and Kremer (2007).

Applicability, Expense, and Political Feasibility

Perhaps the major weakness of using random experiments is that they
can only be applied in certain settings and thus can only answer a limited range of research questions. Although random experiments can be
used to evaluate the educational effects of having a home computer or a
broadband connection, they cannot be used to evaluate many other important and policy-relevant questions. For example, they cannot be used
to examine how a nationwide program providing free computers, Internet
service, or broadband connections to all poor schoolchildren changes
computer use at home, in schools, and among parents. There are many
interrelated effects of changing access to technology at such a broad scale
that cannot be examined with focused experiments.

Random experiments also tend to be very expensive. If a computer or
broadband connection for a year costs $500, generating a sample size of
one thousand students for the experiment would cost $500,000. Unless the
technology is very inexpensive it is often difficult to generate the sample
size needed to find significant effects. In some cases power calculations

based on previous estimates from the literature might suggest substantially larger sample sizes than are affordable by the researcher.

Related to high costs, random experiments often take a long time to implement and gather data. It is not uncommon for a random experiment to take several years from design to data analysis. This could be especially problematic in evaluating rapidly changing technologies.

Random experiments are also not always politically feasible. Often foundations, schools, principals, and teachers would prefer to allocate computers or other technology by need or perceived usefulness. Although researchers often make the argument that randomization is the fairest of all possible allocation methods, practitioners often disagree and prefer to allocate based on income, previous achievement, likely benefits, or another method. Also the inherent need to deny some students the technology in the experiment is often viewed negatively by practitioners. There is also the view that randomly allocating something makes others worse off. In many cases, the researchers bring something new and valuable to disadvantaged students so that no one is made worse off and some are made better off, but this argument does not always work. These issues pose serious problems for researchers, and practitioner concerns need to be addressed carefully and sensitively.

External Validity: Generalizability of Findings

Another major concern of random experiments is the ability of researchers to generalize their results. Often experiments are conducted in narrow and restricted settings to minimize costs, time, administrative burden, and finding participants. They are often conducted in one or a few neighborhoods, cities, or schools and with one or a few age or grade groups. All of these choices affect the external validity of the findings. For example, if an experiment is conducted with students from a wealthy school then the results might not be generalizable to students from poorer schools where technology is used less. In many cases, however, the study is conducted with the group of most interest. For example, many studies focus on students attending low-income, ethnically diverse schools that are exactly the ones most likely to enroll schoolchildren without home computers and be targeted by policies to address inequalities in access to technology (e.g., the E-rate program and individual development accounts (IDAs).

Random experiments also generally have specific participation rules and requirements. For example, in studying the effects of home computers on educational outcomes it is useful to restrict participation to students not having a computer at home. Restricting participation to non-computer owners, however, implies that estimates from an experiment capture the impact of computers on the educational outcomes of schoolchildren whose parents do not buy them on their own and do not necessarily capture the impact of computers for existing computer owners. Schoolchildren without home computers, however, are the population of interest in considering policies to expand access. It would also essentially be impossible to study the effects of having computers for schoolchildren who already have them at home, because the experiment would require removing access to computers.

Participation in a random experiment also implicitly implies some selection, because it is usually voluntary and requires signing up. For example, experiments involving schoolchildren often require students to take home a form, have parents sign it, and bring it back to school. This process creates cases in which students do not participate because they lose or do not bring home fliers for the experiment, their parents do not provide consent to be in the study, or they do not want a computer. Thus, participating students will likely be more interested in receiving computers than non-participating students, affecting the generalizability of the results. But, note that this would also be the case in a real-world voucher or giveaway program.

Another factor affecting the ability to generalize the results is what the specific intervention involves. The results from an evaluation of a new technology that also includes an intervention with some training on how to use the technology do not necessarily generalize to the case where only the new technology is introduced without any training. If the focus of the research project is to estimate the impacts of home computers on educational outcomes and not to evaluate a more intensive technology policy intervention, then no training or assistance should be provided with the technology given in the experiment. Of course, using a much larger random experiment including multiple treatment groups with and without the additional training intervention could be examined, but the costs might be prohibitively expensive. The fundamental tradeoff is between having more power to evaluate a specific policy and being able to evaluate multiple policies.

Overall, it is very important to think carefully about what the intervention is and whether it lines up closely with the research question (i.e., give out free computers and evaluate effects of having home computers), what group the results of the experiment are relevant for (i.e., students without computers and who want one instead of students who already have computers or do not want a computer), and whether participating rules for being in the experiment do not limit the ability to generalize the results to other interesting demographic and ability groups.

Partial Compliance

Another issue that usually needs to be addressed in random experiments is the potential problem of partial compliance in the treatment and control groups. For example, some of the students in the treatment group might not pick up their free computers or sign up for free broadband, and some of the students in the control group will purchase their own computers or broadband on their own during the study period. Estimates of mean differences that do not adjust for noncompliance with the experiment are often referred to as capturing the "intent-to-treat" from the experiment.

The intent-to-treat estimates are relevant for potential policy conclusions drawn from the results. Any technology giveaway or price subsidization program will likely not experience full compliance. There will always be some students in the treatment group who do not participate in a program even though they showed initial interest. The control group also cannot be prevented from purchasing the technology on their own during the study period. This problem of the control group receiving an intervention that potentially has the same effect as the treatment intervention is a similar problem in most social experiments. But, often the researcher is also interested in estimating the effects of the student having access to the technology on educational outcomes. This is sometimes referred to as the "local average treatment effect" (LATE) estimate and is different than the estimate of the effects of the giveaway or subsidization program, which is captured in the intent-to-treat estimates.

In most random experiments, instrumental variable (IV) techniques and information gleaned from a follow-up survey can be used to adjust the estimates for noncompliance and recover the LATE estimate of having the technology. For example, a follow-up survey conducted near the end of the survey period provides information on whether the treatment group still has their free computer and whether the control group purchased their own computer. To implement the IV technique, a first-stage regression of having a computer at follow-up is regressed on treatment status and baseline controls. A second-stage regression of the educational outcome on the predicted value for follow-up computer ownership and baseline controls is estimated to recover the LATE parameter. The IV estimator estimates the effects of having a home computer on educational outcomes using the exogenous variation created by the random experiment. The LATE estimate is a scaled-up version of the original intent-to-treat estimate based on the rates of compliance in the treatment and control groups.

Although noncompliance with the experiment does not affect the intent-to-treat estimates and IV techniques can be used to generate LATE estimates, overall noncompliance essentially weakens the ability to detect treatment-control differences in educational outcomes. Take, for example, the extreme case where everyone in the treatment group does not pick up the technology or everyone in the control group purchases the technology on their own—the estimated effect of the technology will be zero, even if there is an underlying effect. More generally, noncompliance weakens estimation precision.

Differential and Non-Random Attrition on Follow-Up Surveys

In many cases random experiments rely on follow-up surveys to provide information on educational outcomes. In this case, there might be differential (treatment vs. control group) and non-random attrition. Many students do not respond to the follow-up survey, with studies often experiencing a higher response rate among the treatment group than the control group. Although this does not necessarily imply that estimates from the experiment are biased, it is an important issue that needs to be addressed. The main concern is that the students who do not respond to the survey are the ones that benefit the most or the least from the technology. If this is the case, then the effects of the technology are only estimated with the group responding to the follow-up survey and are biased. If attrition is large then this could lead to a high level of bias in the estimates.

One way to address this problem is to obtain administrative data that covers all students. The use of school-provided administrative data on grades and other educational outcomes typically eliminates problems with students not responding to follow-up surveys. Administrative data, however, are not always possible to obtain; in most cases every effort possible should be made with the research budget to reduce attrition from the sample.

To examine how serious a problem attrition is for the estimates a couple of straightforward techniques can be used. First, a dummy variable for whether the student drops out or not can be regressed on all baseline controls to determine if attrition appears to be random or is related to certain student characteristics. If there is some relationship between follow-up survey attrition and student characteristics then two-stage regressions can be estimated in which the second-stage regression includes the predicted probability of attrition as a sample weight. This technique places more weight on "survivors" who look like "attriters," in an attempt to compensate for the attriters' absence. These estimates are often compared to the original estimates to determine sensitivity to attrition. Another technique that can be used is a bounds analysis using various assumptions about the treatment effects for attriters (see Horowitz and Manski 2000 and Lee 2002, 2009).[7] In all of these cases, however, the technique does not fix the problem; they are essentially useful diagnostics for determining how much attrition might be a problem for the main estimates.

Hawthorne and John Henry Effects

As with any random experiment, there exists the possibility that the treatment group has a positive outcome partly because the interest being shown in them by researchers through the experiment leads to a change in their behavior (i.e., Hawthorne effect). This might be of special concern for any self-reported measures on follow-up surveys in which the cost of exaggerating an educational outcome is relatively small. The possibility of Hawthorne effects may be much smaller for grades or graduating with a degree, because these take more effort and are not self-reported. A related issue is that the control group, knowing about their participation in an experiment, might work harder or less hard than otherwise because of participation in the experiment (i.e., John Henry effect).

To reduce these problems researchers can minimize contact with study participants. Handouts of free computers or other technology can be done by other organizations and not by the research team. Surveys can be done by mail, email, or through school packets instead of in-person interviews by research staff. In most cases, no direct contact is required between researchers and students participating in the study. Students participating in the study also do not need to be told that they are specifically going to be compared to other students. Finally, the overall design of the questionnaire and wording of questions should be done to not encourage students to misrepresent educational outcomes. For example, the word "experiment" does not need to be included in the title or any questions on the follow-up survey form.

Opening Up the "Black Box"

Another potential limitation of random experiments is that they cannot always provide direct or even indirect evidence on the underlying causes or mechanisms of an effect of technology on educational outcomes. Usually the first-order priority of an experiment is to evaluate the overall effects of the technology. Additional resources are needed to conduct experiments that directly evaluate underlying mechanisms. In many cases such experiments are very difficult to implement. For example, in studying the impacts of broadband on educational outcomes it might be useful to know whether any positive or negative effects are due to the types of web pages examined (i.e., educational vs. entertainment based). Although information can be collected on the type of web pages examined at follow-up, the only way to directly evaluate the independent effects of the two mechanisms is to create a second treatment group and somehow restrict the broadband use for this group. Restricting website access in this way may be extremely difficult and, of course, more resources will be needed to create additional treatment groups. As already noted, there is a tradeoff between increasing the power to test the main hypothesis and creating multiple treatment groups.

One method of examining different mechanisms is to examine impacts of technology for different subgroups.[8] There are many ways to do this, but often differences in baseline characteristics are used to identify mechanisms. For example, the positive effects of the educational use of broadband might be more prominent for students who already use the Internet extensively to conduct research for school essays. The finding of a positive relative effect for this group is consistent with broadband use for research representing an important mechanism underlying a positive effect of broadband on educational outcomes. Ideally, the distinction between subgroups of students is identified using information from a baseline survey conducted prior to the experiment. In practice, however, suggestive evidence from estimating separate treatment effects for subgroups identified from the follow-up survey is sometimes reported.

Another method is to create multiple treatment groups. For example, to better understand whether computers or specific educational software affects educational outcomes, a random experiment could include a treatment group that only receives a home computer (no special educational software), a second treatment group that receives a home computer and the special educational software, and a control group that receives neither. In this case, a comparison of the two treatment groups provides a method of identifying the effects of the educational software. But creating multiple treatment groups comes at a price. Each additional treatment group reduces statistical power to test hypotheses given a fixed total sample size (because of budget restrictions).

CONCLUSION

Random experiments are useful for examining the impacts of computer, Internet access, and other technology access on the educational outcomes of students. For example, the approach has been used to estimate the impacts of home computers on educational outcomes in a few different settings. Although the strengths of random experiments such as controlling for unobservables (i.e., external validity) and straightforwardness are well known, they also suffer from several weaknesses that need to be considered carefully. These concerns include applicability, costs, time constraints, political feasibility, external validity, attrition, compliance, Hawthorne effects, and understanding mechanisms. Addressing these concerns with experimental design, econometric analysis, and careful interpretation of results, there is much promise for the implementation of random experiments in the evaluation of the impacts of computers, the Internet, and new technologies. With random experiments, we can be more certain that the effects that we see are related to the variable of interest—technology use. The ability to use random experiments to evaluate the effects of new technologies is also not limited to impacts on educational outcomes but has broader applicability to study technology impacts on labor market, health, political, economic, and other outcomes.

NOTES

1. It may instead be the case that the least educationally motivated students and families (after controlling for individual and family characteristics) are the ones that purchase computers, perhaps due to their entertainment value or because they substitute for more traditional and time-consuming forms of learning.
2. A larger and more established literature examines the impacts of computers and computer-assisted software in schools (where use is regulated by teachers, and schools typically make decisions over investment) and finds somewhat mixed results ranging from null to large positive impacts. For example, see Kirkpatrick and Cuban (1998) and Noll et al. (2000) for earlier reviews of the literature. For more recent evidence on computer impacts in schools see Barrera-Osorio and Linden (2009) and Cristia et al. (2012). For evidence on the effects of ICT expenditures and subsidies to schools see Goolsbee and Guryan (2006) and Machin, McNally, and Silva (2007). For evidence on computer-assisted software in schools see Angrist and Lavy (2002); Banerjee et al. (2007); Barrow, Markman, and Rouse (2009); and Carrillo, Onofa, and Ponce (2010).
3. Although the Texas laptop program was initially intended to allow students to take computers home when needed in addition to using them in school, this did not happen in most cases. Damage and theft concerns resulted in many schools not allowing computers to be taken home or restricting their home use. The main effect from this laptop program is therefore to provide one computer for every student in the classroom, rather than to increase home access.
4. Although the one laptop per child program in Peru (Cristia et al. 2012) and the Texas laptop program (evaluated with a quasi-experiment in Texas Center for Educational Research 2009) were initially intended to allow students to take computers home when needed in addition to using them in school, this did not happen in most cases. In Peru, some principals, and even parents, did not allow the computers to come home because of concerns that the laptops would not be replaced through the program if they were damaged or stolen. The result is that only 40 percent of students took the laptops home, and home use was substantially lower than in-school use. In Texas, there were similar concerns resulting in many schools not allowing computers to be taken home or restricting their home use. The main effect from these laptop programs is therefore to provide one computer for every student in the classroom, rather than to increase home access.
5. Recipients of the laptops were also provided with an instruction manual and seven weekly training sessions.
6. The laptops included some tutoring software and one training session was provided.
7. One method following Kling, Liebman, and Katz (2007), Karlan and Valdivia (2011), and Fairlie, Karlan, and Zinman (2015) is to impute to the lower (upper) bound the mean minus (plus) a specified standard deviation multiple of the observed treatment group distribution to the non-responders in the treatment group, and the mean plus (minus) the same standard deviation multiple of the observed control group distribution to non-responders in the control group. A conservative

treatment effect estimate, for example, can be calculated by assuming that treatment group attriters have the mean value for the dependent variable minus 0.05 standard deviations among non-attriting treatment observations, and that the control group attriters have the mean value for the dependent variable plus 0.05 standard deviations among the non-attriting control observations.

8. There is a danger, however, in estimating treatment effects for many subgroups from the total sample in finding a significant treatment effect that is due to chance.

REFERENCES

Angrist, J., and Lavy, V. 2002. "New Evidence on Classroom Computers and Pupil Learning." *Economic Journal* 112: 735–765.

Attewell, P., and Battle, J. 1999. "Home Computers and School Performance." *The Information Society* 15: 1–10.

Banerjee, A., Cole, S., Duflo, E., and Linden, L. 2007. "Remedying Education: Evidence from Two Randomized Experiments in India." *Quarterly Journal of Economics* 122 (3): 1235–1264.

Barrera-Osorio, F., and Linden, L. L. 2009. "The Use and Misuse of Computers in Education: Evidence from a Randomized Experiment in Colombia." Policy Research Working Paper 4836, Impact Evaluation Series 29. Washington, DC: The World Bank.

Barrow, L., Markman, L., and Rouse, C. E. 2009. "Technology's Edge: The Educational Benefits of Computer-Aided Instruction." *American Economic Journal: Economic Policy* 1 (1): 52–74.

Beltran, D. O., Das, K.K., and Fairlie, R. W. 2010. "Home Computers and Educational Outcomes: Evidence from the NLSY97 and CPS." *Economic Inquiry* 48 (3): 771–792.

Beuermann, D. W., Cristia, J. P., Cruz-Aguayo, Y., Cueto, S., and Malamud, O. 2012. "Home Computers and Child Outcomes: Short-Term Impacts from a Randomized Experiment in Peru." Inter-American Development Bank Working Paper No. IDB-WP-382. Washington, DC: Inter-American Development Bank.

Bulman, G., and Fairlie, R. W. 2016. "Technology and Education: Computers, Software, and the Internet." In *Handbook of the Economics of Education*. Vol. 5. Edited by Eric Hanushek, Steve Machin, and Ludger Woessmann, 239–280. Amsterdam: North-Holland Elsevier.

Carrillo, P., Onofa, M., and Ponce, J. 2010. "Information Technology and Student Achievement: Evidence from a Randomized Experiment in Ecuador." Inter-American Development Bank Working Paper. Washington, DC.

Cristia, J. P., Ibarraran, P., Cueto, S., Santiago, A., and Severin, E. 2012. "Technology and Child Development: Evidence from the One Laptop Per Child Program." Inter-American Development Bank Working Paper No. IDB-WP-304. Washington, DC: Inter-American Development Bank.

Duflo, E., Glennerster, R., and Kremer, M. (2007). "Using Randomization in Development Economics Research: A Toolkit." *Handbook of Development Economics*, 4, 3895–3962.

Fairlie, R. W. 2004. "Race and the Digital Divide." *The B. E. Journal of Economic Analysis & Policy* 3 (1): 1–38.

Fairlie, R. W. 2005. "The Effects of Home Computers on School Enrollment." *Economics of Education Review* 24 (5): 533–547.

Fairlie, R. W., Karlan, D., and Zinman, J. (2015). "Behind the GATE Experiment: Evidence on Effects of and Rationales for Subsidized Entrepreneurship Training." *American Economic Journal: Economic Policy,* 7 (2): 125–61.

Fairlie, R. W., and London, R. A. 2012. "The Effects of Home Computers on Educational Outcomes: Evidence from a Field Experiment with Community College Students." *Economic Journal* 122 (561): 727–753.

Fairlie, R. W., and Robinson, J. 2013. "Experimental Evidence on the Effects of Home Computers on Academic Achievement among Schoolchildren." *American Economic Journal: Applied Economics* 5 (3): 211–240.

Fiorini, M. 2010. "The Effect of Home Computer Use on Children's Cognitive and Non-Cognitive Skills." *Economics of Education Review* 29: 55–72.

Fuchs, T., and Woessmann, L. 2004. "Computers and Student Learning: Bivariate and Multivariate Evidence on the Availability and Use of Computers at Home and at School." CESifo Working Paper No. 1321. Munich: Center for Economic Studies.

Goolsbee, A., and Guryan, J. 2006. "The Impact of Internet Subsidies in Public Schools." *The Review of Economics and Statistics* 88 (2): 336–347.

Horowitz, J., and Manski, C. 2000. "Nonparametric Analysis of Randomized Experiments with Missing Covariate and Outcome Data." *Journal of the American Statistical Association* 95 (449): 77–84.

Karlan, D., and Valdivia, M. 2011. "Teaching Entrepreneurship: Impact of Business Training on Microfinance Clients and Institutions." *Review of Economics and Statistics* 93 (2): 510–527.

Kirkpatrick, H., and Cuban, L. 1998. "Computers Make Kids Smarter—Right?" *Technos Quarterly for Education and Technology* 7: 2.

Kling, Jeffrey R., Liebman, J. B., and Katz, L. F. 2007. "Experimental Analysis of Neighborhood Effects." *Econometrica* 75 (1): 83–119.

Lee, D. S. 2002. "Trimming for Bounds on Treatment Effects with Missing Outcomes." NBER Technical Working Paper 277. Cambridge, MA: National Bureau of Economic Research.

Lee, D. S. 2009. "Training, Wages, and Sample Selection: Estimating Sharp Bounds on Treatment Effects." *Review of Economic Studies* 76: 1071–1102.

Machin, S., McNally, S., and Silva, O. 2007. "New Technology in Schools: Is There a Payoff?" *Economic Journal* 117 (522): 1145–1167.

Malamud, O., and Pop-Eleches, C. 2011. "Home Computer Use and the Development of Human Capital." *Quarterly Journal of Economics* 126: 987–1027.

Mo, D., Swinnen, J., Zhang, L., Yi, H., Qu, Q., Boswell, M., and Rozelle, S. (2013). "Can One-to-One Computing Narrow the Digital Divide and the Educational Gap in China? The Case of Beijing Migrant Schools." *World Development,* 46, 14–29.

National Telecommunications and Information Administration (NTIA). 2016. "Digital Nation Data Explorer." https://www.ntia.doc.gov/other-publication/2016/digital-nation-data-explorer

Noll, R. G., Older-Aguilar, D., Rosston, G. L., and Ross, R. R. 2000. "The Digital
    Divide: Definitions, Measurement, and Policy Issues." Paper presented at Bridging
    the Digital Divide: California Public Affairs Forum, Stanford University, May
    1. Stanford, CA.

OECD. 2015. "Students, Computers and Learning: Making the Connection." https://
    www.oecd-ilibrary.org/docserver/9789264239555-en.pdf?expires=1546728675&id=i
    d&accname=guest&checksum=3538B94507D0BFF8C672703DE9E816FD

Schmitt, J., and Wadsworth, J. 2006. "Is There an Impact of Household Computer
    Ownership on Children's Educational Attainment in Britain?" *Economics of Education
    Review* 25: 659–673.

Texas Center for Educational Research. 2009. *Evaluation of the Texas Technology
    Immersion Pilot: Final Outcomes for a Four-Year Study (2004–05 to 2007–08)*. Austin,
    TX: Texas Center for Educational Research.

Vigdor, J. L., Ladd, H. F., and Martinez, E. 2014. "Scaling the Digital Divide: Home
    Computer Technology and Student Achievement." *Economic Inquiry* 52 (3): 1103–1119.

4

Broadband Adoption and Ethnographic Approaches

JESSICA CROWELL

INTRODUCTION

In the fall of 2013, I sat in a faded fabric chair in Sammy's small office, which features one glass window overlooking the streets of central Philadelphia. It would be our final meeting; Sammy had taken a job in a new city, and I was approaching the end of my assignment. I had spent over two years in the health advocacy organization in which Sammy worked, conducting ethnographic fieldwork at the center's computer lab—called a "KEYSPOT"—down the hall. These KEYSPOTs were made possible by two federal Broadband Technology Opportunity Program (BTOP) grants, part of a $7 billion federal initiative to develop broadband infrastructure in the US in the wake of the Great Recession of 2008. The KEYSPOT project was a joint venture of the "Freedom Rings Partnership," a collective that included the City of Philadelphia, the Urban Affairs Coalition, universities, and dozens of community-based organizations. The broader aim of the KEYSPOT program was to serve low-income residents of Philadelphia who were without broadband access or computer skills.

As I scribbled notes into a small book, Sammy reflected on his experience coordinating digital work skills training programs throughout

Jessica Crowell, *Broadband Adoption and Ethnographic Approaches* In: *Transforming Everything?*. Edited by: Karen Mossberger, Eric W. Welch, and Yonghong Wu, Oxford University Press. © Oxford University Press 2022. DOI: 10.1093/oso/9780190082871.003.0005

Philadelphia's KEYSPOTS over the past several years. He explained that although their site had exceeded their "numbers," connecting hundreds of patrons to new jobs, he had begun to question the benchmarks that were being used to evaluate programmatic success and participant outcomes. As an illustration of the deeper concerns he had with the process of BTOP evaluation, Sammy brought up a participant, Dinah, who had recently obtained a job through the KEYSPOTs program. Sammy explained that although Dinah would likely be featured as a KEYSPOT "success story" in an upcoming partnership meeting, her story was more complicated.

To expand on Dinah's story, Sammy called Dinah a "regular" because she visited the lab several times a week, typically on a predictable schedule. Like many participants in Broadband Technology Opportunities Program (BTOP)–funded computer centers and digital training programs across the US, Dinah visited KEYSPOTs to build her digital skills in pursuit of a job. After months of searching, Dinah finally achieved her goal and began work as a security guard in a local hospital. However, to Sammy's surprise, Dinah soon reappeared at the KEYSPOT computer lab. Sammy began to tell Dinah's story:

> So, [Dinah] got this job. Success story. Great. And she was working as—and presumably still is working—as a security guard for some kind of hospital or clinic or something that was open all night, and she needed to get a pay stub. And actually I should say she was working through a contracting company . . . all the universities for example, probably several thousands of jobs, and they are all subcontracted and undoubtedly [they are] paid less and have no unions and no benefits and no retirement. So, [Dinah needed the paystub] to apply for food stamps because despite all that, she is still not making enough money.

In his statement, Sammy explains that while on the surface Dinah is a KEYSPOT "success story" as she obtained a job, a deeper look reveals that this outcome does not offer route out of poverty. In addition to highlighting the structural inequalities that frame urban life in low-income communities, Dinah's story also reveals the challenges digital inequality researchers face in evaluating what "successful" broadband outcomes look like. How do we measure successful outcomes in the context of structural poverty and inequality? Which external factors and what community context should we consider when evaluating program impact?

While measuring outcomes raises important questions about how we conceptualize participant "success" in BTOP programs as outlined in the preceding paragraphs, there are similar complexities in unraveling the factors that shape individual attitudes toward Information Communication Technologies (ICTs). For example, Sammy later admitted that his personal attitudes on the potential of ICTs to change economic conditions in low-income communities had changed over the course of his time working at KEYSPOTs. Using Dinah's story to illustrate these complexities, in his statement Sammy points out the breakdown of durable support structures, like unions, that could have helped bargain and protect workers like Dinah; these structures have been weakened by this new shift to flexible arrangements in the digital information economy. Workers are increasingly isolated from each other. In Dinah's case, she works the night shift alone at a local hospital. As she was not provided Human Resources support from her employer, Dinah came back to the KEYSPOT lab to ask Sammy for help obtaining a paystub online. She needed this paystub so that she could apply—also online—for Supplemental Nutrition Assistance (SNAP).

Later in the same interview, Sammy wondered aloud if new technologies were expanding job prospects for working people in his community, or instead acting as a "tool to help lay off" and suppress wages. Yet, Sammy still emphasized that the programs were necessary and needed. It is important to note the nuance embedded in Sammy's attitudes toward ICTs. His opinions do not fit easily into a single category, and Sammy's attitudes also upend some traditional notions around the economic benefit of ICTs to low-income communities. Sammy likewise remarked that staff often felt pressure to provide straightforward, positive reports, fearing that painting a more complex portrait might starve the center of future funds. Like many other KEYSPOT staff members I interviewed throughout the course of my ethnographic research, Sammy felt pressure to focus on the economic impacts of digital programs, rather than the social, cultural, or political outcomes.

As background, the ethnographic data presented regarding Sammy and Dinah is taken from a larger three-year ethnographic study of the impact of digital access and training programs—or KEYSPOTs—in urban Philadelphia. These KEYSPOTs were made possible by two federal Broadband Technology Opportunity Program (BTOP) grants, one for public computing centers (PCC) and another for sustainable broadband adoption, namely digital training courses (SBA). Approximately four hundred hours of participant observation were completed between 2010 and 2013 in both the public computer centers and broadband adoption training programs. Additionally, eighteen semi-structured interviews were conducted with KEYSPOT program participants and staff, and 150 documents pertaining to the KEYSPOTs were collected and analyzed.[1] In adherence to Institutional Review Board (IRB) protocols, participant names and identifying details have all been changed to preserve confidentiality.[2]

The ethnographic portraits of Sammy and Dinah reveal the potential challenges facing research evaluation of digital training programs like KEYSPOTs serving low-income communities across urban America. Their stories also highlight the complex economic, social, and cultural factors that can shape participant attitudes, interactions, and outcomes with technology. These accounts are also notable, in that digital inequality scholarship has increasingly moved beyond a broadband access and skills literature toward a study of digital attitudes and the "tangible outcomes" of broadband access. However, much of this emerging research remains quantitative in nature and has not offered an extensive sociocultural explanation of why poor attitudes toward digital technology may endure in many marginalized communities, or why broadband outcomes remain stratified by class and race (Blank and Groselj 2015). Given its special attention to understanding everyday activities and sociocultural meanings, ethnographic research is especially well-suited to fill this research gap.

To provide more background on the methodology, ethnography examines social interactions, cultural practices, and local meanings through observing both actions and behaviors over time. To carefully study social practices and cultures, ethnographers conduct extensive field-work, often over many years. In addition to conducting interviews with participants, ethnographers make detailed notes of their observations and social interactions with their participants, or "fieldnotes." In its focus on utilizing semi-structured qualitative interviews—in conjunction with long-term participant observation—ethnographic research can also capture disparities between reported outcomes and actual behaviors. As ethnographic researchers are deeply engaged and trusted in their communities of study, they can also be permitted special insight into behaviors or practices that are ordinarily taboo. As an example, for this reason, urban ethnography has been recognized for its significant contributions to our understanding of unregulated and informal economies in low-income communities. This ability to capture potentially taboo practices or hidden behaviors further underscores ethnography's potential utility to digital inequality research, which is equally invested in the study of practices and behaviors in high-poverty and marginalized communities.

Whereas ethnographic research does not offer "generalizability" or a broad look at how digital inequalities may impact large populations, ethnographic portraits can offer a window into the ways in which policy, poverty, and digital technology intersect on the ground. This chapter first maps out existing research in the areas of digital outcomes and attitudes. Next, we turn to an exploration of ethnographic methodology, including detailing data collection practices and procedures. Finally, this chapter explores the unique contributions ethnographic research has made at the intersection of inequality, sociocultural practices, and ICTs. In offering needed sociocultural context to our understanding of digital attitudes and outcomes, ethnographic research can also help digital inequality researchers further refine research questions, create new categories of measurement, explore new research avenues and directions, and better map complex sociotechnical relationships.

UNDERSTANDING THE DIGITAL DIVIDE: SKILLS, ATTITUDES, AND OUTCOMES

Critical ethnographic research can offer an important contribution to emerging digital inequality scholarship, as this methodology provides a nuanced look at how sociocultural factors shape digital attitudes and broadband outcomes. In the first decades of the 21st century, there has been a shift in the digital inequality literature away from an access and skills framework, toward examining attitudes and "tangible outcomes" of ICTs. Because both social and cultural factors play a key role in shaping both Internet attitudes and outcomes, more qualitative research is needed to help us understand: (1) the range of factors that may impact personal attitudes, and (2) why some groups obtain more beneficial Internet outcomes than others. Given its special attention to detailing everyday activities, local cultures, and social meanings, critical ethnographic research is especially well-suited to fill this research gap. To build the foundation for this argument, this chapter first reviews previous digital divide research, tracing its origin from a focus on digital access to then examining digital skills and digital literacies. Second, the chapter summarizes current research that has revealed the role that individual attitudes play in shaping digital engagement, even as broadband rates have increased. Finally, we turn to scholarship that has focused on digital outcomes; notably, this research has painted a mixed picture of the impact of expanded broadband access and programs in marginalized communities.

Early literature in the digital divide field mapped critical arguments that serve as the basis for later "attitudes" and "outcomes" scholarship. As a frame of reference, the metaphor of the "digital divide" is meant to describe differences in information access, specifically in terms of access to Information Communication Technologies (ICTs). Whereas early digital divide research was primarily concerned with how economic, educational, and geographic factors shape broadband adoption (McConnaughey, Nila, Sloan, Baxter, Alvarez, and Francesconi 1995), research soon turned to an examination of digital skills, digital literacies, and what Jung, Qiu, and Kim (2001) broadly termed "post-adoption" issues (Bertot 2003; Hargittai

2008; Mossberger, Tolbert, and Stansbury 2003; Sevron 2002). Scholars began to advocate for a broader research framework that would situate digital practices within a critique of poverty and inequality (Kvasny 2006; Light 2001; Strover 2003; Warschauer 2003) and would explore how digital access practically impacts individuals in their political, economic, and social lives (Mossberger, Tolbert, and Stansbury 2003; Selwyn 2004). Given this shift in research focus, digital divide scholars critiqued the metaphor of the "divide" as too limited, and some pushed for the term "digital divide" to be replaced with "digital inequality" (DiMaggio and Hargittai 2001; Eubanks 2011; Kvasny and Keil 2006; Warschauer 2003).

Now that broadband adoption rates have continued to rise—aided in part by the global expansion of mobile technology (Napoli and Obar 2014; Perrin 2017)—research has increasingly shifted away from issues of access. For instance, digital inequality scholarship has begun to explore: (1) attitudes toward digital technology, and (2) what Scheerder et al. (2017) have termed the "tangible outcomes" of Internet use. Regarding attitudes research, studies have examined the role that attitudes might play in shaping Internet behaviors along continuums of use (Reisdorf 2012; Reisdorf and Groselj 2017) and how motivations may interact with skills, usage, and materials to influence digital engagement patterns (Ghobadi and Ghobadi 2015). Gonzales (2016) has suggested that the high cost of *maintaining* digital access could play a role in biasing low-income communities toward digital tools (Gonzales 2016). Qualitative studies have offered some potential solutions to these challenges, suggesting that attitudes surrounding digital technologies could be improved if public and private technology programs involve marginalized communities more substantially into program design (Fuentes-Bautista 2014), or if programs clearly articulate the potential political and organizing applications of digital tools for working-class communities (Wolfson et al. 2017). Ultimately, these researchers assert that a deeper understanding of the role attitudes surrounding digital technology may play in adoption is crucial to improving broadband engagement in marginalized communities.

In the second category of outcomes-focused research, this group of scholars expands on digital skills to insist that the goal of broadband interventions should be to promote "meaningful use" of ICTs (Mossberger et al. 2003). While scholars have advocated for broadband programs that can enhance cultural, economic, and social capital for participants (Bach, Shaffer, and Wolfson 2013; Schejter and Nonnecke 2012; Straubhaar 2012), recent quantitative scholarship has painted a mixed picture of digital outcomes among marginalized groups. For example, research has indicated that populations with higher social status use ICTs in more "beneficial ways" (van Deursen and van Dijk 2014; Zillien and Hargittai 2009) and that users with high levels of education or socioeconomic status may continue to reap the greatest rewards from Internet use (Blank and Groselj 2015; van Deursen and Helsper 2015). In short, this scholarship has illustrated that even after access is achieved, online activities and outcomes remain "stratified by both status and class" (Blank and Groselj 2015, 2770). These mixed findings are troubling and underscore the urgency of developing new critical research frameworks to unravel such complexities, helping us understand *how* and *why* digital tools are being used.

In their meta-analysis of quantitative research examining this "third-level" divide, Scheerder et al. (2017) underscore this point. To be more specific, they suggest that because social and cultural factors likely play a role in shaping both Internet attitudes and outcomes, more qualitative research is needed to help us understand "why some Internet users obtain more beneficial Internet outcomes than others" (Scheerder et al. 2017, 1615). Building on those insights, critical ethnographic research is well-tailored toward this line of investigation. Accordingly, to make this case, we will now turn to an introduction to ethnographic research methodology, briefly describing the origins of the methodology. Next, this chapter reviews data collection practices and the role of the ethnographic researcher in their community of study. Finally, we will address the applicability of critical ethnography in the study of social and cultural life in low-income communities, and the ways in which the approach can also provide a nuanced look at the role digital technology plays in everyday life.

METHODOLOGY: THE ETHNOGRAPHIC RESEARCH PROCESS

As previously discussed, the shift in the digital inequality literature toward examining attitudes and "tangible outcomes" of ICT use is an important one, as it marks a turn away from an access and skills framework to a new emphasis on individual Internet use and utility. Yet, these studies have not been able to offer a social or cultural explanation of why poor attitudes surrounding digital technology may endure, or why broadband outcomes remain so stratified. Ethnography examines social interactions, cultural practices, and local meanings through observing both actions and behaviors over time. Thus, critical ethnography offers a useful analytical toolbox for digital inequality scholars, as it also provides a particularized, detailed portrait of social life and firmly roots analysis within a social justice perspective. Further, the methodology emphasizes developing "rapport" and trust with participants, allowing ethnographers insight into social practices that may be ordinarily hidden or taboo (Blumer 1969). This is particularly important in the study of digital inequality, as members of marginalized communities could be hesitant to report honestly on certain behaviors—for example, using digital tools in the unregulated economy—if researchers have not earned their trust. In these ways, ethnography can offer time and space for researchers to map complex behaviors and practices.

Ethnographic research has already made important contributions to our understanding of the digital divide, particularly around public discourse and policy dialogues around digital issues. For example, Clark, Demont-Heinrich, and Webber's (2004) ethnographic research highlights how narratives of individualism and economic self-reliance shape public discussion of digital divide solutions, whereas Kvasny (2006) demonstrates how the same tendencies may shape participants' own understandings of the benefits of ICTs. As a possible solution to these tendencies, ethnographic studies of the digital divide have also argued for more holistic broadband programs that would: (a) include digitally excluded communities in the program design process (Mitchell 2002), and (b) demonstrate how

ICTs can be used to build political power (Wolfson and Crowell 2013). In its focus on utilizing qualitative interviews in conjunction with long-term participant observation, ethnographic research captures disparities between what is *said* and what is *done,* or any inconsistences between reported outcomes and actual behaviors. To showcase the "toolset" ethno-graphic methodology offers, the next section will explore: (1) the previous contributions of ethnographies to the study of the digital divide; (2) the origins of ethnographic methodology and its data collection procedures; (3) critical ethnographic approaches, including research that examines poverty and inequality in low-income US communities; and finally, (4) the contributions of ethnography to our understanding digital life.

What Is Ethnographic Research?

What is ethnographic research? Ethnographic research seeks to study people within their everyday environments (Burawoy 2003). As briefly discussed in this chapter's introduction, the goal of ethnography is to ex-amine cultural practices, social interactions, and local meanings through observing both behaviors and actions. This methodology is unique in that ethnographers conduct extensive fieldwork in their field sites, often over many years, in order to closely study social practices and cultures. As ethnographers observe and interact with their participants over time, researchers catalogue these encounters in extreme detail, utilizing what Geertz (1963) termed a process of "thick description" (Atkinson and Hammersely 2013). These detailed notes or "fieldnotes" form the founda-tion of an ethnographic study. Ethnographers also utilize semi-structured interviews with participants, allowing the ethnographer the flexibility to probe new areas of relevant interest that arise in the course of conversa-tion. Accordingly, the method does not encourage researcher detachment, but rather the goal is to achieve deeper immersion and social engagement (Emerson, Fretz, and Shaw 2011). Additionally, ethnographers may col-lect relevant material documents or artifacts they encounter in the course of their research. In this way, the ethnographer creates a rich, detailed, individualized portrait of everyday life, cataloguing both actions and behaviors.

Although ethnographic research seeks to study people within their environments, it is important to flag here that, "immersion is not merging" (Emerson, Fretz, and Shaw 2011, 43). Researchers unavoidably bring their own life experience or "stance" into the social process, and thus, the research process. Thus, ethnographers must be cognizant of their own position in the social world and use this position as a tool for developing complex reflections and understandings (Wolfinger 2002). This is especially important for digital inequality ethnographers studying marginalized communities, as researchers may share very different economic, educational, or racial privileges from their participants (Liebow 1967). Developing a good "rapport" with participants is therefore critical, as participants are understandably more guarded with outsiders that have not earned their trust (Blumer 1969). Through building rapport, researchers are permitted more nuanced insights into participants' everyday lives. In a similar vein, without this rich on-the-ground knowledge of the communities they study, ethnographers could easily misinterpret messages (Geertz 1973). As referenced earlier, this is particularly important in the study of digital inequality, as members of marginalized communities could be hesitant to report taboo behaviors or practices to researchers who have not earned their trust. In these ways, ethnography can offer time and space for researchers to map complex behaviors and practices.

CRITICAL ETHNOGRAPHY: A HISTORICAL PERSPECTIVE

Whereas ethnography can make important contributions to the study of the digital inequality—especially regarding ICT attitudes and outcomes—it is important to flag possible "pitfalls" and stress the importance of utilizing a *critical* ethnographic approach. Regarding "pitfalls," to offer some historical background, early anthropologists like Malinowski (1979) and Mead (1928) first used ethnographic methods to document social life, systems of economic exchange, and cultural practices among native peoples in South Asia. Given that these early ethnographic studies of native peoples were largely conducted by white Westerners from outside the native cultures, postcolonial scholars have rightly critiqued these works as shaped in part by the racist attitudes and the colonial politics of the period (Clair 2003). It is in the tradition of critical scholars like Antonio Gramsci that ethnographers advocated for a "critical ethnography" that is better suited to the type of critical questions of power digital inequality scholars are likewise invested in. In contrast to early ethnographies, critical ethnography is centered in social justice and thus more attentive to the role that ideologies and socioeconomic structures play in shaping attitudes, cultures, and behaviors (Clark 1977). Accordingly, critical ethnographers actively advocate for the emancipation of oppressed communities in their work and do not strive for values of "objectivity" that may inform other research approaches. As mentioned earlier, ethnographers acknowledge that their research is rooted in a particular set of social relations and values and thus instead strive for self-reflexivity, rather than researcher detachment (Clifford and Marcus 1986). Given that digital inequality scholars are invested in bringing attention to the needs of low-income and minority communities, it is crucial to be mindful of these historical critiques of the methodology when applying it to the study of the digital divide.

Taking into account the investment in social justice and inequality discussed earlier, ethnographers have already made important contributions to our understanding of urban life in high-poverty communities. For instance, due to its ability to uncover hidden practices through rapport and social immersion, urban ethnography has been recognized for its significant contributions to our understanding of economic exchange in low-income communities. This ability to capture potentially taboo practices or hidden behaviors further underscores ethnography's potential applicability to digital inequality research, which is equally invested in the study of practices and behaviors in high-poverty and marginalized communities. To offer some example of the contributions of ethnographies to our understanding of urban life, works by Dow (1977), Lowenthal (1975), and Stack (1974) all highlight the precarious economic lives of the urban poor in the US. More recent scholarship has explored the intersection of domestic life, violence, and policing in low-income urban communities from various perspectives (Anderson 1999; Goffman 2015; Lane 2018). Fairbanks (2009) examines informal drug-recovery houses in Philadelphia, arguing that their emergence is a symptom of a broader urban economic crisis. Edin and Lein (1997) focus on the economic survival strategies of welfare mothers in US cities, whereas Duneier (1999) reveals the informal economic practices of sidewalk book dealers in New York. These ethnographies all paint a vivid picture of the social and cultural attitudes in urban American, in addition to mapping economic lives and outcomes.

While ethnographies like those outlined have contributed nuanced portraits of contemporary urban life, critical ethnographers must take special care to avoid certain "pitfalls" in their research. For instance, Wacquant (2002) has cautioned against glamourizing or sensationalizing urban life at the expense of sincere economic, social, and political critique. To address these challenges, critical ethnographers have argued that researchers could more substantially involve participants in the process of research design, data collection, and analysis (Blomberg and Karasti 2012; Duneier 1999; Spinuzzi 2005). Notably, this could be a promising suggestion for digital inequality scholarship, which has been critiqued by some researchers as too disconnected from community needs (Mitchell 2002). But while ethnographers have long made significant academic contributions to our knowledge of everyday urban life, exploration of digital life is a more recent trend and has become an area of great interest for ethnographic study since the 2010s. We now turn to more recent research that specifically addresses the intersection of culture, social life, and digital technology in everyday life. This research outlines some of the ways that research is already engaging with important questions around digital attitudes, behaviors, and outcomes.

DIGITAL ETHNOGRAPHY

Whereas researchers in fields ranging from information studies, public policy, and education to psychology began to turn their attention to issues surrounding the digital divide in the 1990s, at the same time, few ethnographic studies were specifically engaging with the sociocultural impact of digital technologies (exceptions include Baym 2000; Clark et al. 2004; Danet 2001; Kendall 2002; Kvasny 2005; Mitchell 2002). Given that ethnographic methodology relies on direct, in-person participant observation, ethnographers may have initially been reluctant to see online spaces as a site for potential ethnographic study (Hine 2008; Murthy 2008). However, in the influential article "Ethnographic Approaches to Digital Media" Coleman (2010) helpfully reviews the important contributions that ethnographers have made to the study of digital cultures within the past decade. In this article, Coleman establishes that ethnographers have substantially enriched our understanding of: (1) digital media, politics, and representation (Boyd 2009; Srinivasan 2006); (2) digital cultures and subcultures (Costanza-Shock 2008; Kelty 2008); and (3) digital technology and social practices (Boczkowski 2004; Boellstorff 2015). As ethnographers observe participants within their own environments over long time periods (Moran 2015), they are uniquely positioned to capture overlapping social and online spaces (Hallett and Barber 2014), or the intersections between the digital and the material worlds (Horst and Miller 2013). Dovetailing with this chapter's seminal thesis, Coleman (2010) concludes that ethnography has given greater dimension and nuance to the study of digital technology, as it is grounded within the framework of everyday social and cultural life.

Given these particular methodological strengths and contributions presented in this chapter, ethnographic research on digital inequalities can: (1) enrich our understanding of social attitudes around digital technology, and (2) expand our understanding of the "tangible outcomes" of broadband adoption (Scheerder et al. 2017). In providing sociocultural context to our knowledge of digital attitudes and outcomes, ethnographic research can similarly help digital inequality researchers refine research questions, expose behaviors hidden from other research approaches, create new categories of measurement, explore new research avenues and directions, and map complex sociotechnical relationships. Having addressed how this argument fits within existing digital inequality literature, defined the methodology, and mapped out the contributions of ethnography to our understanding of technology and urban communities, we turn to some concluding thoughts and future research directions.

CONCLUSION

Using Sammy and Dinah's story as a starting point, this chapter demonstrated how ethnographic research can help us better understand complex economic, social, and cultural factors. What is an "effective outcome" of ICT access? What questions do we ask to evaluate effectiveness? Is obtaining employment through ICT access an effective outcome? If yes, does the quality of the job obtained matter? What if, for example, the job obtained will not provide a living wage? How then do we evaluate effectiveness? These questions and more were raised through the ethnographic portrait of two participants in a Philadelphia BTOP-funded broadband training program. Although Dinah obtained a job through a BTOP broadband training program, the job did not offer Dinah a route out of poverty. Sammy, a digital trainer who had worked with Dinah, noted that while ICTs were giving participants like Dinah new job opportunities, ICTs were also enabling greater outsourcing and loosening some worker protections. Remarking that Dinah's "success story" was more complicated than it might initially appear, Sammy felt increasingly conflicted about ICTs. This ethnographic portrait of Sammy and Dinah underscores the challenges facing research evaluation of broadband programs serving low-income communities across urban America. Their stories highlight the complex economic, social, and cultural factors that can shape participant attitudes, interactions, and outcomes with technology.

To establish the relevance of ethnography to digital inequality research, this chapter first reviewed extant scholarship in the field, outlining how digital inequality research has moved toward an investigation of digital attitudes and the "tangible outcomes" of broadband access. Nevertheless, much of this research remains quantitative and has not yet provided a sociocultural explanation of why poor attitudes toward digital technology endure in oppressed communities, or why outcomes remain striated by race and class (Blank and Groselj 2015). Second, we addressed data collection procedures, including how ethnographers take detailed notes—or "fieldnotes"—of their observations and interactions to properly map social behavior and cultural meanings. Third, this chapter advocated for critical ethnographic approaches that center the study of digital inequality in social justice. This chapter illustrated how the methodology can uncover hidden or taboo practices through surveying previous urban ethnographies and then turned to contemporary ethnographies to show how the methodology has already broadened our knowledge of digital cultures and social practices.

As digital inequality research is deeply invested in the issues facing low-income and marginalized communities, engaging those communities in sustained and long-term dialogue about their informational and technological needs will be of vital importance for the field moving forward. In its emphasis on rapport and building networks of trust, ethnographic methodology has a unique role to play in this process. Without methodological approaches like ethnography that center cultural and social life, researchers risk building their proposed solutions to the problems of digital inequality in a techno-deterministic framework. Said differently, if our focus is tilted toward technology rather than culture and community, the answers to the problems of digital inequality will always be technological (Light 2001). However, if the goal of digital inequality research is to develop social justice solutions, a critical ethnographic approach can offer a granular look at how digital tools are being incorporated into the everyday lives of the digitally excluded. A broader methodological framework can only further support the production of quantitative research as well, opening up new lines of inquiry to better capture the shifting features of digital inequality. In short, we propose a methodological intervention in the digital inequality field in order to help us chart new research directions in an ever-shifting digital landscape.

NOTES

1. Following data collection, the fieldnotes from participant observation, transcribed semi-structured interviews, and scanned documents were entered into NVivo qualitative and "coded" through NVivo for themes or categories.
2. Some participants received a $25 gift card for their interview participation.

REFERENCES

Anderson, E. 1999. *Code of the Street: Decency, Violence, and the Moral Life of the Inner City*. New York: W. W. Norton.

Atkinson, P., and Hammersely, M. 2013. "Ethnography and Participant Observation." In *Handbook of Qualitative Research*. Edited by N. K. Denzin and Y. S. Lincoln, 248–261. Thousand Oaks, CA: Sage.

Bach, A., Shaffer, G., and Wolfson, T. 2013. "Digital Human Capital: Developing a Framework for Understanding the Economic Impact of Digital Exclusion in Low-Income Communities." *Journal of Information Policy* 3: 247–266.

Baym, N. K. 2000. *Tune In, Log On: Soaps, Fandom, and Online Community*. New York: Sage.

Blank, G., and Groselj, D. 2015. "Digital Divide Examining Internet Use through a Weberian Lens." *International Journal of Communication* 9: 2763–2783.

Blomberg, J., and Karasti, H. 2012. "Positioning Ethnography within Participatory Design." In *Routledge International Handbook of Participatory Design*. Edited by J. Simonsen and T. Robertson, 86–116. London: Routledge.

Blumer, H. 1969. *Symbolic Interactionism: Perspective and Method*. Englewood Cliffs, NJ: Prentice Hall Press.

Boczkowski, P. J. 2004. "The Processes of Adopting Multimedia and Interactivity in Three Online Newsrooms." *Journal of Communication* 54 (2): 197–213.

Boellstorff, T. 2015. *Coming of Age in Second Life: An Anthropologist Explores the Virtually Human*. Princeton, NJ: Princeton University Press.

Boyd, D. 2009. "Why Youth (Heart) Social Networks Sites: The Role of Networked Publics in Teenage Social Life." In *Hanging Out, Messing Around, Geeking Out: Living and Learning with New Media*. Edited by M. Ito, S. Baumer, M. Bittani, D. Boyd, and R. Cody, 119–142. Cambridge, MA: MIT Press.

Burawoy, M. 2003. "Revisits: An Outline of a Theory of Reflexive Ethnography." *American Sociological Review* 68: 645–679.

Clair, R. P. 2003. "The Changing Story of Ethnography." In *Expressions of Ethnography: Novel Approaches to Qualitative Methods*. Edited by R. P. Clair, 3–28. Albany, NY: State University of New York Press.

Clark, L. S., Demont-Heinrich, C., and Webber, S. A. 2004. "Ethnographic Interviews on the Digital Divide." *New Media & Society* 6 (4): 529–547.

Clark, M. 1977. *Antonio Gramsci and the Revolution That Failed*. New Haven, CT: Yale University Press.

Clifford, J., and Marcus, G. E., eds. 1986. *Writing Culture: The Poetics and Politics of Ethnography*. Berkeley, CA: University of California Press.

Coleman, E. G. 2010. "Ethnographic Approaches to Digital Media." *Annual Review of Anthropology* 39: 487–505.

Costanza-Shock, S. 2008. "The Immigrant Rights Movement of the Net: Between 'Web 2.0' and Commucación Popular." *American Quarterly* 60 (3): 851–864.

Danet, B. 2001. *Cyberpl@y: Communicating Online*. New York: Bloomsbury Academic.

DiMaggio, P., and Hargittai, E. 2001. *From the "Digital Divide" to "Digital inequality": Studying Internet Use as Penetration Increases*. Princeton, NJ: Princeton University Woodrow Wilson Center for Arts and Cultural Policy Studies.

Dow, L. 1977. "High Weeds in Detroit." *Urban Anthropology* 6: 111–128.

Duneier, M. 1999. *Sidewalk*. New York: Farrar, Straus, & Giroux.

Edin, K., and Lein, L. 1997. *Making Ends Meet: How Single Mothers Survive Welfare and Low-Wage Work*. New York: Russell Sage Foundation.

Emerson, R. M., Fretz, R. I., and Shaw, L. L. 2011. *Writing Ethnographic Fieldnotes*. Chicago: University of Chicago Press.

Eubanks, V. 2011. *Digital Dead End*. Cambridge, MA: MIT Press.

Fairbanks, R. 2009. *How It Works: Recovering Citizens in Post-Welfare Philadelphia*. Chicago, IL: University of Chicago Press.

Fuentes-Bautista, M. 2014. "Rethinking Localism in the Broadband Era: A Participatory Community Development Approach." *Government Information Quarterly* 31 (1): 65–77.

Geertz, C. 1963. *Peddlers and Princes*. Chicago: University of Chicago Press.

Geertz, C. 1973. *The Interpretation of Cultures*. New York: Basic Books.

Ghobadi, S., and Ghobadi, Z. 2015. "How Access Gaps Interact and Shape Digital Divide: A Cognitive Investigation." *Behaviour & Information Technology* 34 (4): 330–340.

Goffman, A. 2015. *On the Run: Fugitive Life in an American City*. New York: Picador.

Gonzales, A. 2016. "The Contemporary US Digital Divide: From Initial Access to Technology Maintenance." *Information, Communication & Society* 19 (2): 234–248.

Hallett, R. E., and Barber, K. 2014. "Ethnographic Research in a Cyber Era." *Journal of Contemporary Ethnography* 43 (3): 306–330.

Hargittai, E. 2008. "Digital Inequality: Differences in Young Adults' Use of the Internet." *Communication Research* 35 (5): 602–621.

Hine, C. 2008. "Virtual Ethnography: Modes, Varieties, Affordances." In *The Sage Handbook of Online Research Methods*. Edited by N. Fielding, R. Lee and G. Blank, 257–270. New York: Sage.

Horst, H. A., and Miller, D., eds. 2013. *Digital Anthropology*. London: A & C Black.

Jung, J. Y., Qiu, J. L., and Kim, Y. C. 2001. "Internet Connectedness and Inequality: Beyond the 'Divide.'" *Communication Research* 28 (4): 507–535.

Kelty, C. 2008. *Two Bits: The Cultural Significance of Free Software*. Durham, NC: Duke University Press.

Kendall, L. 2002. *Hanging Out in the Virtual Pub: Masculinities and Relationships Online*. Berkeley, CA: University of California Press.

Kvasny, L. 2005. "The Role of the Habitus in Shaping Discourses about the Digital Divide." *Journal of Computer-Mediated Communication* 10 (2). https://doi.org/10.1111/j.1083-6101.2005.tb00242.x

Kvasny, L. 2006. "Cultural (Re)production of Digital Inequality in a U.S. Community Technology Initiative." *Information, Communication & Society* 9 (2): 160–181.

Kvasny, L., and Keil, M. 2006. "The Challenges of Redressing the Digital Divide: A Tale of Two US Cities." *Information Systems Journal* 16 (1): 23–53.

Lane, J. 2018. *The Digital Street*. Oxford, UK: Oxford University Press.

Liebow, E. 1967. *Tally's Corner: A Study of Negro Streetcorner Men*. New York: Little, Brown.

Light, J. 2001. "Rethinking the Digital Divide." *Harvard Educational Review* 71 (4): 709–733.

Lowenthal, M. 1975. "The Social Economy in Urban Working-Class Communities." In *The Social Economy of Cities*. Edited by G. Gappert and H. M. Ross, 441–469. Newbury Park, CA: Sage.

Malinowski, B. 1922. *Argonauts of the Western Pacific: An Account of Native Enterprise and Adventure in the Archipelagoes of Melanesian New Guinea*. London: Routledge & Kegan Paul.

McConnaughey, J. W., Nila, C. A., Sloan, T., Baxter, D., Alverez, R., and Francesconi, M. 1995. *Falling through the Net: A Survey of the "Have Nots" in Rural and Urban America*. Washington, DC: National Telecommunications and Information Administration, U.S. Department of Commerce. http://www.ntia.doc.gov/ntiahome/fallingthru.html

Mead, M. 1928. *Coming of Age in Samoa: A Psychological Study of Primitive Youth for Western Civilization*. New York: William Morrow.

Mitchell, M. 2002. "Exploring the Future of the Digital Divide through Ethnographic Futures Research." *First Monday* 7 (11).

Moran, M. H. 2015. "The Digital Divide Revisited: Local and Global Manifestations." In *eFieldnotes: The Makings of Anthropology in the Digital World*. Edited by R. Sanjek and S. W. Tratner. Philadelphia, PA: University of Pennsylvania Press.

Mossberger, K., Tolbert, C., and Stansbury, M. 2003. *Virtual Inequality: Beyond the Digital Divide*. Washington, DC: Georgetown University Press.

Murthy, D. 2008. "Digital Ethnography: An Examination of the Use of New Technologies for Social Research." *Sociology* 42 (5): 837–855.

Napoli, P., and Obar, J. 2014. "The Emerging Mobile Internet Underclass: A Critique of Mobile Internet Access." *The Information Society* 30 (5): 323–334.

Perrin, A. 2017. "Smartphones Help Blacks, Hispanics Bridge Some – but Not All – Digital Gaps with Whites." *Fact Tank*. Washington, DC: Pew Research Center. https://www.pewresearch.org/fact-tank/2017/08/31/smartphones-help-blacks-hispanics-bridge-some-but-not-all-digital-gaps-with-whites/

Reisdorf, B. C. 2012. "Internet Non-Use: A Comparative Study of Great Britain and Sweden." PhD dissertation, University of Oxford.

Reisdorf, B. C., and Groselj, D. 2017. "Internet (Non-) Use Types and Motivational Access: Implications for Digital Inequalities Research." *New Media & Society* 19 (8): 1157–1176.

Scheerder, A., van Deursen, A., and van Dijk, J. 2017. "Determinants of Internet Skills, Uses and Outcomes: A Systematic Review of the Second- and Third-Level Digital Divide." *Telematics and Informatics* 34 (8): 1607–1624.

Schejter, A., and Nonnecke, B. M. 2012. "If You Build It – Will They Come? Understanding the Information Needs of Users of BTOP Funded Broadband Internet Public Computer Centers." Paper presented at TRPC 2012: The 40th Research Conference on Communication, Information and Internet Policy, Arlington, VA, September 21–23, 2012.

Selwyn, N. 2004. "Reconsidering Political and Popular Understandings of the Digital Divide." *New Media & Society* 6 (3): 341–362.

Sevron, L. 2002. *Bridging the Digital Divide: Technology, Community, and Public Policy*. Malden: Blackwell.

Spinuzzi, C. 2005. "The Methodology of Participatory Design." *Technical Communication* 52 (2): 163–174.

Srinivasan, R. 2006. "Indigenous, Ethnic & Cultural Articulations of the New Media." *International Journal of Cultural Studies* 9 (4): 497–518.

Stack, C. 1974. *All of Our Kin: Strategies for Survival in the Black Community*. New York: Harper & Row.

Straubhaar, J., ed. 2012. *Inequity in the Technopolis: Race, Class, Gender, and the Digital Divide in Austin*. Austin, TX: University of Texas Press.

Strover, S. 2003. "Remapping the Digital Divide." *The Information Society* 19 (4): 275–277.

van Deursen, A. J., and Helsper, E. J. 2015. "The Third-Level Digital Divide: Who Benefits Most from Being Online?" In *Communication and Information Technologies Annual*. Edited by L. Robinson and J. Schulz, 29–52. Bingley, UK: Emerald Group.

van Deursen, A. J., and van Dijk, J. A. 2014. "The Digital Divide Shifts to Differences in Usage." *New Media & Society* 16 (3): 507–526.

Wacquant, L. 2002. "Scrutinizing the Street: Poverty, Morality, and the Pitfalls of Urban Ethnography." *American Journal of Sociology* 107 (6): 1468–1532.

Warschauer, M., 2003. *Technology and Social Inclusion: Rethinking the Digital Divide*. Cambridge, MA: MIT Press.

Wolfinger, N. 2002. "On Writing Fieldnotes: Collection Strategies and Background Expectancies." *Qualitative Research* 2: 85–95.

Wolfson, T., and Crowell, J. 2013. "Techno-Social Infrastructure: Poverty, Inequality and Broadband Adoption in Urban America." Unpublished research report to the Broadband Technology Opportunities Program. Washington, DC: U.S. National Telecommunications and Information Administration.

Wolfson, T., Crowell, J., Reyes, C., and Bach, A. 2017. "Emancipatory Broadband Adoption: Toward a Critical Theory of Digital Inequality in the Urban United States." *Communication, Culture, & Critique* 10 (3): 441–459.

Zillien, N., and Hargittai, E. 2009. "Digital Distinction: Status-Specific Types of Internet Usage." *Social Science Quarterly* 90 (2): 274–291.

5

Addressing Spatial Inequality in Broadband Use and Community-Level Outcomes

CAROLINE J. TOLBERT, KAREN MOSSBERGER, NATASHA GAYDOS, AND MATTIA CALDARULO

INTRODUCTION

Understanding the effectiveness of broadband programs for creating community-level change is critical for public policy. National data varies in estimating the extent of digital disadvantage in the US: whether twenty-five million lack broadband, according to the Federal Communications Commission, or 162.8 million do not use the internet at broadband speeds, as estimated by Microsoft using data from its products (US Senate 2019). Whatever measure is used, however, reveals that broadband availability, speeds, and use are not evenly distributed across the landscape.

The persistence of spatial disparities in access and use over more than two decades is evident in the first five-year estimates on broadband subscriptions released by the American Community Survey (ACS) for all census tracts for 2017. While 78 percent of the US population had some type of broadband subscription, either fixed or mobile, there were striking differences across neighborhoods, counties, and tribal communities.

Caroline J. Tolbert, Karen Mossberger, Natasha Gaydos, and Mattia Caldarulo, *Addressing Spatial Inequality in Broadband Use and Community-Level Outcomes* In: *Transforming Everything?*. Edited by: Karen Mossberger, Eric W. Welch, and Yonghong Wu, Oxford University Press. © Oxford University Press 2022. DOI: 10.1093/oso/9780190082871.003.0006

Rural Wheeler County, GA had only 24 percent of the population with either fixed or mobile broadband subscriptions, and Navajo Nation had only 27 percent of residents with any type of broadband connection (Mossberger, Tolbert, and LaCombe 2021b). Broadband infrastructure availability is lowest in some rural communities, exacerbating problems of rural poverty that make broadband unaffordable as well (Salemink et al. 2017). But poverty is a significant barrier to adoption in both urban and rural areas (Tomer, Kneebone, and Shivaram 2017). Most unconnected households live in metropolitan areas where infrastructure is available, with wide differences in adoption across neighborhoods (Fishbane and Tomer 2020). The 2017 ACS showed there were zip codes in Memphis with only 26 percent of the population with broadband subscriptions (including smartphones). One-third of Detroit's population had no personal internet access at all, including smartphones or fixed broadband (Mossberger, Tolbert, and LaCombe 2021). There are also suburban census tracts with low rates of broadband subscription in nearly all the one hundred largest metros (Tomer, Kneebone, and Shivaram 2017).

These place-based inequalities in broadband use have consequences for local employment, economic growth, prosperity, educational attainment, and other policy outcomes (Whitacre, Gallardo, and Strover 2014a; Mossberger, Tolbert, and LaCombe 2021b). Policy interventions are often targeted to low-income urban neighborhoods or rural communities with goals for increased local employment, economic investment, educational attainment, or community health (FCC 2010). For program evaluation, it is therefore important to track community-level change in broadband subscriptions and impacts, as well as to gauge outcomes for individual program participants. Outreach and training programs are often evaluated in terms of results for individual participants alone, not for local communities or populations. While most evaluations focus on individual participants, a better understanding of changes in broadband use across different communities is also needed to craft more effective policies.

Such population data can lend significant credibility to evaluations of both infrastructure and adoption programs. For both rural communities experiencing broadband for the first time and urban areas rolling out gigabit networks or 5G, understanding whether broadband *use* has increased as a result of these investments makes a stronger case for broadband as a *cause* of local trends, helping to unpack the "black box" between network inputs and economic outputs. The mere provision of service doesn't mean that the local population will be able to afford broadband subscriptions or will have the skills to use the technology. The Brookings Institution concluded that it was the adoption (or subscription) gap rather than a lack of broadband infrastructure that most affected rural as well as urban communities (Tomer, Kneebone, and Shivaram 2017).

Yet there has been relatively limited emphasis on measuring change in broadband subscriptions for local communities below the state level (see Mossberger, Tolbert, and Franko 2012) or use at the neighborhood or local level in program evaluations. One reason has been the lack of precise data to measure broadband subscriptions for local geographic areas (see Lehr in Chapter 1, and Horrigan in Chapter 2). The first release of tract-level data from the Census's 2017 & 2018 American Community Survey, based on millions of cases, has now opened the way for better community-level evaluation.

Evaluating broadband use (i.e., subscriptions) *over time* in communities can address issues of causation as well as long-term outcomes of use. As we demonstrate here using the example of Chicago's Smart Communities program, it is now possible to measure community-level impacts of neighborhood programs promoting technology use, using quasi-experimental designs to address change over time. Two methodological or research design elements are emphasized here. First, is the need to compare outcomes for treated neighborhoods (that received the policy intervention) to outcomes in control neighborhoods that did not. Second, measuring change over time allows for exploration of long-term impacts, as policy goals such as increases in employment or educational outcomes could be expected to lag initial changes in internet use.

This chapter briefly reviews the significance of place for broadband policy evaluation and examines long-term data on Chicago neighborhoods as an example of a quasi-experimental design. This illustrates the benefits of conducting long-term evaluation, taking advantage of new American

Community Survey data that allows tracking of broadband subscriptions (both fixed and mobile) over time in smaller or less-populated geographies such as neighborhoods or rural communities. Finally, we turn to strategies for expanding such community-level research through use of other quasi-experimental designs and the creation and utilization of community-level data on broadband adoption and use.

INEQUALITY IN BROADBAND SUBSCRIPTIONS BY PLACE

Since the 1980s, income gaps across communities have widened (Giannone 2017), and disparities across cities are accelerating (Moretti 2012, 101). From the metro to the neighborhood level, in rural and urban America, where an individual grows up affects lifelong economic opportunity (Chetty, Friedman, Hendren, Jones, and Porter 2018). Research by Chetty and Hendren (2017) using quasi-experimental design, panel data (where the same individuals are repeatedly studied), and longitudinal data over decades finds that location has a significant and causal relationship to intergenerational mobility in the US. This strong research design employed by Chetty and colleagues to study place-based disparities supports the validity of their findings.

Neighborhood disadvantage in internet connectivity and use is consistent with this and other research on the harmful effects of spatially concentrated poverty in policy areas such as health, education, and employment (Jargowsky 1997; Massey and Denton 1993; Wilson 1987; Bayer, Ross, and Topa 2008; Currie 2011). Broadband disparities clearly affect other place-based inequalities. If many students lack internet access at home, for example, the quality of education may be affected in schools that find it difficult to assign homework and to support student learning outside the classroom. School closures during the 2020 coronavirus pandemic created an educational crisis in urban neighborhoods and rural communities because so many students lacked adequate broadband at home (Romm 2020; Associated Press 2020; Stewart 2020). Communities with low broadband use are more isolated from the larger economy and society. Local governments are unable to fully employ the efficiencies of digital government or to make always-available online access to services and information equitable across neighborhoods (Schartman-Cycyk et al. 2019).

Previous research has shown that neighborhood context influences the prevalence of broadband subscriptions in the population (Mossberger, Tolbert, and Gilbert 2006; Tomer, Kneebone, and Shivaram 2017). More affluent neighborhoods (zip codes) are more likely to have a higher rate of broadband subscriptions across racial and ethnic groups, controlling for both neighborhood and individual factors (Mossberger, Tolbert, and Gilbert 2006). Research on Chicago demonstrated that residence in high-poverty, segregated neighborhoods magnified barriers to technology use, using multilevel models that control for individual characteristics (Mossberger, Tolbert, Bowen, and Jimenez 2012).

Neighborhood environment may matter for many reasons. Goods and services sold in poor communities are often more expensive, with credit and consumer information less available, leading to additional financial burdens beyond individual poverty (Caplovitz 1967; Federal Reserve and Brookings 2008; Dailey et al. 2010). An "ecology of support" (Rhinesmith 2016) in localized social networks and neighborhood institutions may be important for broadband adoption and skills (Rhinesmith 2016; Gangadharan and Byrum 2012). Neighborhood disparities in employment and education may also affect internet skills and learning (Kaplan and Mossberger 2012; Holloway and Mulherin 2004). The quality of broadband may be slower and less reliable in some urban neighborhoods (Dailey et al. 2010), though problems with availability tend to be more common in rural areas and more lightly populated suburbs (Tomer, Kneebone, and Shivaram 2017). While it has been difficult to study systematically pricing differences across communities, some research in Washington, DC found that options in low-income neighborhoods were more expensive for the speeds delivered (Dunbar 2011).

Overall, broadband in the US ranks among the most expensive in the developed world, well above international averages (Tomer et al. 2017; OECD 2017).[1] Low-income census tracts, whether urban or rural, have a lower proportion of the population with broadband subscriptions because cost is a primary barrier (see Figure 5.1 from the Brookings Institution).

But it is also possible that policy interventions in high-poverty neighborhoods or rural communities can create environments that promote change. Goolsbee and Klenow's (2002) study of computer diffusion revealed localized spillover effects encouraging adoption within neighborhoods. Surveys have shown that sharing of technology resources with friends and family is more common in low-income communities (Mossberger, Kaplan, and Gilbert 2008) and this may encourage informal learning and spillovers. Chicago's Smart Communities program relied on a theory of change that training and outreach programs could create such spillovers at the neighborhood level. In the following section, we demonstrate how place-based evaluation over time can capture community-level changes in broadband adoption and use, as well as longer-term economic outcomes for communities. Following this example, we discuss more general strategies for addressing issues in place-based research—dealing

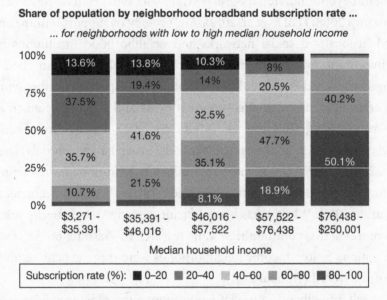

Figure 5.1 Share of Population by Neighborhood Broadband Subscription Rate
SOURCE: Tomer, Kneebone, and Shivaram (2017).

with causation using observational data throughout quasi-experimental designs and using longitudinal data.

THE SMART COMMUNITIES: EVALUATING
THE POTENTIAL FOR COMMUNITY CHANGE

The City of Chicago received a $7 million grant from the federal Broadband Technology Opportunities Program (BTOP) to implement training and outreach initiatives in nine of Chicago's seventy-seven official community areas between 2010 and January 2013. The Smart Communities program aimed to create a culture of digital excellence, or information technology use, in low- and moderate-income neighborhoods (neighborhood effect), as well as to increase internet skills and use among program participants (individual effect) (LISC Chicago 2009). The program featured multiple training and outreach efforts: technology skills training in English and Spanish and public access at six FamilyNet Centers with computers and staff, digital summer jobs for high school students, training and technical assistance for internet use by small businesses, Civic 2.0 classes for neighborhood groups, and digital media programs for youth. One of the most common activities at FamilyNet Centers was support for online job search and resumes. One neighborhood introduced modules for online banking as an alternative to expensive check cashing and payday loans. Civic 2.0 classes showed community groups how to access government information and services online (author interviews; Mossberger 2012).

The Smart Communities did not provide home internet access for participants, though in Fall 2011, midway through the program, Comcast began to offer discounted broadband to eligible Chicago households. The FamilyNet Centers promoted the Comcast program and helped participants sign up. Outreach encouraging purchase of a broadband subscription was conducted through Tech Organizers, neighborhood portals, and advertising on buses and transit shelters, and such outreach was geared toward expanding the impact of the program beyond the training participants.

Panel Data and Quasi-Experimental Design

This chapter examines immediate impacts for broadband subscriptions and activities online at the close of the program (January 2013), and longer-term economic outcomes at the neighborhood level (2008–2017). The initial program evaluation, supported by the John D. and Catherine T. MacArthur Foundation and the Partnership for a Connected Illinois, included three Chicago citywide telephone surveys over five years used for a pre-post analysis (2008, 2011, 2013). We have extended this evaluation with newly available data from the 2017 Census American Community Survey that permits a time series analysis over a ten-year period. Broadband subscriptions for Chicago's seventy-seven community areas are measured from 2008 to 2017, creating a panel design with repeated measurement for the same units.

Data over time improves empirical rigor for program evaluation with measures before (pre) and after (post) a policy's implementation (treatment), creating a quasi-experiment. This change is then compared to the change pre and post for Chicago neighborhoods that do not receive the policy, as a control group. Statistical controls and multivariate regression work to make the two groups equivalent. Such panel data designs are powerful in program evaluation and are part of a group of methods referred to as causal inference, including difference in difference designs (Angrist and Pischke 2009).

This study compares places with the Smart Communities programs (the treatment) vs. Chicago community areas with no program (control cases) holding constant demographic and economic changes over this period across the neighborhoods. Key research questions included: *Was the Smart Communities program effective at stimulating increased broadband adoption and activities online at the community level, even though they provided outreach, training, and skills rather than internet access? Did growth in broadband subscriptions lead to economic benefits for the neighborhoods ten years later?*

Measuring Neighborhood-Level Broadband Subscriptions and Online Activities

Estimates for broadband subscriptions and activities online were based on citywide random sample telephone surveys (landline and mobile) conducted prior to the program in 2008 (3,500 respondents), midway through implementation in 2011 (2,500 respondents) and at the end of the program in 2013 (2,400 respondents). The Eagleton Institute at Rutgers University conducted the random sample telephone survey, with similar questions all three years. Interviews were conducted in English and Spanish. The random sample telephone surveys used a geographic sampling frame that drew respondents from each of Chicago's seventy-seven community areas in a stratified sample.

To generalize from a small sample to an entire neighborhood can be problematic and lead to bias. To overcome this problem, hierarchical linear modeling was used to estimate broadband subscriptions for Chicago's seventy-seven neighborhoods controlling for individual-level demographic factors and census tract demographic factors. This method creates geographic estimates of critical outcome variables but leverages the neighborhood-level socioeconomic data to improve estimates based on individual-level data (Mossberger, Tolbert, and Franko 2012; Mossberger, Tolbert, and Anderson 2014). This method has been shown to work well with a small number of cases in each geographic area (Lax and Phillips 2009; Raudenbush and Bryk 2002; Snijders and Bosker 2011; Steenbergen and Jones 2002; Pacheco 2011).

We used random intercept multilevel statistical modeling with post-stratification weights (a form of statistical simulation) to generate geographic estimates of broadband access and online activities for neighborhoods in Chicago.[2] Respondents in the three surveys were asked to identify their cross-streets, and each participant was geocoded in a census tract. The survey data were merged with aggregate-level census tract information from the American Community Survey for the appropriate citywide survey (2008, 2011, or 2013). (See discussion of the 2017 data in the section on Long-Term Evaluation.) The statistical models were based on data that combined individual and aggregate variables. Leveraging the neighborhood-level data provides more accurate and representative estimates than could be obtained from the individual-level data alone.

Short-Term Evaluation: Comparing Change for Treated and Non-Treated Neighborhoods, 2008–2013

With the new data measuring broadband subscriptions and use for Chicago neighborhoods, multivariate regression analysis was used to assess change in the Smart Communities compared to non-treated neighborhoods over the five-year period (see Mossberger, Tolbert, and Anderson 2014). The primary predictor variable was a binary variable that measured whether the neighborhood had a Smart Communities program or not. The outcome or dependent variable was created by taking the difference in our estimates from 2013 minus 2008 (Mossberger and Tolbert 2009), measuring neighborhood-level change in internet use anywhere, broadband subscriptions, or online activities. To account for other factors that might lead to changes in technology use for neighborhoods over time, the models controlled for change in population, percent in poverty, high school graduates, and the race, ethnicity, and age of the population (2008 and 2012 American Community Survey).[3] The models therefore control for change in neighborhood socioeconomic status, racial and ethnic diversity, and age.

Results

An initial analysis comparing changes in the Smart Communities to other neighborhoods between 2008 and 2011 showed that there were significantly higher rates of internet use in any location in the Smart Communities, including use at libraries or the homes of friends and relatives. There was no difference in subscription rates or activities online in 2011, after less than a year of implementation.

By the end of the two-year project, however, the Smart Communities had higher rates for home broadband subscriptions and internet use for jobs, health, and mass transit as well. These differences were statistically and substantively significant, ranging between 9 and 11 percentage points higher than the non-treated neighborhoods, controlling for changing demographic and economic conditions. Holding change constant at mean values for all demographic and economic factors, internet use in any location increased by 4.5 percent in control communities and 13 percent in the Smart Communities (a nearly 9 percentage point difference). At the close of the program in 2013, the Smart Communities also had a 14.7 percent increase in home broadband adoption compared with only 6 percent in other Chicago community areas (again an almost 9 percentage point difference), controlling for economic and demographic change (see Figures 5.2).

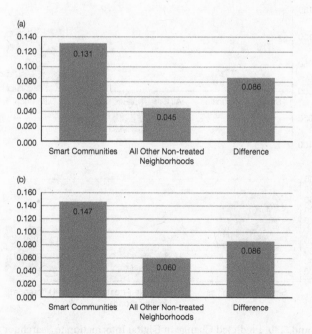

Figure 5.2a and 5.2b Predicted Change in Internet Use (Left) and Change in Broadband Subscriptions (Right), 2008–2013 (Predicted Probability of Percent Change)
NOTE: Estimates are based on multivariate statistical models with other neighborhood-level factors (change in poverty rates, demographic factors, etc.), held constant at mean values.

By 2013, the rate of increase for online job search was 11 percentage points higher in the Smart Communities than other Chicago neighborhoods (see Figure 5.3a).[4] Change in use of the internet for health information was 17 percentage points in the Smart Communities, whereas the increase was only 6.6 percentage points in other neighborhoods—a 10-point difference (see Figure 5.3b). Similarly, the increase in use of the internet for mass transit information was 17 percentage points in the Smart Communities and was 6 percentage points in other Chicago neighborhoods, an 11 percentage point difference comparing the treated and non-treated neighborhoods (see Figure 5.4). This suggests a measurable effect not only for increasing internet access and broadband use, but for a range of important economic and social activities online. Other online activities included in the surveys

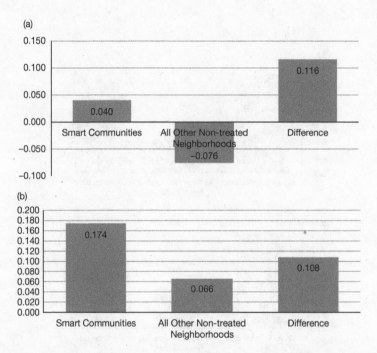

Figure 5.3a and 5.3b Predicted Change in Digital Information to Search for a Job (Left) and Find Health Information Online (Right), 2008–2013 (Predicted Probability Percent Change)

NOTE: Estimates are based on multivariate statistical models with other neighborhood-level factors (change in poverty rates, demographic factors, etc.), held constant at mean values.

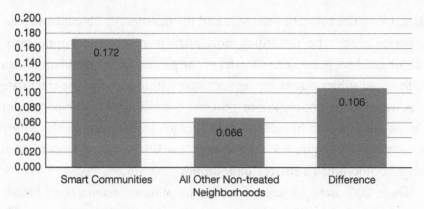

Figure 5.4 Predicted Change in Digital Information for Transportation, 2008–2013
(Predicted Probability Percent Change)
NOTE: Estimates are based on multivariate statistical models with other neighborhood-
level factors (change in poverty rates, demographic factors, etc.), held constant at mean
values.

did not demonstrate statistically significant differences in change over the
five-year period.

LONG-TERM EVALUATION: MEASURING BROADBAND SUBSCRIPTIONS ACROSS CHICAGO'S COMMUNITY AREAS TEN YEARS LATER

To what extent were these gains in home broadband subscriptions sustained
over time? Did the Smart Communities increase in internet use more than
the non-treated areas? Given the increases in broadband subscriptions
and activities such as searching for information on jobs, transportation,
and health, do we see greater change in economic outcomes in the Smart
Communities, compared to other neighborhoods in Chicago? Did proximate outcomes lead to longer-term impacts?

In December 2018 the U.S. Census released tract data for the five-year
American Community Survey (ACS) for all seventy-three thousand tracts,
making possible for the first time the generation of broadband subscription data for neighborhoods within large urban areas based on government

data. Using the 2017 five-year ACS and the question on "broadband sub-scription of any type" (including mobile data plan, cable, fiber optic, satel-lite, or DSL) we generated estimates of the percent of the population with high-speed subscriptions for census tracts within the city. The tract data was weighted by population to generate the estimates of the percent of the population with broadband for Chicago's seventy-seven community areas shown in Figure 5.5. On the map, the Wi-Fi icon indicates which neighborhoods had a Smart Communities program.

These 2017 data are compared to the authors' estimates of broad-band subscriptions for community areas from the 2008 citywide survey discussed in the previous section—an earlier time period when

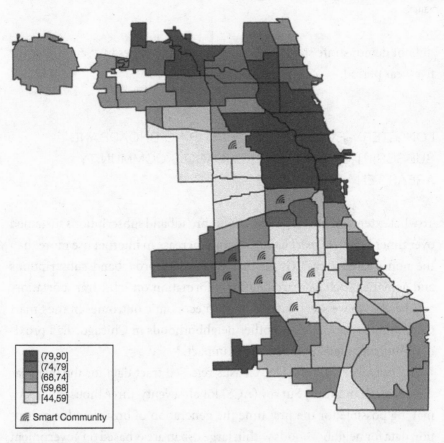

Figure 5.5 Chicago Broadband Subscriptions by Community Area, 2017

government data was not available. This nearly ten-year evaluation of Chicago's Smart Communities is assessed using change models (i.e., lagged panel models) and multivariate regression. Our expectation is that the "treated" neighborhoods with the Smart Communities will exhibit better outcomes across a range of indicators almost a decade later.

Our study includes two important outcome variables. The outcome variable is either (1) broadband subscriptions of any type in 2017, and the lagged term for broadband adoption in 2008, or (2) direct measures of change in broadband subscriptions from 2008 to 2017. The primary predictor variable is binary, measuring the treatment, coded 1 if the neighborhood was a Smart Community and 0 if not.

Results, 2008–2017: Broadband Subscription Rates Grew More in Treated Communities

Neighborhoods targeted for the Smart Communities programs (again, shown on the map with the Wi-Fi symbol) on average had lower rates of adoption in 2008 than more affluent parts of the city. Table 5.1 shows the change in broadband subscription rates for the nine treated

Table 5.1 CHANGE IN BROADBAND ADOPTION 2008–2017, SMART COMMUNITY NEIGHBORHOODS

Community Area	CCA Name	2008 Broadband Rate (%)	2017 Broadband Rate (%)	Change (%)
23	Humboldt Park	43	60	17
31	Lower West Side	39	73	34
62	West Elsdon	62	75	13
63	Gage Park	38	67	29
65	West Lawn	56	73	17
66	West Englewood	35	49	14
68	Englewood	56	44	−12
71	Auburn Gresham	38	53	15

community areas from 2008 to 2017, the study's time window. The increase in broadband subscription rates from 2008 to 2017 was found across most neighborhoods that participated in the Smart Communities program, although one community lost ground over the longer period.

In 2017, nine years after the baseline survey and seven years after program implementation began, neighborhoods with Smart Communities (noted on the map by the wired icon) continued to have lower than average broadband connectivity; on average 62 percent of the population had high-speed internet subscriptions, compared to 71 percent for the non-treated neighborhoods (see Figures 5.6).

But when we look at the change in broadband subscriptions, shown in Figures 5.7, there was a 15.3 percent increase for the Smart Communities compared to 8.1 percent for the non-treated neighborhoods. *The Smart Communities experienced almost double the citywide increase in broadband adoption.* The nine-year change in broadband subscription rates is shown in Figure 5.7b with the Smart Communities designated by the wireless icon. These differences are statistically significant. But, these simple differences between the two groups don't control for other factors that may have changed in the neighborhoods over the decade.

Table 5.2 shows the change in broadband subscription rates for the Smart Communities (treated) compared with all other communities (control group) in column 1. This is compared to the average change in unemployment rates (column 2) and in the percent college-educated (column 3) for the two groups. While there is a large difference in the change in broadband subscriptions, the two groups (treated and untreated) have similar change in unemployment rates and in the growth of the college-educated population. This suggests the differences we see in the Smart Communities may be robust to adding statistical controls.

To control for other factors that might have changed in the Chicago neighborhoods over the decade, including gentrification, we use multivariate regression and include controls for demographic variables, population change, median income, and the percent college-educated, a measure of human capital that has been strongly associated with economic outcomes for communities (Moretti 2012). Our measure of college education includes

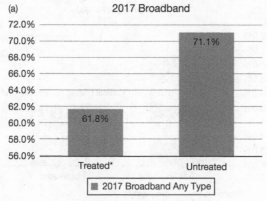

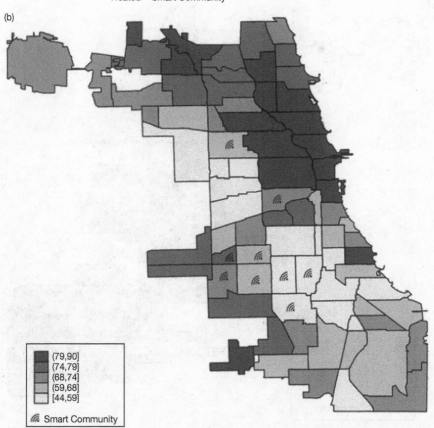

Figure 5.6a and 5.6b Broadband Subscription Rates in 2017 Compared: Treated and Non-Treated Neighborhoods

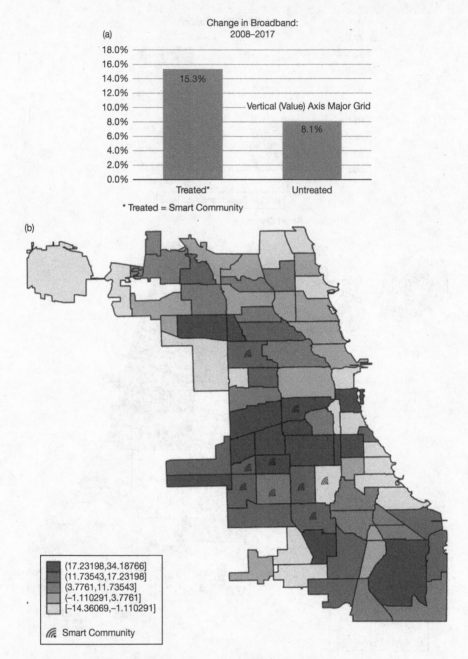

Figure 5.7a and 5.7b Change in Broadband Subscriptions across Chicago Neighborhoods, 2008–2017

Table 5.2 Treated vs. Untreated Communities/Neighborhoods, 2008–2017

	Avg. Broadband Rate Change (%)	Avg. Change in Unemployment (%)	Avg. Change in % College Educated
Smart Communities	15.3	−8.7	2.0
All Other Communities	8.1	−7.1	4.0

associate degrees as well, given that these are low- and moderate-income communities. We include a lagged term for broadband subscriptions in 2008 to predict broadband rates in 2017. This lagged panel design means that the outcome variable is the *change in broadband subscriptions rates*. The unstandardized regression coefficients significance tests are reported in Table A5.1 on the left. Once we control for other factors, we don't see a statistically significant difference between the treated and untreated neighborhoods in the long term.

While the collective differences between the Smart Communities and similar neighborhoods aren't statistically significant in the long run, we explore whether there was some factor that predicted the variation we observed in outcomes across the communities over time. Shown in Table A5.1 (on the right) is the same regression model including an interaction term of the Smart Communities program and the percent college-educated (including associate degrees). This coefficient is positive and statistically significant, meaning that in places with more educated populations and a Smart Communities program, broadband adoption rates increased the most.

Figure 5.8 shows the predicted rate of broadband adoption in 2017 for the Smart Communities (gray line) and other Chicago community areas (black line) based on the interaction model shown in Table A5.1 (right) with all other factors in the multivariate regression model held constant. While the Smart Communities started off lower than non-treated neighborhoods in broadband subscriptions, as the percent of the population with at least an associate degree increases, there is a difference between the two groups. But the confidence intervals cross, so the results are not significant over

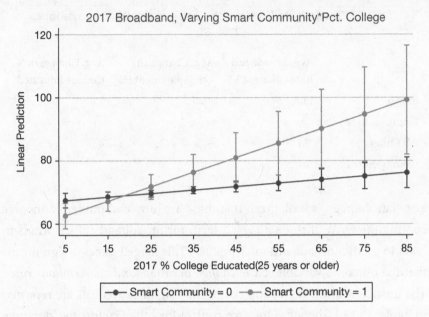

Figure 5.8 Predicted Broadband Subscriptions in 2017 Using Lagged Term

much of the range. This graph provides some evidence that growth in broadband subscriptions continued in Smart Communities when the population overall had higher education. Some neighborhoods included in the program were more socioeconomically mixed than others at the outset and had different experiences over time. The statistical controls for race and ethnicity, income, and education control for gentrification.

Table A5.2 and associated Figure 5.9 model these data more simply and directly, where the outcome variable is now change in broadband adoption rates from 2008 to 2017 and there is no lagged term. Again, the interaction term for a Smart Community neighborhood and percent college-educated (associate, bachelor, or postgraduate degrees) is statistically significant (see Table A5.2, right). The predicted probabilities displayed in Figure 5.9 show a stronger relationship. Holding other demographic and economic factors constant, Smart Communities with over 15 percent of the population with at least an associate degree experienced much more change in broadband adoption over the ten-year period (gray line). Smart Community neighborhoods with 15 percent of the population with

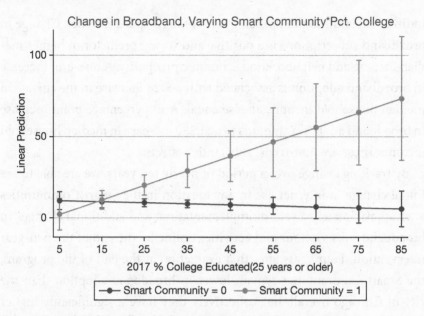

Figure 5.9 Predicted Broadband Subscriptions in 2017 Using Lagged Term

an associate degree or more also experienced higher increases in broadband adoption than those without a Smart Community. This suggests that there may have been some long-term effects of the intervention, but that this was less likely in neighborhoods with the least-educated populations. Access to higher education, including community colleges, may be necessary to fully exploit the economic advantages of broadband for neighborhood prosperity. The findings suggest future rates of connectivity and digital access are contingent on efforts and resources aimed at reducing the digital divide *and* the gap in education.

We also conducted a preliminary analysis of whether increasing broadband subscription rates in Chicago neighborhoods has long-term beneficial economic impacts. The primary predictor variable then becomes the change in broadband subscriptions from 2008 to 2017 for each community area, while the outcome variable is the change in median household income from 2010 to 2017. The models include variables measuring demographic factors in absolute terms and the change in demographic factors over the ten-year period. The Smart Communities program has an indirect effect through increasing rates of high-speed internet. Change in broadband subscriptions is a positive and strong predictor of higher median income and neighborhood economic prosperity. A one-unit increase in broadband adoption is associated with a $128 increase in the change in median household income, all else equal. A 10 percentage point increase in broadband adoption amounts to a $1,280 increase in median household income. These are non-trivial substantive effects.

By tracking change over a period of nearly ten years, we are able to see initial change in internet use in any location in the Smart Communities after approximately a year of implementation, and additional changes in broadband subscriptions and activities online by the end of the two-year intervention. Four years after that evaluation at the end of the program, the Smart Communities remain lower in broadband adoption than the city of Chicago overall, but collectively they have a significantly higher rate of change than the average of the city's community areas. Controlling for other factors, however, it is only the Smart Communities with higher rates of college education (including associate degrees) that have higher broadband subscription rates over the entire period, compared to other Chicago neighborhoods. Community areas with greater change in broadband subscriptions also experienced significant increases in median income over this period, suggesting long-term outcomes for some of the Smart Communities, despite the relatively short two-year intervention. This is strong empirical evidence that the Smart Communities program not only increased internet use but is associated with improved economic outcomes. Because the evaluation compared a program/policy to control neighborhoods using a pre- and post-design (quasi-experiment) with panel data, we have increased confidence in the results.

OTHER CAUSAL INFERENCE METHODS AND LESSONS FOR PLACE-BASED EVALUATION

There have been relatively few quantitative evaluations of the effects of government or nonprofit policy programs on community outcomes (but see Manlove and Whitacre 2019; Hauge and Prieger 2015). Most quasi-experimental studies of broadband's impacts explore the effects of broad-band diffusion through the market rather than place-based interventions. Both types of place-based broadband research share similar challenges for causal inference because of the use of observational data and the lack of random assignment in the treatment (i.e., markets or policy choices).

Researchers evaluating the spatial impacts of broadband infrastructure or training programs face what has been called the "fundamental problem of causal inference" (Holland 1986, 947). That is, scholars who want to assess the effects of a broadband intervention in a city, county, neighbor-hood, or state are usually not able to measure what would have occurred if the intervention had not taken place, assuring them that the broadband program or policy is the cause of the changes they observe. One method for solving this problem is the use of randomized experiments (see Fairlie's discussion of experiments in Chapter 3). However, randomization rarely occurs in the selection of sites for broadband programs. Grants are often awarded on a competitive basis by governments and foundations, and so there may be selection bias; places that participate in programs may have more favorable conditions than other eligible communities. Moreover, places that decide to compete for the grant might be different from those that choose not to compete. Market decisions are not random, either, as internet providers choose more profitable communities first. Thus, due to this self-selection phenomenon (Wheelan 2012), comparisons might lead to biased results. To account for selection bias, quasi-experimental designs of various types can be used (see Cook and Campbell 1979).

One strategy for causal analysis with observational data leverages quasi-experiments where treatment and control groups are not randomized, but outcomes for the treated unit can be compared to similar units that did not receive the policy. Panel data (repeated observations from the same unit, i.e., a within-subjects experiment) and longitudinal data—as in the Smart Communities example—can be used to address causation with a high degree of accuracy, even outside of randomized experiments.

A closely related statistical and research design method for broadband evaluation is the difference-in-differences method (Card and Krueger

1994; Angrist and Pischke 2009; Hanmer 2007). Difference-in-difference is a method able to address and minimize both selection bias and omitted variable bias, the two fundamental problems faced by researchers working with observational data because of the lack of randomization (Angrist and Pischke 2015). Difference in differences (DID) statistically attempts to mimic an experimental research design using observational data to study the differential effect of a treatment (policy, law, program) on a treatment group. It calculates the effect of a treatment (i.e., an explanatory variable) on an outcome variable by comparing the average change (pre vs. post) over time in the outcome variable for the treatment group, compared to the average change (pre vs. post) over time for the control group. Stated more directly, it measures the difference or change in the treated group divided by the change in the control group.

Broadband policies often are natural experiments that impact only specific states, counties, cities, or neighborhoods. For example, Manlove and Whitacre (2019) used difference-in-differences in order to evaluate the broadband adoption-oriented program Connected Nation, while Kim and Orazem (2017) used fixed effects and difference-in-differences to estimate the effects of broadband availability on new firms' locational decisions. The main assumption of difference-in-difference is a parallel trend between the treated and control groups; we assume that the units not affected by the policies are a counterfactual for the treated ones (Cunningham 2018). The method is a strong approach if the control units are carefully selected.

Statistical matching is another technique to develop causal arguments with observational data. Propensity Score Matching (PSM) consists of estimating and assigning to each unit in the sample a score representing the probability of receiving the treatment, given the observable variables (Rosenbaum and Rubin 1983). Both treated and non-treated units are matched on their propensity score. The closer the matched units' propensity score, the more the differences between treated and non-treated units will be minimized, thus, the more plausible will be the hypothesis that the differences in outcomes between the two groups were caused by the treatment.

This method is used in some notable broadband policy evaluations. To measure the impact in rural communities of higher levels of broadband on economic variables such as salaries, job growth, employment growth, and nonfarm private earnings, Stenberg et al. (2009) matched control and treated counties on demographic and economic factors (Stenberg et al. 2009). PSM is used by Whitacre, Gallardo, and Strover (2014a) to measure the effects of both broadband adoption and broadband availability on several economic growth dimensions of rural counties. Although statistical matching tries to overcome the selection bias that characterizes nonrandom experiments, a failure to include the confounding variables can lead to biased results (Heckman and Hotz 1989).

One of the best methods for overcoming threats to selection bias is time series data where the same units are measured repeatedly and the outcome measures change (as well as often in the predictor variable). For time series or longitudinal data, fixed effects are a popular tool to minimize omitted variable bias (Angrist and Pischke 2009, 223; Cunningham 2018, 245). Fixed effects are able to reduce bias in the estimation of causal effects by controlling for time or geographic units (see examples in Atasoy 2013; Mummolo and Peterson 2018). In studies of the fifty states, for example, researchers included forty-nine binary variables for each state (with one state as a reference category) as fixed effects. The idea is that anything influencing the outcome that is specific to an individual state (i.e., NY, CA, or FL) will be held constant. The same logic applies to isolating events that might occur in one year or one time period. Hauge and Prieger (2015) used fixed effects to evaluate whether BTOP managed to increase the broadband adoption rate in counties. A limitation is if the source of bias cannot be isolated to a geographic unit or time period or something measurable.

Instrumental variable regression (two-stage regression models) are often used to develop causal arguments with observational data to address an endogenous predictor variable—defined as an explanatory variable that is caused by something else (Angrist and Pischke 2009, 2015). The idea is the researcher needs to remove or strip out of the predictor variable other factors that are causing it, so the predictor variable becomes exogenous (this is necessary to limit selection bias). To be defined as an instrument, a variable must impact the outcome variable only through the action of the independent variable. Moreover, the instrument should be unrelated to any omitted variable and must not directly be related to the outcome variable. Once scholars have found a suitable instrumental variable (i.e., rainfall, elevation change, geographic area, temperature), they estimate the impact of a policy by using a two-stage least squares method.

Kolko (2012) used this method to study the effects of broadband availability on local economic growth at both county and zip code levels, while LaCombe et al. (2021) used the method to study the effects of broadband subscriptions on state policy innovations and diffusion since the 1980s. In the latter example, a two-stage probit uses three geographic variables (state geographic area, average elevation in a state, and Dobson and Campbell's [2014] measure of the percentage of a state's area that is flat) to predict rates of broadband subscriptions. These three geographic variables affect broadband subscription rates but not state policy innovations. Sovey and Green (2011) developed a checklist for instrumental variable regression. This checklist includes establishing "that an instrumental variable be correlated with an endogenous variable, but not causally related to" it, and the exclusion restriction, that the instrumental variable have no direct effect on the outcome variable. They also recommend using a Wald test of exogeneity.

Alternatively, researchers have also adopted spatial econometrics models such as spatial lag models and spatial error models to estimate broadband impacts. As an example, Mack and Faggian (2013) analyzed whether broadband availability increases productivity, while Whitacre, Gallardo, and Strover (2014b) adopted spatial error models and first differenced regressions to analyze the relationship existing between broadband availability/broadband adoption and jobs and income in rural counties.

As this discussion reveals, it is often difficult with place-based research, as with other evaluation research, to isolate the causal role of broadband in producing outcomes of interest. Despite this uncertainty, prior studies on broadband show that there are a variety of tools that might be applied in program evaluations in order to increase confidence in the results. As Whitacre, Gallardo, and Strover (2014a) argue, the use of quasi-experimental methods can bring us closer to such claims of causation.

CONCLUSION

Disadvantage in the United States is increasingly sorted by place or local geography (Moretti 2012) and it affects lifelong opportunity (Chetty and Hendren 2017). Spatial inequalities in broadband subscriptions and use require that we gain a better understanding of community-level solutions and impacts. Place-based evaluation of broadband's impacts is important for public policy, to understand whether and how interventions create benefits for communities and the larger society. To what extent can programs bring about community-level change in broadband use? And how does that matter for outcomes such as economic development, or the health and well-being of communities? To address such questions, we need place-based evaluations that examine broadband use and do so over time.

Examining trends over time improves our ability to discern causation, as most place-based evaluations involve quasi-experimental designs rather than randomized experiments. Additionally, long-term evaluations allow us to understand dynamic relationships in communities: are gains expanded or sustained; and how do they matter for long-term benefits in communities? The Smart Communities evaluation offers an example of long-term evaluation with data at several different points in time, and insights that varied across time. Measuring broadband subscriptions at the neighborhood level demonstrated that community-level change occurred during implementation, producing higher and substantively significant gains for the Smart Communities, compared with other similarly situated Chicago community areas. While those gains were sustained only in treated neighborhoods with relatively higher rates of college attainment (at least 15 percent with an associate degree or more), places that did experience higher continued growth reaped significant increases in annual median household income, estimated at $128 for each one-point increase in broadband subscriptions (controlling for other factors). Place-based evaluations can provide better guidance for policy—suggesting the role of education as well as broadband adoption, for example, or the need for programs beyond the short time frame of many government- and grant-funded efforts (especially in communities with lower levels of education).

Central to the improvement of evaluation research on community-level impacts is a greater focus on quasi-experimental designs and longitudinal data that can yield more confidence about the causal role of interventions. Community-level measures of adoption and use are critical for evaluating programs designed to boost adoption, such as training and outreach programs, but they are also necessary to more accurately understand how infrastructure investments affect surrounding communities. With the American Community Survey, new data on mobile and fixed broadband subscriptions is now available for all census tracts in the US. Yet there are still significant gaps for longitudinal data on subscriptions. There is no subnational data on activities online, which could serve as proximate outcomes for infrastructure or training interventions. Estimates based on multilevel modeling of citywide surveys (as in the Chicago study) provides one solution for estimating data on adoption or activities online at the scale of interventions, whether they are in urban neighborhoods, rural counties, or Tribal communities. "Big data" generated through activities online may be another source for researchers in the future. Microsoft has gathered data from Xbox and other products to study broadband speeds, and data on the density of domain name websites has been used as a measure of broadband use in communities (Mossberger, Tolbert, and LaCombe 2021a).

Place-based evaluations are important for revealing distinctions in needs and potential solutions across communities. Barriers to technology use in urban neighborhoods vary between African American and Latino communities (Mossberger, Tolbert, Bowen, and Jimenez 2012). Rural communities with older and less-educated populations may experience different benefits from broadband investments than places that primarily lack infrastructure (Stenberg et al. 2009; see Strover in this volume).

Strategies for increasing connectivity or adoption in Tribal communities must also recognize the unique challenges and goals of each nation (Duarte 2017). Place matters in varied and complex ways, and we need evaluations and policy recommendations that provide evidence in a diversity of communities.

NOTES

1. https://www.oecd.org/sti/broadband/broadband-statistics/
2. The method is commonly referred to as Mr. P, for post-stratification.
3. The data were downloaded from the Census website at the tract level and then aggregated to the neighborhood level, weighted by community area population size. As with the dependent variables, the independent variables used in this analysis are the differences between the 2008 and 2013 neighborhood-level values.
4. The coefficient for the treatment (Chicago Smart Communities) is positive and statistically significant with a 95 percent confidence interval.

REFERENCES

Angrist, J. D., and J.-S. Pischke. 2009. *Mostly Harmless Econometrics: An Empiricist's Companion*. Princeton, NJ: Princeton University Press.

Angrist, J. D., and J.-S. Pischke. 2015. *Mastering 'Metrics: The Path from Cause to Effect*. Princeton, NJ and Oxford: Princeton University Press.

Atasoy, H. 2013. "The Effects of Broadband Internet Expansion on Labor Market Outcomes." *Industrial & Labor Relations Review* 66 (2): 315–345.

Bayer, P., S. Ross, and G. Topa. 2008. "Place of Work and Place of Residence: Informal Hiring Networks and Labor Market Outcomes." NBER Working Paper 11019. https://www.nber.org/papers/w11019.

Caplovitz, D. 1963. *The Poor Pay More: Consumer Practices of Low-Income Families*. New York, NY: Free Press.

Card, D., and A. Krueger. 1994. "Minimum Wages and Employment: A Case Study of the Fast-Food Industry in New Jersey and Pennsylvania." *The American Economic Review* 84 (4): 772–793.

Chetty, R., J. N. Friedman, N. Hendren, M. R. Jones, and S. R. Porter. 2018. "The Opportunity Atlas: Mapping the Childhood Roots of Social Mobility." NBER Working Paper 25147. https://opportunityinsights.org/paper/the-opportunity-atlas/.

Chetty, R., and N. Hendren. 2017. "The Impacts of Neighborhoods on Intergenerational Mobility II: County-Level Estimates." http://www.equality-of-opportunity.org/assets/documents/movers_paper2.pdf

Cook, T. D., and D. T. Campbell. 1979. *Quasi-Experimentation: Design and Analysis Issues for Field Settings*. Chicago: Rand McNally College.

Cunningham, S. 2018. *Causal Inference: The Mixtape (V. 1.8)*. New Haven, CT: Yale University Press.

Currie, J. 2011. "Health and Residential Location." In *Neighborhood and Life Chances: How Place Matters in Modern America*, edited by H. B. Newburger, E. L. Birch, and S. M. Wachter, 3–17. Philadelphia: University of Pennsylvania Press.

Dailey, D., A. Bryne, A. Powell, J. Karaganis, and J. Chung. 2010. "Broadband Adoption in Low-Income Communities." Social Science Research Council. https://pdfs.semanticscholar.org/dde5/13083ed19e7187e833cd41ae421a35d7064c.pdf

Dobson, J. E., and J. S. Campbell. 2014. "The Flatness of US States." *Geographical Review* 104 (1): 1–9.

Duarte, M. E. 2017. *Network Sovereignty: Building the Internet across Indian Country*. Seattle, WA: University of Washington Press.

Dunbar, J. 2011. "Wealthy Suburbs Get Best Broadband Deals; D.C., Rural Areas Lag Behind." Washington, DC: Investigative Reporting Workshop.

Federal Communications Commission. 2010. "Connecting America: The National Broadband Plan." Washington, DC. https://transition.fcc.gov/national-broadband-plan/national-broadband-plan.pdf

Federal Communications Commission. 2019. "2019 Broadband Deployment Report." Washington, DC. https://docs.fcc.gov/public/attachments/FCC-19-44A1.pdf

Federal Reserve, and Brookings. 2008. "The Enduring Challenge of Concentrated Poverty in America: Case Studies from Communities across the U.S." Washington, DC: The Brookings Institution.

Fishbane, L., and A. Tomer. 2020. "Neighborhood Broadband Data Makes It Clear: We Need an Agenda to Fight Digital Poverty." Washington, DC: The Brookings Institution. https://www.brookings.edu/blog/the-avenue/2020/02/05/neighborhood-broadband-data-makes-it-clear-we-need-an-agenda-to-fight-digital-poverty/

Gangadharan, S. P., and G. Byrum. 2012. "Introduction: Defining and Measuring Meaningful Broadband Adoption." *International Journal of Communication* 6: 2601–2608.

Giannone, E. 2017. "Skilled-Biased Technical Change and Regional Convergence." In *2017 Meeting Papers* (No. 190). Society for Economic Dynamics. https://www.semanticscholar.org/paper/Skill-Biased-Technical-Change-and-Regional-Giannone/b1b53539bce99180796cd99f3afec2be8b9a7ac7

Goolsbee, A., and P. J. Klenow. 2002. "Evidence on Learning and Network Externalities in the Diffusion of Home Computers." *Journal of Law and Economics*, 45 (2): 317–343.

Hanmer, M. J. 2007. "An Alternative Approach to Estimating Who Is Most Likely to Respond to Changes in Registration Laws." *Political Behavior* 29: 1–30. https://doi.org/10.1007/s11109-006-9022-5

Hauge, J. A., and J. E. Prieger. 2015. "Evaluating the Impact of the American Recovery and Reinvestment Act's BTOP on Broadband Adoption." *Applied Economics* 47 (60): 6553–6579.

Heckman, J. J., and V. J. Hotz. 1989. "Choosing among Alternative Nonexperimental Methods for Estimating the Impact of Social Programs: The Case of Manpower Training." *Journal of the American Statistical Association* 84 (408): 862–874.

Holland, P. W. 1986. "Statistics and Causal Inference." *Journal of the American Statistical Association* 81 (396): 945–960.

Holloway, S. R., and S. Mulherin. 2004. "The Effect of Adolescent Neighborhood Poverty on Adult Employment." *Journal of Urban Affairs* 26 (4): 427–454.

Jargowsky, P. A. 1997. *Poverty and Place*. New York, NY: Russell Sage Foundation.

Kaplan, D., and K. Mossberger. 2012. "Prospects for Poor Neighborhoods in the Broadband Era: Neighborhood-Level Influences on Technology Use at Work." *Economic Development Quarterly* 26 (1): 95–105.

Kim, Y., and P. F. Orazem. 2017. "Broadband Internet and New Firm Location Decisions in Rural Areas." *American Journal of Agricultural Economics* 99 (1): 285–302.

Kolko, J. 2012. "Broadband and Local Growth." *Journal of Urban Economics* 71 (1): 100–113.

LaCombe, S. J., Tolbert, C., and Mossberger, K. 2021. "Information and Policy Innovation in U.S. States." *Political Research Quarterly*. April 2021. doi:10.1177/10659129211006783.

Lax, J. R., and J. H. Phillips. 2009. "How Should We Estimate Public Opinion in the States?" *American Journal of Political Science* 53 (1): 107–121.

LISC Chicago. 2009. "A Platform for Participation and Innovation." Chicago. http://archive.lisc-chicago.org/uploads/lisc-chicago/documents/scpmasterplan.pdf

Mack, E. A., and A. Faggian. 2013. "Productivity and Broadband: The Human Factor." *International Regional Science Review* 36 (3): 392–423.

Manlove, J., and B. Whitacre. 2019. "An Evaluation of the Connected Nation Broadband Adoption Program." *Telecommunications Policy* 43 (7): 1–11.

Massey, D. S., and N. A. Denton. 1993. *American Apartheid: Segregation and the Making of the Underclass*. Cambridge, MA: Harvard University Press.

Moretti, E. 2012. *The New Geography of Jobs*. New York: First Mariner Books.

Mossberger, K. 2012. "Smart Communities: Formative Evaluation." University of Illinois at Chicago. https://techdatasociety.asu.edu/sites/default/files/uploads/smartcommunitiesformativeevaluation.pdf

Mossberger, K., D. Kaplan, and M. Gilbert. 2008. "Going Online without Easy Access: A Tale of Three Cities." *Journal of Urban Affairs* 30 (5): 469–488.

Mossberger, K. and C. J. Tolbert. 2009. "Digital Excellence in Chicago: A Citywide View of Technology Use." https://www.chicago.gov/content/dam/city/depts/doit/supp_info/DEI/Digital_Excellence_Study_2009.pdf

Mossberger, K., C. J. Tolbert, and C. Anderson. 2014. "Measuring Change in Internet Use and Broadband Adoption: Comparing BTOP Smart Communities and Other Chicago Neighborhoods [Updated 2014]." https://techdatasociety.asu.edu/sites/default/files/uploads/smartcommunities_measuringinternetchangeinchicago.pdf

Mossberger, K., C. J. Tolbert, D. Bowen, and B. Jimenez. 2012. "Unraveling Different Barriers to Internet Use: Urban Residents and Neighborhood Effects." *Urban Affairs Review* 48 (6): 771–810.

Mossberger, K., C. J. Tolbert, and W. Franko. 2012. *Digital Cities: The Internet and the Geography of Opportunity*. New York, NY: Oxford University Press.

Mossberger, K., C. J. Tolbert, and M. Gilbert. 2006. "Race, Place, and Information Technology." *Urban Affairs Review* 41 (5): 583–620.

Mossberger, K., C. J. Tolbert, and S. LaCombe. 2021a. "Measuring Digital Entrepreneurship at the Grassroots: What Role Will It Play in Community Resilience?" In *Big Data Directions in Entrepreneurship Research: Researcher Viewpoints*, 21–25. Kansas City, MO: Ewing Marion Kauffman Foundation. https://www.kauffman.org/wp-content/uploads/2021/05/Big-Data-Directions-in-Entrepreneurship-Research.pdf

Mossberger, K., C. J. Tolbert, and S. LaCombe. 2021b. *Choosing the Future: Technology and Opportunity for Communities*. New York, NY: Oxford University Press.

Mummolo, J., and E. Peterson. 2018. "Improving the Interpretation of Fixed Effects Regression Results." *Political Science Research and Methods* 6 (4): 829–835.

OECD. 2017. "OECD Broadband Portal." 2017. https://www.oecd.org/sti/broadband/broadband-statistics/

Pacheco, J. 2011. "Using National Surveys to Measure Dynamic U.S. State Public Opinion: A Guideline for Scholars and an Application." *State Politics & Policy Quarterly* 11 (4): 415–439.

Raudenbush, S. W., and A. S. Bryk. 2002. *Hierarchical Linear Models: Applications and Data Analysis Methods (Advanced Quantitative Techniques in the Social Sciences)*. Thousand Oaks, CA: Sage.

Rhinesmith, C. 2016. "Digital Inclusion and Meaningful Broadband Adoption Initiatives." Benton Institute. https://www.benton.org/publications/digital-inclusion-and-meaningful-broadband-adoption-initiatives.

Romm, T. 2020. "'It Shouldn't Take a Pandemic': Coronavirus Exposes Internet Inequality among U.S. Students as Schools Close Their Doors." *The Washington Post*, March 16, 2020. https://www.washingtonpost.com/technology/2020/03/16/schools-internet-inequality-coronavirus/

Rosenbaum, P. R., and D. B. Rubin. 1983. "The Central Role of the Propensity Score in Observational Studies for Causal." *Biometrika* 70 (1): 41–55.

Salemink, K., D. Strijker, and G. Bosworth. 2017. "Rural Development in the Digital Age: A Systematic Literature Review on Unequal ICT Availability, Adoption, and Use in Rural Areas." *Journal of Rural Studies* 54: 360–371.

Schartman-Cycyk, S., K. Mossberger, B. Callahan, S. Novak, A. Sheon, A. Siefer, E. Mancinas, and S. K. Cho. 2019. "Connecting Cuyahoga Investment in Digital Inclusion Brings Big Returns for Residents and Administration." https://static1.squarespace.com/static/59d3bca38dd041c401d9ed80/t/5d5c448f6fede80001a75334/1566328034944/Connecting+Cuyahoga_2019.pdf

Snijders, T. A., and R. J. Bosker. 2011. *Multilevel Analysis: An Introduction to Basic and Advanced Multilevel Modeling*. Thousand Oaks, CA: Sage.

Sovey, A. J., and D. P. Green. 2011. "Instrumental Variables Estimation in Political Science: A Readers' Guide." *American Journal of Political Science* 55 (1): 188–200.

Steenbergen, M. R., and B. S. Jones. 2002. "Modeling Multilevel Data Structures." *American Journal of Political Science* 46 (1): 218–237.

Stenberg, P., M. Morehart, S. Vogel, J. Cromartie, V. Breneman, and D. Brown. 2009. "Broadband Internet's Value for Rural America." U.S. Department of Agriculture.

Economic Research Service. Economic Research Report No. 78. https://www.ers.usda.gov/webdocs/publications/46200/9335_err78_1_.pdf?v=41056.

Stewart, N. 2020. "She's 10, Homeless and Eager to Learn. But She Has No Internet." *The New York Times*, March 26, 2020. https://www.nytimes.com/2020/03/26/nyregion/new-york-homeless-students-coronavirus.html

The Associated Press. 2020. "School Shutdowns Raise Stakes of Digital Divide for Students." *PBS News Hour*, March 30, 2020. https://www.pbs.org/newshour/education/school-shutdowns-raise-stakes-of-digital-divide-for-students

Tomer, A., E. Kneebone, and R. Shivaram. 2017. "Signs of Digital Distress: Mapping Broadband Availability and Subscription in American Neighborhoods." Washington, DC. Brookings Institution. https://www.brookings.edu/wp-content/uploads/2017/09/broadbandreport_september2017.pdf

US Senate. 2019. "Broadband Mapping: Challenges and Solutions." US Senate. 2019. https://www.commerce.senate.gov/2019/4/broadband-mapping-challenges-and-solutions

Wheelan, C. 2012. *Naked Statistics: Stripping the Dread from the Data*. New York, NY: W. W. Norton.

Whitacre, B., R. Gallardo, and S. Strover. 2014a. "Broadband's Contribution to Economic Growth in Rural Areas: Moving towards a Causal Relationship." *Telecommunications Policy* 38 (11): 1011–1023.

Whitacre, B., R. Gallardo, and S. Strover. 2014b. "Does Rural Broadband Impact Jobs and Income? Evidence from Spatial and First-Differenced Regressions." *The Annals of Regional Science* 53 (3): 649–670.

Wilson, W. J. 1987. *The Truly Disadvantaged: The Inner City, the Underclass, and Public Policy*. Chicago, IL: University of Chicago Press.

APPENDIX

Table A5.1 MULTIVARIATE REGRESSION ESTIMATING CHANGE IN 2017
BROADBAND SUBSCRIPTION RATES, LAGGED PANEL MODELS

Lagged Model 1: Broadband Rates, 2017		Lagged Model 2: Broadband Rates, 2017	
	2017 Broadband		2017 Broadband
2008 Broadband	0.1404*	2008 Broadband	0.1578*
	(0.0686)		(0.06666)
Population Change, 2010–2017	0.0005	Smart Community	−6.6318*
	(0.0003)		(2.5752)
Smart Community	−2.3961	Percent College	0.1100*
	(1.6696)		(0.0433)
Median Income	0.0002***	Smart Community x Percent College	0.3495*
	(0.0000)		(0.1355)
Percent Over 65 Yrs.	0.0295	Population Change, 2010–2017	0.0005
	(0.1348)		(0.0003)
Percent White	−0.6861	Median Income	0.0002***
	(0.5538)		(0.0000)
Percent Black	−0.6778	Percent Over 65 Yrs.	0.0118
	(0.5449)		(0.1308)
Percent Hispanic	−0.5556	Percent White	−0.7075
	(0.5416)		(0.5596)
Percent Asian	−00615	Percent Black	−0.6957
	(0.5482)		(0.5511)
Percent College	0.1339**	Percent Hispanic	−0.5803
	(0.0466)		(0.5481)
		Percent Asian	−0.6208
			(0.5543)
Constant	110.4438*	Constant	111.9580*
	(53.8377)		(54.5267)
N	77	*N*	77

Standard Errors in parentheses   Standard Errors in parentheses
*p<0.05, **p<0.01, ***p<0.001   *p<0.05, **p<0.01, ***p<0.001

Table A5.2 OUTCOME VARIABLE CHANGE IN BROADBAND SUBSCRIPTIONS
RATHER THAN USING THE LAGGED TERM

Change Model 1 Change in Broadband (Any Type), 2008–2017		Change Model 2 Change in Broadband (Any Type), 2008–2017	
Population Change, 2010–2017	0.0000 (0.0006)	Smart Community	−13.238* (6.273)
Smart Community	−1.6159 (3.6799)	Percent College	−0.062 (0.099)
Median Income	0.0002 (0.0001)	Smart Community x Percent College	0.9553** (0.309)
Percent Over 65 Yrs.	0.1307 (0.3270)	Population Change, 2010–2017	0.0001 (0.0006)
Percent White	0.3526 (1.4751)	Median Income	0.0002 (0.0001)
Percent Black	0.5515 (1.4228)	Percent Over 65 Yrs.	0.077 (0.324)
		Percent White	0.237 (1.469)
Percent Hispanic	0.7400 (1.4242)	Percent Black	0.435 (1.417)
Percent Asian	0.3458 (1.4409)	Percent Hispanic	0.601 (1.420)
Percent College	−0.0044 (0.1091)	Percent Asian	0.241 (1.434)
Constant	−53.1010 (139.9650)	Constant	−39.944 (139.509)
N	77	N	77
Standard Errors in parentheses *p<0.05, **p<0.01, ***p<0.001		Standard Errors in parentheses *p<0.05, **p<0.01, ***p<0.001	

PART III

Asking the Right Questions

PART II

Asking the Right Questions

6

Broadband for Telemedicine and Health Services

SHARON STROVER

INTRODUCTION

Advances in communications infrastructure have been linked to the delivery of healthcare for many decades. Communication technologies' advantages for extending information and expertise across geographic distances, and their ability to give health providers potential cost savings, have been highly attractive. Health services in the US face rising expenses even as the populations in need of services continue to grow. In the case of rural health providers particularly, rural retrenchment of medical services means shrinking physical facilities, for which communications services can substitute in certain ways. The onset of broadband specifically, as a high capacity and low latency transmission service as well as a way to connect many people or consumers to Internet-based information and health services, brings tremendous opportunities.

Research into telecommunications applications to health has been ongoing for decades. Some broad categories of communication-based interactions have developed. One comprises campaigns and programs to improve health or health information; anti-smoking, obesity prevention, and anti-cancer campaigns are common domains that use various

Sharon Strover, *Broadband for Telemedicine and Health Services* In: *Transforming Everything?*. Edited by: Karen Mossberger, Eric W. Welch, and Yonghong Wu, Oxford University Press. © Oxford University Press 2022. DOI: 10.1093/oso/9780190082871.003.0007 communications techniques and technologies including the Internet, social media, wearables, and smartphone functions to promote certain behaviors. Another category of communication technology interventions might best be labeled innovations to improve doctor-patient or health service provider/user interactions and outcomes. This category receives a great deal of attention squarely within the medical domain and invokes a wide range of systemic factors such as the organizational qualities of hospitals or clinics, for example, or the risk aversion of patients and doctors with respect to trying new techniques or technologies. Examinations of the process for transmitting diagnostics to distant experts, systems used for remote diagnosis, cost effectiveness, and sensors that can quickly relay time-sensitive health indicators are representative of this type of focus. Finally, maintaining a capable and ubiquitous broadband network that is not only technically reliable and adequate in quality but also one that geographically reaches the appropriate users, clinics, hospitals, and other medical facilities has been a national goal for many years, arguably since Universal Service was written into the 1996 Telecommunications Act. The Federal Communications Commission (FCC) and several scholars have examined the suitability of broadband network connections, policies, and shifts for telemedicine purposes.

From the time of radio onward, communication technologies have penetrated health services delivery and organization with the promise of extending resources to remote or rural regions as well as to trim the costs of service delivery. With the arrival of broadband networks operating at a 25 Mbps download and 3 Mbps upload standard, possibly abetted by wireless 5G services in the future, and populations accustomed to using smartphones and their apps, we are on the cusp of the latest generation of applications and services capable of enhancing both the campaign and information seeking models as well as direct service delivery models within the healthcare ecosystem.

This chapter considers the role of telecommunications services in healthcare, particularly the prospects for broadband networks' potential contributions. The 2020 pandemic represented a surge in telehealth use nationwide, and funding through multiple relief programs. The FCC's

$100 million Connected Care Pilot Program is supporting new initiatives nationwide.[1] Yet, as this history demonstrates, efforts have been underway for many years. We focus especially on some of the opportunities to evaluate the broadband-based innovations in healthcare. As is the case in many applications domains, optimism around using communications systems to improve healthcare is high, but evidence-based proof and strong research designs are less common than is desirable.

We will briefly review some of the language and intent of broadband-related health services regulations and federal agency programs, and then present some detail on broadband infrastructure availability and adoption. We single out rural broadband and health needs since less populated regions lag in both infrastructure and health services. Some notable projects that have linked broadband capabilities and health services infrastructure include the FCC's early mHealth panel's work, as well as its Pilot Health Care projects, which were recast into four Universal Service programs: the Healthcare Connect Fund, the Rural Health Care Telecommunications Program, the Rural Health Care Internet Access Program, and the Rural Health Care Pilot Program (FCC 2018a). The national push toward electronic health records and meaningful use criteria initiated in 2010 also are relevant to a discussion of the role of broadband networks. Finally, we comment on measurement and evaluation issues with respect to having broadband connectivity in the equation. The health field has a long history of medical clinical trials, and examining the ways that broadband connectivity can affect patient care, clinic and hospital operations, and how it might interact with service habits and standards presents important questions.

HEALTHCARE AND BROADBAND

Cost factors have figured prominently in new interest in using broadband-based services for healthcare. The healthcare costs in the US approached $3.8 trillion as of 2019, according to the Centers for Medicare and Medicaid Services (Centers for Medicare and Medicaid Services 2020).

Most analysts acknowledge that healthcare systems' costs are skyrocketing (ibid.; FCC 2010, 199). The US has been rated as 37th in healthcare system performance internationally, but spends more money per capita and per GDP on health than other countries (Sawyer and Cox 2018; FCC 2010). The US also faces an aging population whose healthcare needs will escalate, compounded by a geographic misdistribution of health services. Not only are healthcare services more limited in rural regions, they also are less affordable for lower income populations who often are concentrated in rural or highly urban regions; the Affordable Care Act may have changed that situation at least somewhat. Finally, substantial health disparities exist across ethnic and racial groups and also within rural regions. According to one source, "rural communities have higher rates of preventable conditions (such as obesity, diabetes, cancer, and injury) and higher rates of related high-risk health behaviors (such as smoking, physical inactivity, poor diet, and limited use of seatbelts)" (see Basiu, Negussie, and Geller 2017 for health disparities in rural places). One report sponsored by a healthcare company notes that rural dwellers find accessing care more difficult for reasons of cost and distance (UnitedHealth Center 2011). The Kaiser Family Foundation also notes that rural populations depend more heavily on Medicaid and federal sources of healthcare support compared to urban regions (Foutz, Artiga, and Garfield 2017). These locational differences suggest that technology-based healthcare economies targeting this population could be an important priority.

Cost factors alone have prompted many to seek ways to economize on healthcare services, and in that context the possibilities for using telecommunications to reduce certain costs and to expand geographic reach are receiving more attention. In part this can be attributed to the tremendous 21st-century spread of both wireline and wireless infrastructure, ubiquitous devices such as smartphones, and the explosion of Internet-based applications in the US and elsewhere. As well, a series of explicit technical and service innovations and policy changes that facilitated the application of broadband to health problems have emerged in the Internet environment. The American Telehealth Association maintains a useful listing of state-specific policies around different telehealth services and

chronicles important policy-related developments that affect reimbursement for telemedicine (American Telemedicine Association n.d.). The
literature is replete with rosy predictions for telemedicine within broadband environments. For example, one U.S. Chamber of Commerce Report
states "Broadband is facilitating the development of a number of cutting-
edge approaches to healthcare, many of which are expected to lead to vast
individual and national cost savings and to an increase in the availability
of quality health solutions. Moreover, broadband-enabled telemedicine
services are shifting the healthcare paradigm by, among other things, enabling in-home care and real-time patient monitoring and focusing on
disease prevention by enhancing personal wellbeing" (Davidson and
Santorelli 2009, 3). However, an early assessment of the evaluation literature on telemedicine in general illustrates a lack of strong research
designs and limited evidence regarding telemedicine's positive impact
on clinical outcomes (Ekeland, Bowes, and Flottorp 2010). Nevertheless,
broadband-related health technologies are constantly evolving, and they
reside in an environment in which more people are comfortable using in-
home technologies for various purposes, including health monitoring or
health reminders, and one in which the provider community too becomes
smarter regarding the most suitable systems and applications. A broadband environment that can eventually support various remote monitoring
apparatuses from wearable sensors to mobile diagnostic systems could
dramatically increase care opportunities while limiting costs (Dorsey and
Topol 2016).

Standardizing Language and Services

Developing policy around broadband and health services will depend on
generating a consistent language to describe services. One issue facing
the entire healthcare industry as it intersects communication and information technologies concerns the lack of standardized terms to describe
health communications applications. Both the literature on and the practice of healthcare associated with communication technologies invoke

different terminology to describe their domains. For example, terms such as mHealth (for mobile health), e-care, telehealth, telemedicine, and Health IT are often used interchangeably; this causes difficulties among formal programs run by state or federal agencies or insurance companies expected to reimburse for services because they require standard definitions. Consistent terminology among providers, institutions, and users/patients also will be necessary in order to develop adequate legal frameworks governing services. For example, *telemedicine* is a multidimensional concept that sometimes means the process of faxing records or diagnostic test results and sometimes continuing education for health professionals using a videoconference network. To the extent that its components are defined consistently, one can assess different applications and installations: standard definitions are required for assessments in terms of cost, quality, and effectiveness (Shaw et al. 2017). Since we can probably expect that some communication-mediated interaction will become a routine component of "normal" healthcare practices, generating consistent terms to describe those services or applications will be essential for record keeping, intra-institutional practices, and reimbursements.

Bashshur et al. (2011) develop the framework illustrated in Figure 6.1 to explore telemedicine dimensions, addressing the *health service/ user* categories mentioned earlier. Their breakdown of functionalities, applications, and technologies begins to map a taxonomy that brings together elements of the technological mediation with types of healthcare activities. These three aspects of technologically based services suggest some of the variations in how one characterizes telemedicine as well as the specific sorts of tasks and domains in which that term can be used. With respect to broadband and Internet-related aspects, network capabilities—including speed or capacity as well as reliability—are critical. This typology breaks "technology" into three categories, usefully noting that the type of network, its specific connectivity imprint, and whether it is asynchronous or synchronous can affect the sorts of telemedicine services offered; indeed, the geographical range and type of connectivity and its use characteristics, such as whether it links to home-based sensors monitoring blood sugar levels or entails networks enabled with real-time, two-way video for

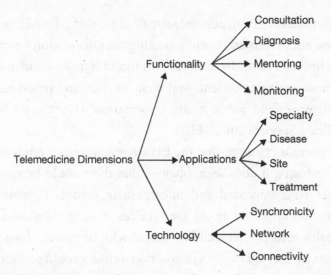

Figure 6.1 Telemedicine Dimensions
SOURCE: Bashshur et al. (2011).

visual diagnostic and treatment purposes, can vary greatly. Their typology begins to sketch out the levels of specification that could be necessary to use a term like "telemedicine" with precision.

Electronic Health Records

Another related policy concerns the federal effort to incorporate electronic records (electronic health records or EHRs) into the national health infrastructure. Electronic records would facilitate the processing of insurance and reimbursements associated with healthcare, and presumably also help to manage patients' care by multiple caregivers. Moving toward electronic health records has been accompanied by a "Meaningful Use standard" that establishes certain criteria and incentives for reimbursement of the efforts to transition to electronic records (ARRA 2009). Several federal agencies established financial incentives amounting to $19 billion as of 2012 to motivate practices and institutions to adopt the standards. The federal definition of "meaningful use" of electronic records is: "electronically capturing health information in a structured format, using that information to track key clinical conditions and communicating the information for care coordination, implementing decision support tools for disease and medication management, engaging patients and their families, and reporting clinical quality measures and public health information" (Centers for Medicare and Medicaid Services 2010, 44321).

While there is criticism that the EHR emphasis was unduly fueled by the data industry, it does seem obvious that there could be savings and efficiencies with improved and interoperable records (Creswell 2013). Like using standardized terms for services, having standardized electronic health records that could be shared with or passed along to other institutions such as pharmacies or additional clinics could provide savings and enhance care, and they could be especially useful for telehealth services where several remote providers may need access to health records. The utility of such records clearly would rely on information technology as well as broadband networks—and resolving all the security concerns that go along with sharing any personal digital data. In the wake of various deep and broad security breaches across numerous public and private data holders, it is unclear that the federal effort to motivate the medical industry to adopt electronic health records has been accompanied by comparable efforts to insure those records' privacy.

The FCC's 2012 assessment of its Rural Health Care Pilot Program (discussed further in the following paragraphs), notes the significance of broadband networks for facilitating the exchange of EHRs, explicitly linking them to improving the quality and reducing the costs of delivering healthcare in rural areas (FCC Wireline Competition Bureau 2012). Implementing EHR systems has been fraught with controversy insofar as different types of organizational arrangements (well resourced, university-based hospitals, for example) in different geographic regions, notably urban, are better equipped to make this transition and consequently to profit from the incentives offered by the government (Jamoom and Yang 2016). It seems clear that the backbone of any system must be an acceptable internal network on which appropriate software can run, as well as a secure network connection for external filesharing. However, achieving these technical standards and incorporating government-defined standards such as patient access to health records are challenging.

Creating the most effective telemedicine applications invokes concerns regarding the ubiquity and quality of broadband networks. If contemporary broadband connectivity around the US affects how telemedicine services will evolve, it bears examination. While detailed analysis of the quality of US broadband is beyond the scope of this chapter, there are some salient aspects that should be noted.

BROADBAND INFRASTRUCTURE CAPABILITIES: METRO AND NONMETRO CONSIDERATIONS

The National Telecommunications and Information Administration (NTIA) initiated state-by-state broadband mapping as part of its infrastructure development program under the American Reinvestment and Recovery Act of 2009, expanding the efforts that the FCC had made since 1996 to document the state of the US broadband infrastructure. NTIA's mapping represented an improvement over the FCC data gathered from vendors under form 477. However, as of 2013 this improved mapping effort was transferred back to the FCC. Both the FCC and NTIA data repeatedly illustrate deficits in rural broadband infrastructure as well as adoption and use. Moreover, criticism of the FCC's mapping efforts is widespread, with many alleging that their estimate of households lacking broadband access is too low (Whitacre, Strover, and Rhinesmith 2018; Lohr 2018; Microsoft 2018). However, as of 2021 the FCC remains the only national broadband data repository.

The broadband maps collect information about the types of networks available for business and residential use, their advertised speeds, the providers who own them, and their coverage. Broadband maps illustrate coverage gaps and begin to suggest where service alternatives or competition exist. What is most pertinent to the impact of broadband on healthcare options is that rural regions generally have fewer providers and less robust infrastructure. One NTIA report noted that rural-urban network disparities increase as speeds increase, so that rural regions that might require high speeds for certain telehealth applications would be incapable of supporting them from a network perspective (Beede and Neville 2013). Confirming this, Whitacre, Wheeler, and Landgraf (2017) used national FCC broadband connection data for anchor institutions to compare nonmetro to metro health-related institutions and concluded that speeds used in nonmetro health facilities from 2010 through 2014 were far less robust than their urban counterparts.

From the perspective of home-based health applications, from 2000 to 2010 there was a consistent 13 percent gap in household broadband subscription between metro and nonmetro regions (Whitacre, Gallardo, and Strover 2014). Limited household-based Internet access can affect information health seeking as well as certain types of service delivery. While currently the status of a household connection quality may be most pertinent to campaign-style information and certain smartphone- or text-based applications—information one can read, videos one can view, for example—connection quality may be essential in the future for home-based monitoring, diagnosis, and even treatment. The 2018 FCC Broadband Deployment Report reports fixed 25 Mbps download/3 Mbps upload quality terrestrial connections as 69.3 percent, 97.9 percent, and 64.6 percent for rural, urban, and tribal percentages of the population, respectively (FCC 2018b, 50), clearly illustrating disparities in rural and tribal environments; tribal lands have especially poor service. Microsoft reports even greater disparities, claiming that 162.8 million people lack broadband service compared to the FCC's estimate of 24.7 million people (Microsoft 2018).

Both telecommunications companies and the FCC respond that wireless connectivity rather than wireline may be most appropriate for rural services, since that infrastructure is intrinsically less expensive, faster to build, and provides mobility. However, most wireless cellular services do not reach broadband thresholds of service. The 2018 Broadband Deployment Report notes that availability of mobile LTE at speeds of at least 10 Mbps down and 3 uploading are available to 70.1 percent of the rural population, compared to 90.5 percent of the urban population.

Tribal populations are covered by such services at even lower percentages, 63.7 percent (FCC 2018b, 52). At this writing, debates about the substitutability of wireless for wireline and the equity implications of one service standard for rural regions and another for metro regions are lively and charged. The FCC's current broadband standard of 25/3 Mbps guides its assessments of network capacity and its funding allocations through the Connect America Fund.

As wireless networks supporting widespread mobile connectivity through smartphones and other devices developed, wireless broadband services in various application domains including health became viable. Even if wireless speeds do not match those of terrestrial networks as is the case for rural regions, they can be useful for certain applications. The FCC and several health-related institutions have singled out health services as a highly significant service domain for broadband, highlighting that the bandwidth requirements of various conventional telemedicine applications range from fairly low bandwidth requirements of text to the much greater requirements of graphics and streaming video (Figure 6.2). The 2010 National Broadband Plan from the FCC reported that for 60 percent of doctors, the fax machine was the dominant clinician

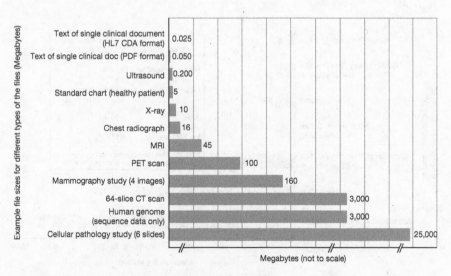

Figure 6.2 Megabyte Requirements for Various Applications
SOURCE: FCC National Broadband Plan (2010, 210).

communication, and that only 20 percent of doctors used a smartphone for work. It also noted then that only 36 percent of medical offices use electronic health records (with adoption lower among providers serving minority patients, the uninsured, and Medicaid patients), and that electronic medical record use also was lower in smaller practices, which are predominantly rural (FCC 2010).

The prevalence of smaller practices in rural settings corresponds to fewer technology-enabled capabilities, including lower bandwidth connections as well as fewer technological innovations such as electronic health records within the facilities themselves (Figure 6.3). Inasmuch as telemedicine may entail supporting or maintaining a technical capability that is outside of the normal healthcare worker toolkit, the need for upgrading bandwidth can add costs. Whether locally available networks can support typical office or service needs is a related issue. Because signal quality is especially important for certain types of applications, the reliability and quality of local connectivity may be an issue (Steele and Lo 2013). As new broadband-based health applications develop, assessing the utilities and impacts of different speeds and technical configurations will provide useful information.

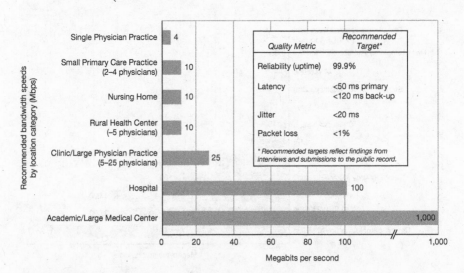

Figure 6.3 Bandwidth Needs by Facility Type
SOURCE: FCC National Broadband Plan, 2010.

Health Services, Infrastructure, and the FCC

The FCC has recognized for many years that a high-quality broadband network could transform health services. It established a Rural Health Care Program in 1997 pursuant to the 1996 Telecommunications Act and supported it via universal service funds. By subsidizing public and non-profit healthcare providers' telecommunications service rates, offering a 25 percent to 50 percent discount on Internet access costs that funded capital costs of new dedicated networks, the agency hoped to encourage broadband adoption and equalize some of the higher costs associated with healthcare in rural regions. However, that program was not heavily utilized, and the National Broadband Plan recommended its reformulation (FCC 2010).

One well-received component was its Rural Health Care Pilot Program, which supported projects that used networks to link resources across rural and urban hospitals and clinics (FCC Wireline Competition Bureau 2012). This program is especially significant in that evaluations were a prominent component. The Rural Health Care Pilot Program initiated sixty-nine projects, and its 2012 evaluation examined fifty projects costing $364 million and operating in thirty-eight states and territories (see Figure 6.4). The thrust of the program was to explore the applications of broadband capabilities to various healthcare providers, and especially to support coalitions of providers that could share resources and expertise in order to benefit rural regions. Several participants were networks composed of several operations and multiple locations (FCC 2012). Forty-four of the fifty projects included urban healthcare providers, and the leaders of many projects were housed in large medical institutions and universities and most purchased connections exceeding typical speeds purchased in the FCC's normal programs.

After conducting the pilot from 2006 to 2012, the agency came to several significant conclusions, including:

- Broadband healthcare networks improve the quality and reduce the cost of delivering healthcare in rural areas.

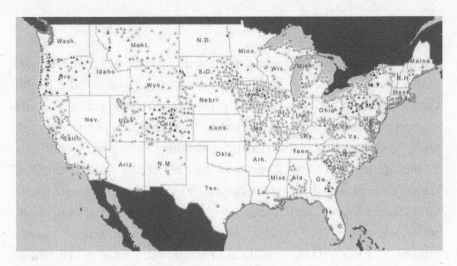

Figure 6.4 Locations of FCC Pilot Health Care Networks, 2012
Source: FCC Wireline Competition Bureau (2012, 22).

- Consortium applications are more efficient.
- Bulk buying plus competitive bidding is a powerful combination.
- Urban sites are key members of rural healthcare provider networks.
- Most healthcare providers do not have the technical expertise to manage broadband networks and do not want to own such networks.
- Funding challenges remain for rural healthcare providers.

Its evaluation report released in August 2012 considers factors such as the leadership of the projects, what sorts of broadband services were needed by the healthcare providers, the role of rural versus urban locations, types of healthcare facilities (i.e., whether they are university-affiliated institutions), costs, and a range of benefits, among other variables (FCC 2012).

Based on the results of its evaluation of the Pilot Program, the FCC determined that a permanent Healthcare Connect Fund should be established, and the 2013 Federal Register language authorizing this program states "Broadband connectivity has become an essential part of 21st century medical care. Whether it is used for transmitting electronic health records, sending X-rays, MRIs, and CAT scans to specialists at a distant hospital, or for video conferencing for telemedicine or training, access to broadband for medical providers saves lives while lowering healthcare costs and improving patient experiences" (FCC 2013). That Fund targeted access to broadband and continued the Pilot Program's successful cultivation of regional networks and links between urban and rural health providers. Funds match broadband services or facilities used for healthcare purposes on a two-for-one basis (initially requiring that the healthcare provider absorb 35 percent of the cost), and the enabling language includes clear performance goals and measures. The Rural Health Care program experienced significant increases in demand after 2015, attributable to more services and providers becoming eligible for support alongside new types of telehealth technology dependent on improved broadband networks (FCC 2018a). In response, the FCC increased the Rural Health Care program funding in 2018 by 43 percent, although its actions fell short of some commenters' request that the program budget be doubled.

Park et al. report that telehealth use escalated dramatically in 2013–2016 (2018). Their investigation of four years of data from nationally representative consumer surveys illustrates a rapid uptick in using live chat, mobile, texting, and video, but it also underscores that rural, poor, and Medicaid populations used telehealth services less often. They emphasize the need to think about incentives among both providers and users to address these disparities.

Mobile Health Initiatives

The FCC initiated an examination of new health opportunities provided by mobile technologies after it released the National Broadband Plan. Expanding prospects for incorporating mobile devices into healthcare prompted the creation of the mHealth Task Force, which issued a 2012 report exploring some of the ideas for accelerating the adoption of mobile health infrastructure (FCC 2012). The Task Force report included recommendations for federal agencies as well as the private sector and charts a future for health services that widely utilizes a variety of devices in order to both improve health outcomes and reduce costs. It includes a lengthy list of promising mobile health innovations, including remote patient monitors, health software apps for users, body sensors to capture and forward physiological data, medical implants for neuromuscular simulation, displaying medical data through various devices, and mobile diagnostic imaging, among other ideas (mHealth Task Force 2012). In response to the Task Force recommendations, the FCC Chairman announced Orders to promote wireless "test beds" so that mHealth technologies could be studied and that the agency would work to make needed spectrum available (FCC 2012). As more private sector and publicly funded mobile health applications and trials emerge, evaluations will help to assess successes and failures.

ADOPTION AND USE ISSUES: HEALTH ORGANIZATIONS, INDIVIDUALS, AND BROADBAND

Adoption and use issues for telemedicine applications using broadband invoke many different questions regarding the settings (type of health institution or home-based setting), health/medical personnel, patients involved, as well as the specific health problem or target. Matters of organizational cultures and values, clinical operational practices, as well as classic diffusion factors pertinent to individual adoption decisions comprise some of the issues that enter into the existing literature examining how people and institutions adopt technology-based innovations. Insofar as broadband joins many earlier innovations as a "new" technology offering new affordances to the healthcare community and to users, many of the same variables and questions are helpful to assessing adoption and use. For example, substantial issues of workflow for staff and disincentives for adopting new practices, whether for treatment or record keeping or other aspects, impede telemedicine's development. Hence even with offers for new infrastructure, practical matters of local expertise or interest can

affect adopting telecommunications services or broadband: reimbursement definitions that omitted "delivering services via networks" from eligible expenses can mean that staff may not go out of their way to use
telemedical techniques even if they might result in superior care. The telemedicine literature includes several studies that illustrate practical and operational disincentives of adopting new technology of all sorts. One 2013
survey of hospitals reports on the challenges of transitioning to electronic
health records and notes a range of technological, cultural, and organizational adoption and use impediments (Harle et al. 2013). In that particular
study, the usability of technology and demonstrated clinical usefulness
were among the factors that prevent hospitals from adopting new systems.
Since providers are "crucial gatekeepers" in telemedicine, technology must
provide solid evidence of its effects on medical care, workflow, the quality
of care delivered, internal productivity, and of course on cost effectiveness,
all factors that any medical institution would consider in adopting a new
technology or new practice (Bashshur et al. 2011, 486).

Adoption barriers extend to individual physicians, staff, and patients.
Lack of trust, technical problems, confusing instructions, fear of technology, physical disabilities, technological literacy, and privacy concerns
can contribute to reduced enthusiasm for telemedicine. One emerging
set of practices, however, illustrates keen adoption and interest among
patients/users: people with smart devices (phones, tablets, and other mobile media) and computers are using health-relevant applications that
incorporate social networking components. Commercial or nonprofit services ranging from fitness apps like Strava to condition-specific monitoring
such as the QoC Health Inc. mobile app illustrate a new type of healthcare
practice that unites easy, household-based access to broadband networks
with applications that incorporate monitoring, feedback, and reward (QoC
2019). Systems such as those on the platform *Patientslikeme.com* may invoke
social contacts as sources of information and support. Losing weight, stop-
ping smoking, maintaining disease support groups, and achieving fitness
goals are among some of the health behaviors that have captured developers'
and users' interest. Motivated individuals can benefit from using these apps.
As well, health providers are using apps to communicate with patients in

order to gather data and do checkups and virtual assessments, sometimes saving costs and patient time (de Jong et al. 2018). In one trial, surgery patients used a mobile app for follow-up care and successfully minimized the need for in-person visits without compromising outcomes (Armstrong et al. 2017). The service QoC Health offers an example of such platform-based, customizable innovations. This new style of health practice foretells a generation of devices, platforms, and programs capable of offering people direct services anywhere, anytime as long as they are willing to engage them. They depend on ubiquitous, real-time connectivity and sometimes require broadband capacity. Mobile technologies are additionally valuable in reaching minority users or patients inasmuch as cellphone penetration is very high among that population. Their clear utility for assisting with mo-bility and access limitations for people in rural or remote areas, or people whose diseases may limit their travel and hence continuity of care, has prompted enthusiasm around the globe (Cannon 2018).

Basic Internet access to health information also has spawned a great deal of information seeking about health-related subjects among the population at large. Statistics from the Pew Research Center provide reasons to be optimistic about this category of health information, sup-port, and care. For example, their 2014 Social Life of Health Information study, which focused on individual behavior and attitudes toward health behaviors, reported that people were actively seeking online health in-formation and sharing their own experiences and notes on dealing with health situations (Pew Research Center 2014). Some findings include that 72 percent of adult Internet users searched online for health infor-mation, and 26 percent read or watched someone's else's health posts in the past year. People with chronic diseases and caregivers were especially likely to use the Internet for various health-related purposes. Pew Internet investigated how family caregivers use the Internet, finding this group is highly engaged in searching for and sharing information offline and on-line (Pew Internet 2013).

Another study examining health information seeking trends across four waves of the national Health Information National Trends Survey found that more people go to the Internet before they seek health information from family and friends or healthcare professionals and traditional media (Jacobs, Amuta, and Jean 2017). It sounds the alarm regarding the relationships between age, socioeconomic status, and ethnicity as they bear on digital disparities in health information seeking. Being older, having less Internet literacy, and being Hispanic were related to using traditional print media or seeking information from a healthcare provider; they conclude that the uneven diffusion and use of digital health information may disadvantage certain populations because they do not use the Internet. Younger users and people from higher income brackets and with greater Internet skills were most likely to search for health information online.

MEASUREMENT AND EVALUATION ISSUES

This brief review raises several issues with respect to assessing broadband's application to healthcare and healthcare environments. An aging population, new healthcare laws and rules, opportunities to exploit mobile technologies, broadband networks, as well as powerful Internet-based social networking options are reshaping healthcare priorities and possibilities. However, healthcare practitioners, institutions, and "users"— the patients, those seeking information or care—live in an environment of incentives and motivations that may be untouched by new technologies. Identifying best infrastructures, best practices, and the features that yield the best outcomes will challenge researchers in this domain.

First, the technological horizon is always changing: not only is broadband connectivity improving—attaining greater speed and reliability—it also facilitates new applications. With respect to rural areas, there is ample evidence that the technological capabilities of both the networks and the local medical facilities will lag those of urban areas. These two qualities mean that it is incumbent on evaluators to adequately document and appraise the qualities of the extant technological capabilities, and to be cognizant of access barriers and inequities in the research setting.

Second, the broader context of technological competence and motivations of users and support personnel in rural regions should enter into any assessment of using broadband for health purposes. Although there are readily apparent incentives for developing telemedicine as a means of trimming the time and energy costs associated with having to travel great distances for healthcare and as a means of obtaining expertise available from nonlocal facilities, if the location cannot support the innovation, its use will fail. The reasons for not supporting it—whether they rest in incentive structures, unfamiliarity with the technology, workflow, and so forth—should enter into the research. We need national datasets that assess technology competence and readiness for telehealth applications.

Third, researchers must understand what constitutes "meaningful use" of broadband-based technologies among target populations. From the individual perspective, because rural populations are in general somewhat older, lower income, and because they are characterized by the presence of more chronic (and hence costly) diseases, the challenges as well as the possible benefits for broadband to enhance telemedicine outcomes are very apparent. Nonetheless, on the downside older populations in general, irrespective of location, exhibit less broadband adoption and use and lower digital literacy. As those same users have less access to broadband in the home, they may be less educated in how to use digital information or applications and lack the social support system for learning the requisite skills. Consequently, while online health information and support systems are expanding quickly, their potential may be depressed by location-based factors such as network quality or a population's disinclination to use computer-based knowledge and transactions. More research on the latter phenomenon could help planners to target the specific needs of older populations and the family- and friend-based social environments that can influence broadband use.

Various hurdles have been identified with respect to implementing EHR systems, and evaluation research may help to identify strategies that can ease their introduction. Federal guidelines on EHR specify thresholds to ease institutions toward "meaningful use" of the records, and each threshold could raise new intra-institutional issues. At the institutional and inter-institutional level, handling and exchanging medical records (interoperability) and figuring out appropriate workflow models clearly need attention, and strong research designs that identify core factors and approaches could be useful. We need to explore and identify best practices for security, authentication, and encryption needs. Even more broadly, identifying reimbursement and insurance bottlenecks to integrate broadband and mobile options with healthcare coverage and offering recommendations for new definitions, practices, and language would be welcome.

Finally, measurement and evaluation issues in this field require strong research designs (McIntosh and Cairns 1997). We need strong research designs that will allow causal inferences using controls in order to accurately assess telemedicine conditions and practices and the way that broadband may make a difference. National datasets would be helpful to yield a better understanding of how certain categories of health institutions can or cannot use broadband, and what quality or level of service demands are appropriate. Longitudinal data are lacking in general. While the literature shows that there is a solid and theoretically informed understanding of individual behaviors, especially health information seeking and attitudes to health-related behaviors, a great deal of the research on telemedicine more generally is either anecdotal or composed of single case studies, with little attention to outcomes, especially long-term outcomes. More information on costs, outcomes, and usable business models is needed in order to realize the best potential of these systems (Bergmo 2015). Researchers have called attention to the paucity of randomized or comparative studies, which limits causal claims. Institutional facets—the size, resource base, setting, culture—have not been well studied with respect to introducing new practices and technologies, and the federal push toward EHRs and meaningful use provides excellent focus for next-generation work in this domain. Investigating the connectivity needs of all providers, especially those in rural regions, and including practical factors such as affordability and pricing should be a priority as new networks are constructed. Because some researchers have questioned the clinical outcomes associated with telemedicine's technologically mediated health practices, researchers would do well to address these basic and important questions using panel studies and rigorous research designs.

NOTE

1. https://www.fcc.gov/wireline-competition/telecommunications-access-policy-division/connected-care-pilot-program

REFERENCES

American Recovery and Reinvestment Act of 2009 (ARRA). 2009. Pub. L. No. 111-5, 123 Stat. 115.

American Telemedicine Association. N.d. https://www.americantelemed.org/

Armstrong, K., P. Coyte, and M. Brown. 2017. "Effect of Home Monitoring via Mobile App on the Number of In-Person Visits Following Ambulatory Surgery: A Randomized Clinical Trial." *Journal of the American Medical Association Surgery* 152 (7): 622–627. http://jamanetwork.com/article.aspx?doi=10.1001/jamasurg.2017.0111

Bashshur, R., G. Shannon, E. Krupinski, and J. Grisgsby. 2011. "The Taxonomy of Telemedicine." *Telemedicine and E-Health* 17 (6): 484–494. https://doi.org/10.1089/tmj.2011.0103

Basiu, A., Y. Negussie, and A. Geller, eds. 2017. *The State of Health Disparities in the United States: Communities in Action; Pathways to Health Equity; National Academies of Sciences, Engineering, and Medicine; Health and Medicine Division; Board on Population Health and Public Health Practice; Committee on Community-Based Solutions to Promote Health Equity in the United States.* Washington, DC: National Academies Press. https://www.ncbi.nlm.nih.gov/books/NBK425844/

Beede, D., and A. Neville. 2013. "Broadband Availability beyond the Rural/Urban Divide." Broadband Brief 2. Washington, DC: U.S. Department of Commerce. https://www.ntia.doc.gov/files/ntia/publications/broadband_availability_rural_urban_june_2011_final.pdf

Bergmo, T. S. 2015. "How to Measure Costs and Benefits of EHealth Interventions: An Overview of Methods and Frameworks." *Journal of Medical Internet Research* 17 (11): e254. https://doi.org/10.2196/jmir.4521

Cannon, C. 2018. "Telehealth, Mobile Applications, and Wearable Devices Are Expanding Cancer Care beyond Walls." *Seminars in Oncology Nursing* 34 (2): 118–125. https://doi.org/10.1016/j.soncn.2018.03.002

Centers for Medicare and Medicaid Services. 2010. "Medicare and Medicaid Programs: Electronic Health Record Incentive Program; Final Rule." Federal Register 75, no. 144. July 28, 2010. 44321. http://edocket.access.gpo.gov/2010/pdf/2010-17207.pdf

Centers for Medicare and Medicaid Services. 2020. https://www.cms.gov/Research-Statistics-Data-and-Systems/Statistics-Trends-and-Reports/NationalHealthExpendData/NationalHealthAccountsHistorical

Creswell, J. 2013. "A Digital Shift on Health Data Swells Profits in an Industry." *The New York Times*, February 19, 2013. https://www.nytimes.com/2013/02/20/business/a-digital-shift-on-health-data-swells-profits.html

Davidson, C. M., and M. Santorelli. 2009. *Barriers to Broadband Adoption: A Report to the Federal Communications Commission.* The Advanced Communications Law & Policy Institute, New York Law School. https://www.ncleg.gov/documentsites/committees/HSCHSIARUA/10-28-2009/Barriers%20to%20Broadband%20Adoption%20Report.pdf

De Jong, J. M., P. Ogink, C. van Bunningen, R. Driessen, L. Engelen, B. Heeren, S. Bredie, and T. van de Belt. 2018. "A Cloud-Based Virtual Outpatient Clinic for Patient-Centered Care: Proof of Concept Study." *Journal of Medical Internet Research* 20 (9): 1–12. http://dx.doi.org/10.2196/10135

Dorsey, E. R., and E. J. Topol. 2016. "State of Telehealth." *New England Journal of Medicine* 375 (2): 154–161. https://doi.org/10.1056/nejmra1601705

Ekeland, A. G., A. Bowes, and S. Flottorp. 2010. "Effectiveness of Telemedicine: A Systematic Review of Reviews." *International Journal of Medical Informatics* 79 (11): 736–771. https://doi.org/10.1016/j.ijmedinf.2010.08.006

Federal Communications Commission. 2010. *Connecting America: The National Broadband Plan.* Washington, DC: FCC. https://transition.fcc.gov/national-broadband-plan/national-broadband-plan.pdf

Federal Communications Commission. 2012. "Fact Sheet: MHealth Task Force Recommendations." https://www.fcc.gov/document/fact-sheet-mhealth-task-force-recommendations

Federal Communications Commission. 2013. "Rural Health Care Support Mechanism." 47 CFR Part 54 [WC Docket No. 02-60; FCC 12-150]. *Federal Register* 78 (41): 54967–54968. https://www.govinfo.gov/content/pkg/FR-2013-03-01/pdf/2013-04040.pdf

Federal Communications Commission. 2018a. "Promoting Telehealth in Rural America." 47 CFR 54 [WC Docket No. 17-310; FCC 17-164]. *Federal Register* 83 (2): 30573–30584. https://www.federalregister.gov/documents/2018/06/29/2018-14073/promoting-telehealth-in-rural-america

Federal Communications Commission. 2018b. *2018 Broadband Deployment Report.* https://docs.fcc.gov/public/attachments/FCC-18-10A1.docx

Federal Communications Commission Wireline Competition Bureau. 2012. *Evaluation of Rural Health Care Pilot Program Staff Report.* WC Docket No. 02-60. https://docs.fcc.gov/public/attachments/DA-12-1332A1.pdf

Foutz, J., S. Artiga, and R. Garfield. 2017. "The Role of Medicaid in Rural America." https://www.kff.org/medicaid/issue-brief/the-role-of-medicaid-in-rural-america/

Fox, S. 2011. "The Social Life of Health Information, 2011." Washington, DC: Pew Internet & American Life Project. http://www.pewinternet.org/2011/05/12/the-social-life-of-health-information-2011/

Fox, S., and M. Duggan. 2012. "Mobile Health 2012." Washington, DC: Pew Research Center's Internet and American Life Project. http://www.pewinternet.org/2012/11/08/mobile-health-2012/

Harle, C., T. R. Huerta, E. Ford, M. L. Diana, and N. Menachemi. 2013. "Overcoming Challenges to Achieving Meaningful Use: Insights from Hospitals That Successfully Received Centers for Medicare and Medicaid Services Payments in 2011." *Journal of the American Medical Informatics Association* 20 (2): 233–237. https://doi.org/10.1136/amiajnl-2012-001142

Jacobs, W., A. Amuta, and K. Jean. 2017. "Health Information Seeking in the Digital Age: An Analysis of Health Information Seeking Behavior among US Adults." *Cogent Social Sciences* 3: 1302785. http://dx.doi.org/10.1080/23311886.2017.1302785

Jamoom, E. W., and N. Yang. 2016. "State Variation in Electronic Sharing of Information in Physician Offices: United States, 2015." NCHS Data Brief No. 261. Hyattsville, MD: National Center for Health Statistics. https://www.cdc.gov/nchs/data/databriefs/db261.pdf

Lohr, S. 2018. "The Digital Divide Is Wider than We Think, Study Says." *New York Times*, December 4, 2018. https://www.nytimes.com/2018/12/04/technology/digital-divide-us-fcc-microsoft.html

mHealth Task Force. 2012. "mHealth Task Force Findings and Recommendations: Improving Care Delivery through Enhanced Telecommunications." http://www2.itif.org/2012-mhealth-taskforce-recommendations.pdf?_ga=2.145861046.368572733.1554075782-2139826135.1554075782

McIntosh, E., and J. Cairns. 1997. "A Framework for the Economic Evaluation of Telemedicine." *Journal of Telemedicine and Telecare* 3 (3): 132–139. https://doi.org/10.1258/1357633971931039

Microsoft. 2018. "An Update on Connecting Rural America: The 2018 Microsoft Airband Initiative." https://blogs.microsoft.com/uploads/prod/sites/5/2018/12/MSFT-Airband_InteractivePDF_Final_12.3.18.pdf

Park, J., C. Erikson, X. Han, and P. Iyer. 2018. "Are State Telehealth Policies Associated with the Use of Telehealth Services among Underserved Populations?" *Health affairs* 37 (12): 2060–2068. https://doi.org/10.1377/hlthaff.2018.05101

Pew Research Center. 2013. "Family Caregivers and Health Care Info." Washington, DC: Pew Research Center. http://www.pewinternet.org/2013/06/20/family-caregivers-and-health-care-info/

Pew Research Center. 2014. "The Social Life of Health Information." https://www.pewresearch.org/fact-tank/2014/01/15/the-social-life-of-health-information/

QoC Health. N.d. https://qochealth.com/

Sawyer, B., and C. Cox. 2018. "How Does Health Spending in the U.S. Compare to Other Countries?" https://www.healthsystemtracker.org/chart-collection/health-spending-u-s-compare-countries/

Shaw, T., D. McGregor, M. Brunner, M. Keep, A. Janssen, and S. Barnet. 2017. "What Is EHealth? Development of a Conceptual Model for EHealth: Qualitative Study with Key Informants." *Journal of Medical Internet Research* 19 (10): e324. https://doi.org/10.2196/jmir.8106

Singh, M. 2008. *Chronic Care Driving a Fundamental Shift in Health Care Supply Chains*. Boston, MA: MIT Center for Transportation & Logistics. https://ctl.mit.edu/sites/ctl.mit.edu/files/library/public/whitepaper_singh_chroniccarehealthcareSC.pdf

Steele, R., and A. Lo. 2013. "Telehealth and Ubiquitous Computing for Bandwidth-Constrained Rural and Remote Areas." *Personal Ubiquitous Computing* 17: 533–543. http://dx.doi.org/10.2196/10135

Telecommunications Act of 1996. 1996. Pub. L. No. 104–104, 110 Stat. 56.

UnitedHealth Center for Health Reform & Modernization. 2011. "Modernizing Rural Health Care: Coverage, Quality and Innovation." http://www.unitedhealthgroup.com/~/media/UHG/PDF/2011/UNH-Working-Paper-6.ashx

Weinstein, J. N., A. Geller, Y. Negussie, A. Baciu, and National Academies of Sciences Engineering and Medicine. 2017. "The State of Health Disparities in the United States." In *Communities in Action: Pathways to Health Equity*, edited by Weinstein, J., A. Geller, Y. Negussie, and A. Baciu, 57–97. Washington, DC: National Academies Press. https://doi.org/10.17226/24624

Whitacre, B., R. Gallardo, and S. Strover. 2014. "Broadband's Contribution to Economic Growth in Rural Areas: Moving towards a Causal Relationship." *Telecommunications Policy* 38 (11): 1011–1023. https://doi.org/10.1016/j.telpol.2014.05.005

Whitacre, B., S. Strover, and C. Rhinesmith. 2018. "Broadband Speed: FCC Map vs. Experience on the Ground." *Daily Yonder*. July 25, 2018. https://www.dailyyonder.com/tag/by-brian-whitacre-sharon-strover-colin-rhinesmith/

Whitacre, B., D. Wheeler, and C. Landgraf. 2017. "What Can the National Broadband Map Tell Us about the Health Care Connectivity Gap?" *Journal of Rural Health* 33 (3): 284–289. https://doi.org/10.1111/jrh.12177

7

Opportunities and Challenges in Advancing Broadband-Enabled Government Services

ALFRED T. HO

INTRODUCTION

Since the mid-1990s, policymakers and researchers have been exploring the promise and implications of broadband networks for e-government services, as the technology not only allows the rapid download and upload of data but also provides a platform that encourages more interactive communication among government agencies, between government service providers and citizens, and among citizens themselves. The potential impact is especially significant for certain communities, such as rural towns, and in certain public services, such as healthcare, education, and economic development. The purpose of this chapter is to re-examine the potential impact of the technology on public services and suggest a framework that evaluates the "knowns" and the "unknowns" of the success of e-government from both governmental and citizen perspectives. The chapter emphasizes that e-government "success" cannot be viewed purely from the supply side or be based primarily on how many e-government services are made available to the public. Policymakers and e-government

Alfred T. Ho, *Opportunities and Challenges in Advancing Broadband-Enabled Government Services* In: *Transforming Everything?*. Edited by: Karen Mossberger, Eric W. Welch, and Yonghong Wu, Oxford University Press. © Oxford University Press 2022. DOI: 10.1093/oso/9780190082871.003.0008 observers should also look at the demand side by examining who may use and benefit from the services and the implications of usage patterns.

The first section of the study defines broadband technologies and discusses some of its potential implications for e-government development. The second section of the study suggests a "stakeholder-logic model" to evaluate the implications of e-government strategies for elected officials, public employees, service users, and the community-at-large. It also examines the potential risk and challenges of deploying broadband-enabled e-government tools for these stakeholders. The third section of the study examines how various local governments have already begun to implement new e-government tools under the broadband environment. At the same time, it points out some of the known "broken promises" of e-government, and some of the unknowns about the potential benefits of broadband-enabled e-government services that require more future research and policy attention. Then in the final section, the study concludes by raising some important questions that may help policymakers and public managers evaluate how they should plan for the future of broadband-enabled government services and socioeconomic development.

BROADBAND IMPLICATIONS FOR
E-GOVERNMENT DEVELOPMENT

Since the internet became available to the general public in the 1980s, speed and bandwidth have been the major constraints on how much the internet can do and what services users and citizens can access online. Dial-up modem services in the 1980s only offered 1.2 to 2.4 kb of data transfer per second. The speed improved dramatically to 56 kb of data transfer per second in the 1990s, but it was still very limiting. It was not until the arrival of broadband internet access that online services began to take off. From ADSL and cable to the newer technologies such as VDSL[1] and optical fiber networks, broadband internet access can now reach beyond 1 Gb per second of data transfer. It is also available to wireless and mobile devices, such as through WiMAX and 3G and 4G LTE. According to the U.S. Federal Communications Commission (2018), approximately 98.1 percent of the US population had access to either fixed terrestrial services at 25 Mb per second/3 Mb per second or mobile LTE at speeds of 10 Mb per second/3 Mb per second by the end of 2016. In rural areas, that number was about 89.7 percent. In addition, some urban communities in the US had begun to offer 5G services by the end of 2019, which have a potential download speed of 20 Gb per second and a 10 Gb per second upload speed (Fisher 2019).

Because of its speed advantage, broadband is likely to stimulate the usage of e-government services (Hitt and Tambe 2007; Trkman and Truk 2009). It also opens up new possibilities for e-government services (Grant and Chau 2005), which can be characterized as faster, data-intensive, interactive, participatory, integrated, intelligent, and more cost-effective.

Broadband-Enabled E-Government Services Are Faster and More Data Intensive

Because of the rapid data transfer speed, the government can put a lot of graphics, data, and information on its website, and citizens can browse and download them instantly twenty-four hours a day, seven days a week. As a result, broadband technology empowers government officials and politicians to push for greater transparency. President Obama's "Open Government Initiative" and the data.gov web portal are earlier examples for this. Many state and local governments also have electronic newsletters, online videos of public meetings, and downloadable maps and public records of service results to allow citizens to use these tools to hold the government accountable. In the early 21st century, many state and local governments have also launched their own open data initiatives and allow the public to freely download public documents, administrative records, service performance data, and maps to understand the operations and outcomes of local services (Ho and McCall 2016).

Broadband-Enabled E-Government Services Are More Interactive and Participatory

The increase in capacity and speed in broadband networks also allows the government to offer more interactive services. In the late 1990s and early 2000s, some federal, state, and local government agencies already offered online transaction services, such as online payment of fees and online document uploads (Ho 2002). However, the speed and relia- bility of the network at that time constrained how much these services could be offered. Now, with broadband services, government agencies can offer a variety of interactive services, from online payment, online complaints and service requests (with pictures), and document submis- sion, to interactive chats, twitter, and video conferencing with citizens and constituencies. All these allow government agencies to tailor their services and communication more to individual citizen needs. They also give citizens more opportunities to participate directly in the govern- mental decision-making process. For example, the fiber network can be used to conduct interactive, real-time online meetings between officials and individual citizens when they are at home or in multiple gathering places, conduct instant online polling, and organize mass simulations to understand possible individual responses to certain policies or programs and assess their potential impact. Also, citizens may or- ganize and interact with each other more conveniently, and govern- ment agencies can crowd-source to networks of individuals to identify problems, come up with solutions, and solve policy problems jointly. None of these could be done easily or cheaply in traditional face-to- face meetings. Online interactivity is especially useful for government agencies at the national or state level, which are more distant from the public and cannot easily organize community town-hall meetings. With fiber networks, for example, Congressional representatives and federal officials in Washington, DC can reach out to individual citizens in the nation more directly and regularly, bypassing a lot of intermediate lobby and interest groups.

Broadband-Enabled E-Government Services Are More Integrated

Partly because of the rising importance of user-focus and the idea of "one-stop" portals in web development (Hagen and Kubicek 2000; Ho 2002; Gouscos et al. 2007), and partly because of the capacity to transfer significantly more data due to broadband technologies, governmental services can become more integrated virtually among departments and service providers (Fountain 2001). As a result, citizens can now go to most government websites and request a variety of services or conduct a number of online transactions without the need to visit multiple departmental websites. Also, broadband connections allow multiple departments in multiple jurisdictions to communicate and coordinate more easily in real-time. As a result, many public services, especially in the area of law enforcement, emergency management, homeland security, and healthcare, will have greater potential to benefit from this more integrated approach to service planning and delivery.

Broadband-Enabled E-Government Services Are More Intelligent

Because broadband capacity allows easy real-time transfer of a large amount of data, public officials can now deploy a lot of data collection devices in different locations, monitor service provision closely, and then use data-driven analytical models to examine the changing situations and respond accordingly. This is especially useful in traffic management, crowd control in public spaces, emergency response, energy consumption control, and infrastructure maintenance if government agencies can connect sensor technologies with the local broadband network (Ho and McCall 2016; Jaeger et al. 2007; IBM 2012; Tang and Ho 2019).

Broadband-Enabled E-Government Services Can Be More Cost-Effective

With better planning and more responsive delivery tailored to situational changes and citizen demand, public services can be more user-friendly and effective. More importantly, public services can benefit from economies of scale and overcome cost disadvantages due to geographic constraints. For example, rural communities often have great difficulties hiring qualified teachers and professionals to offer specialized services, such as foreign language training, information technology services, or medical consultation for citizens. With broadband technologies, rural areas can now access service providers outside their communities easily and provide similar services that would have been available only to major metropolitan areas in the past. As a result, technology may break down geographical and cost barriers and can potentially empower disadvantaged and rural communities to get access to a greater variety of services in a more competitive environment.

APPLYING A STAKEHOLDER-LOGIC MODEL TO EVALUATE E-GOVERNMENT STRATEGIES

Given these advantages, broadband-enabled e-government tools can be used in different operations and policymaking stages of the government and are likely to impact different stakeholders (Gouscos et al. 2007). Table 7.1 provides a stakeholder-logic framework that can be used to evaluate these potential benefits and implications. The framework categorizes four types of stakeholders—elected officials, governmental managers and employees, service users, and the community-at-large. It also specifies five stages of the policymaking process—understanding public demand and expectations, budgeting and policymaking, budget execution and service provision, realization of service output and outcome goals, and program evaluation. In each of these stages, the four types of stakeholders may have different expectations of broadband-enabled e-government tools.

Table 7.1 A STAKEHOLDER LOGIC MODEL

	Understanding public expectations and demand	Budgeting and policymaking	Budget execution and service provision and realization of service output and outcome goals	Program evaluation and citizen feedback
Potential contributions of broadband-enabled e-government tools	• online surveys • interactive online meetings • social media • online policy simulation	• web-based reporting • webcast of meetings • reporting and feedback through social media tools • online voting	• "smart-government" tools to refine service demand analysis and improve production technologies • web-based reporting of results to citizens • constant feedback from citizens through web-based and social media tools	• online surveys • reporting and feedback through social media tools • more responsive tools (e.g., web-based tools and apps) to track service demand and complaints
What do elected officials expect?	• new ways to reach out to more citizens • more direct and instant communication with citizens • 24-7 engagement	• greater transparency • greater sense of being informed among the public • greater sense of informed decision-making	• more cost-effective and efficient operations that lead to cost savings • offering more services with less input, a "smarter" government	• more responsive services • new ways to reach out to more citizens, especially the young

What do program managers/ employees expect?	• greater sense of participation among the public • greater trust in the government • new ways to solicit user demand • new ways to mobilize support for programs/ services • 24-7 engagement • the public being more informed	• greater pressure to communicate with and engage the public • 24-7 engagement • the public being more informed	• greater responsiveness to citizen demand and service requests • greater citizen satisfaction • greater pressure to enhance cost-effectiveness and efficiency • greater pressure to enhance service responsiveness and citizen satisfaction • greater desire to enhance the operational environment and job satisfaction • new opportunities to enhance intergovernmental, interdepartmental, and public-private collaboration	• greater pressure to communicate with and engage the public • 24-7 engagement • competency shifts to more analytical work and communication management

(continued)

Table 7.1 CONTINUED

	Understanding public expectations and demand	Budgeting and policymaking	Budget execution and service provision and realization of service output and outcome goals	Program evaluation and citizen feedback
What do service users/ customers expect?	• new ways to provide feedback and make service requests • new opportunities to participate and influence policy decisions • greater sense of participation	• greater transparency in decision-making • greater sense of being informed • greater sense of ownership of the services or programs	• competency shifts to more analytical work and communication management • sense of professional pride and accomplishments • greater cost-effectiveness, efficiency, responsiveness in services • more convenient access to services • more choices/variety of services • more equitable access to services • new opportunities of co-production • greater sense of ownership of the services or programs	• greater cost-effectiveness, efficiency, responsiveness in services

What does the community-at-large expect?

- more widespread participation
- greater transparency and democratic accountability
- greater voice for the young
- greater trust in the government

- greater transparency in decision-making
- more proactive solicitation of customer feedback
- more accountability reporting
- greater trust in the government

- better quality of life that helps attract residents and businesses
- more transparency and accountability in the government
- greater sense of community pride and progressiveness

- new tools to solicit user feedback more cost-effectively, conveniently, and instantly

For example, in soliciting public input and trying to understand public expectations and demand for services, elected officials may want to use broadband-enabled e-government tools to reach out to a wider scope of the public and have direct interaction with individual citizens (Scott 2006). Tools such as online surveys, online policy simulation tools, interactive online meetings, and social media will allow elected officials to accomplish these goals (Hudson-Smith et al. 2005). Service users and the community-at-large may also welcome these tools, since they can potentially lead to greater transparency and participatory opportunities, especially for the young who are more technology-savvy. Public managers may also enjoy new opportunities to listen to the public and rally political support for their programs. They may also hope that these e-government tools can keep the public more informed about policy and budgetary constraints in thinking about the demand for services.

In the budgeting and policymaking stage, broadband-enabled e-government tools can play a significant role in keeping the public informed. Online reporting, webcasts of meetings, and constant feedback from citizens and users through social media tools can certainly lead to a stronger sense of transparency, accountability, and being informed among service users and the community-at-large (Bertot et al. 2010). If the online communication is well managed, this may lead to greater trust in the government, which is what elected officials may want to achieve.

Among all stages of policymaking, broadband-enabled e-government tools will probably have the largest potential impact on budget execution and service delivery (Gouscos et al. 2007; Government of Alberta 2009). The availability of better, faster, and more accurate information about user demand and use patterns of services, better customer-provider communication, and greater potential for inter-organizational collaboration in service delivery may allow the government to do more with less and provide services more cost-effectively. To elected officials, this may eventually mean greater potential for cost-savings, which is critically important in public sector fiscal environments. From the customer's perspective, these tools offer more choices and more convenient access to services. They may also find new opportunities to coproduce some services with government officials and develop a stronger sense of ownership of the services and programs. For the community-at-large, better public services should enhance the quality of life and help attract more residents and businesses. Also, the use of more sophisticated technological tools to engage the public and deliver more effective services may lead to a sense of pride and progressiveness among public managers and the community-at-large, and they may try to project this image outside their organization or their community.

Finally, broadband-enabled e-government tools can enable public managers to solicit faster feedback from more citizens in a cost-effective way. From online service requests, special apps in mobile devices, to social media tools, service users and the community-at-large can provide feedback on policy results and service outcomes and quality very conveniently.

THE FULFILLED AND UNFULFILLED PROMISES, AND THE KNOWN AND UNKNOWN ACCOMPLISHMENTS, OF BROADBAND-ENABLED E-GOVERNMENT TOOLS

Some of the potential advantages and expectations of these broadband technologies have already been realized in some local communities in the US over the past few years. In addition to new possibilities of real-time distance learning and telemedicine services, many communities now take advantage of the broadband environment by offering new platforms to inform and communicate with the public. For example, many communities now webcast their budget and city council meetings so that the public can watch them online in real time or asynchronously and submit questions to elected officials by email or on the city website during or after the meetings. This provides greater transparency and accountability of the policymaking process.

Many communities also try to "democratize" their data (Mossberger and Wu 2012). For example, in many cities, such as San Francisco, citizens can now access data on all business contracts a government has entered into in recent years to ensure public accountability in these transactions.

Many governmental agencies also offer web portals that integrate all kinds of data for citizens to download, such as climate and environmental data, GIS map data about public facilities and nonprofit organizations, public transportation routes and service schedules, local road condition and congestion data, and crime data at the neighborhood level (Ho and McCall 2016). Citizens can now use these data to monitor service delivery results, social entrepreneurs and businesses can develop apps and on-line platforms to help citizens use the data intelligently to improve their quality of life, and community organizers, think tanks, academics, and even individual citizens may analyze the data and come up with new ideas to help solve public policy problems. An example was flyontime.us in the mid-2010s, which was launched by the Sunlight Foundation using open data from the Federal Aviation Administration (FAA) to map out average delay times of flights by cities.

Many communities have also used broadband technologies to improve internal operations and Government-to-Government (G2G) services. For example, fiber networks allow more governmental workers to telecommute. Broadband also empowers officials to manage energy usage in government buildings according to hours, environmental changes, and energy demand in the community, and to monitor equipment and vehicle usage to optimize the cost-effectiveness and responsiveness of public service delivery. Furthermore, with wireless broadband, police officers in many communities can now access fingerprint information in a national database instantly and identify an individual on site when they are performing law enforcement duties. Also, with fiber networks in major streets, local public works, transportation, and police departments can monitor traffic flows jointly in real time and coordinate traffic light signaling and traffic enforcement more responsively according to road usage. For example, in the mid-2000s, Fort Collins, Colorado deployed an optical fiber network ring around the city and crisscrossed it in all major streets. Chattanooga, Tennessee also provides broadband services throughout the city. In addition to the benefits of offering very reasonably priced cable TV and internet services to residents, the fiber network allows the Chattanooga police department to manage traffic flow interactively and intelligently.

These are the known benefits of broadband-enabled e-government services. At the same time, there are different sets of risks and challenges faced by policymakers in using these e-government tools to engage the public (see Table 7.2). For example, public officials need to think about the cost and workload implications of using these tools because of the time and information processing demands. Public managers may be especially concerned about their organization's staff and analytical capacity to process the data. Also, past research has shown that there is a greater tendency for social media tools to be negatively biased and ideologically driven. Greater and faster access to information and data may also empower the rich and the educated disproportionally in shaping policy agendas. All these issues have led to growing concerns about power imbalance in the decision-making process if only a small fragment of the population has access to these e-government tools and have a louder voice in the policymaking process.

Furthermore, government officials and the community-at-large may have to embrace the potential risk of more diffuse and fragmented preferences in the policymaking process. This may force public managers to invest more time and effort on informational clarification and damage control if biased and misinformed opinions spread rapidly in the online world, especially through social media. With broadband technologies, the social damage of biased information and "fake news" can be especially serious if the information is empowered and reinforced by images and videos, which can have lasting emotional effects on people. These are some of the governing challenges and social risks that officials and policymakers need to face more frequently in the new era of broadband-enabled society.

In response to these challenges, public managers need to broaden their competency training. In addition to pushing for greater efficiency and effectiveness in service delivery, public managers today also need to deal with many governance and public communication challenges in the new world of "24-7 engagement." Also, broadband technologies have created new possibilities of public-private partnership, such as cloud-sourcing new ideas and coproducing public services with the public and businesses.

Table 7.2 POTENTIAL RISK AND DRAWBACKS OF BROADBAND-ENABLED E-GOVERNMENT DEVELOPMENT

	Understanding public expectations and demand, budgeting, and policymaking	Budget execution and service provision, realization of service output, and outcome goals	Program evaluation and citizen feedback
Potential risks and drawbacks of broadband-enabled e-government tools	• financial cost • capacity and time demand to process the information and respond • domination of a few • the danger of social media negativism and self-selection in formulating policy consensus • conflict between transparency and confidentiality, the danger of unauthorized sharing of information and data, and the ambiguity of individual employees' rights and responsibilities in the social media world • digital divide that may reinforce the power of the rich and the educated • potential battle with telecommunication and cable companies • potential for more intense debate • potential for more diffused and fragmented preferences in formulating policy decisions	• digital divide that gives the rich and the educated more access to services • digital divide that gives the rich and the educated greater voice in budget execution and program implementation, which may shape the service output and outcomes	• financial cost • capacity and time demand to process the information and respond • digital divide that gives the rich and the educated a greater voice, which may shape the service output and outcomes in their favor • building trust or destroying trust?

As a result, public managers need to become more data literate, more sensitive to technological trends, and understand the organizational, social, and political implications of technological development.

Furthermore, policymakers and public managers need to recognize many potentially unknown broken promises and unknown benefits that may happen in the future (see Table 7.3). For example, while many communities have made significant progress over the past decade in using web-based services and broadband-enabled tools to enhance their web portal informational features, improve customer services, and increase the use of online transactions, there has been very limited progress in e-democracy, such as the use of interactive townhall meetings, online voting, or online citizen committee meetings.

In addition, while significant progress has been made in offering cable, DSL, and 4G LTE broadband networks in many communities over the past few years, most cities still lack fiber optic networks that allow ultrafast uploads and downloads that can enable real-time, interactive communication among multiple players. Within communities, there are still concerns about computer literacy among low-income groups, less-educated residents, and among minority groups (Horrigan and Rainie 2002; Lloyd and Bill 2003; Dugdale et al. 2005).

Another equity concern and a potentially broken promise of broadband-enabled society is the urban-rural digital divide. The latest FCC data about broadband access show that the gap in broadband access between urban and rural areas is still significant (see Table 7.4). While significant progress in closing the gap has been made over the past decade and more rural areas now have good access to fixed terrestrial services and 4G LTE mobile data services, many rural communities, that is, those in counties that have a lower urban population ratio, still lag behind in the quality of services and the availability of fixed broadband and LTE services. For example, for counties that have at least 90 percent of population living in rural areas, the average percentage of the rural population with fixed broadband and mobile LTE is only 57 percent. This contrasts sharply with urban counties—for counties that have at least 90 percent of population living in urban areas, the average percentage of the urban population with fixed

Table 7.3 THE KNOWNS AND UNKNOWNS OF BROADBAND-ENABLED
E-GOVERNMENT PROMISES

	Fulfilled Promises	Unfulfilled/Broken Promises
Known	• more variety of services for those who have access • easier access to specialized services for rural communities/smaller cities • more user-provider interaction and direct contacts • more data and information available to the public • potential for cloud-sourcing new ideas and service delivery • reduction of digital divide among urban and rural areas	• more interactive, direct participation in decision-making • slow progress in offering optical fiber broadband services • significant digital divide and gap in computing literacy among socioeconomic classes, and significant gap in computing literacy
Unknown	• building a greater sense of public trust in government? • greater cost-effectiveness and responsiveness in service delivery? • the implications of mobile computing for the usage of e-government services • the implications of social media for the job responsibilities and individual rights of employees	• new possibilities to actualize participatory democracy, or a reinforcing mechanism for the privileged and the educated?

Table 7.4 THE URBAN-RURAL GAP IN BROADBAND ACCESS, 2016

	% Population with fixed broadband & mobile LTE, urban areas	% Population with fixed broadband & mobile LTE, rural areas	Urban-rural
Urban Population Ratio <= 10%			
Mean	84.9%	57.2%	27.8%
N	62	62	62
Std Dev	30.4%	26.6%	32.4%
Maximum	100.0%	99.3%	93.8%
Minimum	0.0%	0.4%	−67.4%
Urban Population Ratio, 10.01% – 25%			
Mean	85.7%	53.5%	32.1%
N	315	315	315
Std Dev	27.1%	25.3%	27.3%
Maximum	100.0%	100.0%	90.1%
Minimum	0.0%	0.0%	−86.1%
Urban Population Ratio, 25.01% – 50%			
Mean	88.0%	57.9%	30.1%
N	841	841	841
Std Dev	26.0%	27.0%	26.4%
Maximum	100.0%	100.0%	95.7%
Minimum	0.0%	0.0%	−66.6%
Urban Population Ratio, 50.01% – 75%			
Mean	93.6%	67.4%	26.3%
N	691	691	691
Std Dev	18.4%	26.0%	22.8%
Maximum	100.0%	100.0%	96.4%
Minimum	0.0%	0.0%	−29.2%

(continued)

Table 7.4 CONTINUED

	% Population with fixed broadband & mobile LTE, urban areas	% Population with fixed broadband & mobile LTE, rural areas	Urban-rural
Urban Population Ratio, 70.01% – 90%			
Mean	95.5%	74.9%	20.6%
N	297	297	297
Std Dev	14.0%	24.2%	20.7%
Maximum	100.0%	100.0%	82.8%
Minimum	0.0%	0.0%	−13.1%
Urban Population Ratio, > 90%			
Mean	98.7%	83.8%	14.9%
N	210	210	210
Std Dev	1.6%	22.1%	21.8%
Maximum	100.0%	100.0%	99.9%
Minimum	91.6%	0.0%	−4.1%

SOURCE: Author's calculation based on U.S. FCC (2018), Appendix F2.

broadband and mobile LTE is almost 99 percent. A fixed-effect regression model shows that after controlling for the state fixed effects and the broadband access condition in urban areas, counties with less population and a lower urban population ratio, which are basically rural counties, are more likely to demonstrate a wider gap in broadband service availability (see Table 7.5). Hence, the digital divide between urban and rural areas has largely persisted, and this gap may even get worse when more urban areas in the US begin to deploy 5G network services while rural areas are still stuck with older technologies due to low population density and insufficient market incentive to invest in these areas (Hart 2018).

Besides the "known" broken promises, there are also many "unknowns" about the promises and challenges of future e-government development.

Table 7.5 REGRESSION ANALYSIS OF THE URBAN-RURAL GAP IN BROADBAND
ACCESS IN COUNTIES

Dependent Variable: Urban-rural gap in fixed & LTE access (the percentage of population in urban areas of a county with broadband access—the percentage of population in rural areas of the same county with broadband access)	Parameter estimate	Standard error	
Intercept	0.433	0.045	***
Log (total county population)	−0.052	0.005	***
Urban population ratio of a county	−0.099	0.024	***
% of population with fixed and mobile LTE in urban areas	0.491	0.021	***

NOTES: R-square = 0.22; N = 2,415; State fixed effects are controlled for.

*** statistically significant at the 1-percent level.

As suggested in Table 7.1, broadband-enabled e-government services are supposed to improve the cost-effectiveness of service delivery and provide significant cost savings for communities over time. Nonetheless, most communities do not have any cost accounting tools, such as activity-based costing, or well-designed program evaluation, to demonstrate cost savings, cost effectiveness improvement, or return of investment. This problem is especially challenging as broadband infrastructure investment tends to be huge in initial years, while the benefits may be diffuse and spread over a long period of time. Without these cost analysis tools or value analyses, many e-government purchasing or capital investment decisions are likely to be supply-side driven without much information on who benefits most from these services, how these services have and will be used, whether there is real demand and willingness to pay for these services, and whether taxpayers' money is put to the best use.

There is also some uncertainty about the impact of broadband-enabled e-government services on citizens' perception of being informed, their satisfaction with the government's communication efforts

and engagement results, their trust in the government, and their satisfaction with the performance of government services. West (2004) has
found that e-government usage has no significant impact on citizens' trust
in government. However, Welch et al. (2005) have shown that usage of
government websites is linked to citizen satisfaction with e-government,
which is then indirectly linked to greater trust in government. At the same
time, they have also found general dissatisfaction with the interactivity
of government websites, which is exactly what broadband technologies
can help overcome. Scott (2006) has shown that many communities do
not offer much in the way of interactive engagement tools, such as online
policy forums and e-consultations that broadband technology can potentially empower citizens to do. More studies are needed to investigate if
broadband-enabled e-government services really enhance greater direct
and discursive democracy as well as citizen satisfaction and public trust
in the government.

In addition, there is a lot of ambiguity about what individual employees
can and cannot do using social media, what constitutes individual free
speech, and which communications should be regarded as governmental
records and therefore properly archived under the current legal framework
(Bertot et al. 2010). For example, many governments have encouraged
their departments to set up social media tools to get in touch with citizens
and customers more directly. However, it is unclear if employees are doing
these on their own personal initiative, or whether they are representing
their organizations officially. Also, many organizations may not have clear
guidelines on what information and data they can publish through social media, and the extent to which the opinions and information released
through social media platforms represent official policies, since many "instant" remarks may not have been approved through the formal communication channels of the organization. Some organizations also struggle
with the decision of whether there should be a centralized approach in
handling social media, which has the potential risk of stifling the sponta-
neity and authenticity of these tools, or should instead use a decentralized

approach, which has the risk of creating unorganized and fragmented messaging. Hence, how to reconcile the competing values of transparency, individual freedom of expression, accountability, and participatory democracy is another uncertainty that organizations have to wrestle with in a broadband-enabled society.

Furthermore, there are some criticisms of broadband-enabled e-government services that have not been thoroughly tested. For example, some have claimed that given the digital divide among socioeconomic classes, broadband technologies will benefit mostly the educated and the high-income households disproportionally because they have the means to access the technologies. As a result, as more services are shifted to online platforms and as more participatory opportunities are done through web-based technologies or mobile device apps, some hypothesize that these social groups will have an even more significant influence on policy agenda setting and service delivery planning of a community, thus reinforcing further their ruling power in the current governance structure. However, some past studies dispute this and suggest the opposite—that the internet has expanded political participation, especially among the young, and created more equal access to the government among those who have less traditional power and access to information (Kiesler et al. 2000).

Given prior research, how broadband technology will affect digital equalization trends is unclear. Kwak et al. (2004) found a small positive impact on political discussion among broadband users in contrast to narrowband internet users, but they also show that broadband users tend to be more educated, have higher incomes, and have greater political interest than narrowband users and non-users of the internet. Krueger (2002) has found some limited positive impact of broadband technology on political participation. However, he also cautions that this finding is uncertain, given the gradual diffusion of broadband technology among communities and across socioeconomic groups. It is possible that in the long run, broadband technology may in fact reverse the promise of power equalization for all. Hence, this potentially broken promise has yet to be tested carefully.

PROPOSING AN EVALUATIVE FRAMEWORK FOR E-GOVERNMENT SERVICES IN THE BROADBAND ERA

Given the knowns and unknowns about the benefits and challenges of broadband-enabled e-government services, public managers and policymakers need to gather more data and conduct more evaluative analysis to understand how broadband-enabled services should be organized and what policies should be pursued to promote greater efficiency, equity, responsiveness, and accountability in the public sector. At a minimum, more evidence-based evaluative studies are needed to measure the economic and social benefits of broadband-enabled services. Also, greater understanding is needed to understand the implications for public service delivery (see Table 7.6). For example, do governmental agencies provide more online services as a result of technological change, and do they begin to substitute traditional face-to-face interactions with the public by online services? If so, what are the administrative benefits and challenges? Do they see more or less opportunities for public participation among different groups of citizens? Do government agencies realize more cost savings because of these trends?

From elected officials' perspective, they may need to think about the implications for governing in the broadband-enabled environment. For example, do elected officials feel more empowered to engage the public because of the new technology platforms? Do citizens become more satisfied with government performance given the new possibilities of broadband-enabled delivery options and participatory channels? Are citizens becoming more informed, and do they trust the government more? At the same time, do policymakers and program managers experience more time pressure and public demand and are they equipped to respond to these challenges?

From the citizen perspective, public managers and policymakers should also explore whether citizens actually use online platforms to interact more with the government and fellow citizens and feel more informed and engaged. Also, do different socioeconomic and neighborhood groups have the same experience? Do citizens feel that the government has become

Table 7.6 POTENTIAL QUESTIONS FOR EVALUATING THE IMPACT OF BROADBAND-
ENABLED E-GOVERNMENT SERVICES

For City Governments	• Do city governments provide more web-based services after broadband services are in place?
	• After broadband services are in place, can city governments cut back on traditional channels of service delivery, such as mailing, call center services, and neighborhood meetings?
	• After broadband services are in place, are city services, such as parks and recreation, library, and neighborhood services, able to reach out to a wider range of residents?
	• After broadband services are in place, are city departments able to use more sophisticated technologies to organize their internal operations, planning, and service delivery more responsively and cost-effectively?
	• How much cost savings do city governments experience in service delivery after they are able to shift some of the services online?
	• Do city governments provide more interactive, direct participation opportunities in decision-making after broadband services are in place?
For Elected Officials	• Do elected officials feel that they are more empowered to understand citizens' concerns after broadband services are in place?
	• Do elected officials feel that they are more empowered to reach out to and interact with citizens after broadband services are in place?
	• Do elected officials receive more citizen contact and service requests online after broadband services are in place?
	• Do elected officials shift more citizen interaction from face-to-face meetings to online meetings after broadband services are in place?

(continued)

Table 7.6 CONTINUED

| For the General Citizenry | • Do citizens who have broadband access use government services online more frequently and widely than those who do not?
• Do citizens who have broadband services use web-based channels to interact with government officials more frequently and on a wider scope of issues?
• Are citizens who have broadband services better informed about community and public policy issues?
• Do citizens interact online more frequently and on a wider scope of issues with their neighbors and fellow citizens after they have broadband services?
• Do citizens who have broadband access participate more actively in public affairs, such as watching the webcast of government meetings and participating more in public and community services?
• Do citizens who have broadband access feel that the government is more transparent, responsive, accountable, effective, and trustworthy?
• Do citizens who have broadband access feel that they lose some degree of privacy?
• Do the answers to these questions differ significantly by race, neighborhoods, educational background, and income groups? |

more transparent, accountable, cost-effective, and trustworthy because of the online services and participatory opportunities empowered by broadband technologies? These are some of the questions worth exploring in the near future so that policymakers and broadband advocates can understand more comprehensively the impact of broadband technology on e-government and society. Since many governments lack reliable and sufficient data to answer these questions, evaluate the economic and social benefits of broadband technologies in a particular community, and demonstrate the cost savings for public organizations and the citizenry, more evidence-based research is still needed.

CONCLUSION

Much progress has been made in the US to offer faster and better broadband services in various communities. Indeed, broadband technology can offer many empowering possibilities to those who have access and know how to use it. It also opens up a completely new dimension of interactivity and public participation and has raised a lot of new potential for cost-effective solutions in government-to-citizen (G2C), citizen-to-government (C2G), government-to-business (G2B), and government-to-government (G2G) services (Dugdale et al. 2005). At the same time, there are still many unknowns and potentially broken promises about its benefits. Also, how to bridge the digital gap between urban and rural areas and how public-private partnership should be leveraged more to address this equity concern are issues that remain unresolved, despite some progress made (Gillett et al. 2003).

To address some of these policy concerns effectively, the future development of broadband-enabled e-government requires not only more infrastructure investment but also new thinking and strategies of governing. If broadband-enabled technology is intended to shift the focus to users and empower them to generate more information and applications, government officials in the new technological era may have to shift their thinking from the mentality of provider and regulator to that of a market creator, coordinator, facilitator, community organizer, and network builder (Svara and Denhardt 2010; Nabatchi 2012). Instead of producing and managing service delivery, government officials may need to take a stronger role in convening, connecting, and fostering collaboration among individual citizens, nonprofits, and businesses so that broadband technology can deliver its potential benefits desired by different communities (Lynne Bradley, in FCC 2009a).

Finally, it should be emphasized that some of the potential social benefits of broadband-enabled e-government services can only be realized if public officials and policymakers embrace the principles of openness, transparency, and accountability and are willing to post information and data online (Jansen 2005). If officials resist the open data movement because of political risk or are concerned about too much open interaction with the public in real-time to answer potentially embarrassing questions online, then the premium broadband network is still insufficient to advance the democratic ideal and participatory ethos. As John Wonderlich of the Sunlight Foundation remarked in an FCC testimony, "Just as successful national broadband policy is necessary to fulfill our shared vision for a transparent and connected democracy, government transparency is necessary to allow digital citizenship to develop its full potential" (FCC 2009a, 117). As broadband technologies continue to evolve and improve, the principles of democratic governance will also need to be transformed and strengthened to keep up with the new technological possibilities and their related social, economic, and political challenges.

NOTE

1. ADSL is asymmetric digital subscriber line and VDSL is very high-speed digital subscriber line.

REFERENCES

Bertot, J. C., Jaeger, P. T., Munson, S., and Glaisyer, T. 2010. "Social Media Technology and Government Transparency." *Computer* 43 (11): 53–59.

Dugdale, A., Daly, A., Papandrea, F., and Maley, M. 2005. "Accessing E-Government: Challenges for Citizens and Organizations." *International Review of Administrative Sciences* 71: 109–118.

Fisher, T. 2019. "5G: The Latest News and Updates." *Lifewire.* https://www.lifewire.com/5g-news-4428066

Fountain, J. E. 2001. *Building the Virtual State: Information Technology and Institutional Change.* Washington, DC: Brookings Institution Press.

Gillett, S. E., Lehr, W. H., and Osorio, C. 2003. "Local Government Broadband Initiatives." Working paper of the Program on Internet and Telecoms Convergence. Cambridge, MA: Massachusetts Institute of Technology.

Gouscos, D., Kalikakis, M., Legal, M., and Papadopoulou, S. 2007. "A General Model of Performance and Quality for One-Stop E-Government Service Offerings." *Government Information Quarterly* 24: 860–885.

Government of Alberta, Canada. 2009. *Broadband as a Catalyst for e-Government: A Case Study of Five Rural Municipalities in Alberta.*

Grant, G., and Chau, D. 2005. "Developing a Generic Framework for E-Government." *Journal of Global Information Management* 13 (1): 1–30.

Hagen, M., and Kubicek, H. 2000. *One-Stop Government in Europe: Results of 11 National Surveys.* Report of COST Action A14: Government and Democracy in the Information Age; Working Group "ICT in Public Administration." Bremen, Germany: University of Bremen.

Hart, Kim. 2018. "How 5G May Widen the Rural-Urban Digital Divide." *Axios.* https://www.axios.com/5g-digital-divide-19b70d34-4978-44df-a1cb-ae9222d113ef.html

Hitt, L., and Tambe, P. 2007. "Broadband Adoption and Content Consumption." *Information Economics and Policy* 19 (3–4): 362–378.

Ho, A. T.-K. 2002. "Reinventing Local Governments and the E-Government Initiative." *Public Administration Review* 62 (4): 410–420.

Ho, A. T.-K., and McCall, B. 2016. *Ten Actions to Implement Big Data Initiatives: A Study of 65 Cities.* Washington, DC: IBM Center for the Business of Government.

Horrigan, J., and Rainie, L. 2002. "The Broadband Difference: How Online Americans' Behavior Changes with High-Speed Internet Connections at Home." *Pew Internet and American Life.* https://www.pewresearch.org/internet/2002/06/23/the-broadband-difference-how-online-behavior-changes-with-high-speed-internet-connections/

Hudson-Smith, A., Evans, S., and Batty, M. 2005. "Building the Virtual City: Public Participation through E-Democracy." *Knowledge, Technology, and Policy* 18 (1): 62–85.

IBM. 2012. IBM Intelligent Operations Center. http://www-01.ibm.com/software/industry/intelligent-oper-center/

Jaeger, P. T., Shneiderman, B., Fleischmann, K. R., Preece, J., Qu, Y., and Wu, P. F. 2007. "Community Response Grids: E-Government, Social Networks, and Effective Emergency Management." *Telecommunications Policy* 31: 592–604.

Jansen, A. 2005. "Assessing E-Government Progress: Why and What." Working paper. Department of E-Government studies, Oslo, Norway: University of Oslo.

Kiesler, S., Zdaniuk, B., Lundmark, V., and Kraut, R. 2000. "Troubles with the Internet: The Dynamics of Help at Home." *Human-Computer Interaction* 15: 323–351.

Krueger, B. S. 2002. "Assessing the Potential of Internet Political Participation in the United States: A Resource Approach." *American Politics Research* 30 (5): 476–498.

Kwak, N., Skoric, M. M., Williams, A. E., and Poor, N. D. 2004. "To Broadband or Not to Broadband: The Relationship between High-Speed Internet and Knowledge and Participation." *Journal of Broadcasting and Electronic Media* 48 (3): 421–445.

Lloyd, R., and Bill, A. 2003. *Digital Divide? Who Uses Computers and the Internet in Australia Today?* Canberra: NATSEM.

Mossberger, K., and Wu, Y. 2012. *Civic Engagement and Local E-Government: Social Networking Comes of Age.* Chicago, IL: UIC Institute for Policy and Civic Engagement.

Nabatchi, T. 2012. *A Manager's Guide to Evaluating Citizen Participation.* Washington, DC: IBM Center for the Business of Government.

Scott, J. K. 2006. "'E' the People: Do U.S. Municipal Government Web Sites Support Public Involvement?" *Public Administration Review* 66 (3): 341–353.

Svara, J. H., and Denhardt, J., eds. 2010. *The Connected Community: Local Governments as Partners in Citizen Engagement and Community Building.* White paper. Alliance for Innovation.

Tang, T., and Ho, A. T.-K. 2019. "A Path-Dependence Perspective on the Adoption of Internet of Things: Evidence from Early Adopters of Smart and Connected Sensors in the United States." *Government Information Quarterly* 36 (2): 321–332.

Trkman, P., and Truk, T. 2009. "A Conceptual Model for the Development of Broadband and E-Government." *Government Information Quarterly* 26 (2): 416–424.

U.S. Federal Communications Commission. 2009a. *National Broadband Workshop: Open Government and Civic Engagement (August 6).* Washington, DC: FCC.

U.S. Federal Communications Commission. 2009b. *National Broadband Plan Workshop for State and Local Governments: Toolkits and Best Practices.* Washington, DC: FCC.

U.S. Federal Communications Commission. 2018. *Broadband Deployment Report.* 2018. Washington, DC: FCC. https://www.fcc.gov/reports-research/reports/broadband-progress-reports/2018-broadband-deployment-report

Welch, E., Hinnant, C. C., and Moon, M. J. 2005. "Linking Citizen Satisfaction with E-Government and Trust in Government." *Journal of Public Administration Research and Theory* 15 (3): 371–391.

West, D. M. 2004. "E-Government and the Transformation of Service Delivery and Citizen Attitudes." *Public Administration Review* 64 (1): 15–27.

8

Digital Media's Impact on Civic Engagement

Challenges and Opportunities for Evaluation Research on Broadband Technologies, Young People, and Citizen Engagement

MICHAEL A. XENOS

INTRODUCTION

In the late 1960s, communication theorist James Carey suggested that a major consequence of technological advances in information technologies would be the heightened significance of age or generational membership relative to other social categories. In doing so he was drawing on Harold Adams Innis's notion that a central feature of electronic media is their spatial bias, meaning that they tend to influence society by obliterating physical space and distance, as compared to other media of communication such as stone tablets, which are hard to transport but provide stable storage of information across time and influence traditional cultures accordingly. Along these lines, Carey predicted that over time future

Michael A. Xenos, *Digital Media's Impact on Civic Engagement* In: *Transforming Everything?*. Edited by: Karen Mossberger, Eric W. Welch, and Yonghong Wu, Oxford University Press. © Oxford University Press 2022. DOI: 10.1093/oso/9780190082871.003.0009 advances in communications technology would further erode cultural and regional differences in comparison to *generational* variation in "language and values, symbols and meanings" (Carey 1967, 31).

To be sure, social and cultural differences have hardly receded into the background, and indeed some would argue that our current media structures even work to exacerbate them in important ways, while adding in a host of new issues surrounding the erosion of truth and civility in public discourse (Pariser 2012; Rainie, Anderson, and Albright 2017). Scholarly research on digital media and citizen engagement, however, has tended to emphasize the generational components of widespread advances in communications technologies. For a variety of reasons, researchers in communication, political science, and allied fields have paid considerable attention to the impacts of digital media on civic and political engagement among young people. In contrast to the tenor of most contemporary popular discussion surrounding digital politics, this work has taken on a distinctly positive and at times exuberant posture toward the prospects for broadband technologies to usher in a new age of democracy led by a new generation of technologically savvy young citizens.

It is not difficult to understand how a variety of contemporary factors could lead to an optimistic faith that efforts to combine greater broadband infrastructures, political and civic content, and young people cannot help but lead to positive and worthwhile outcomes. The first premise in this line of thinking is typically the observation that citizens of advanced democracies across the age spectrum have become increasingly disengaged from political processes since the early 21st century, and that this growing disengagement is concentrated among the young (Bennett 2008; Martin 2012; Norris 2001; Putnam 2000). This provides a problem in search of a solution that, while involving phenomena that are relatively less foundational than economic activities like finding a job or negotiating health services, can hardly be ignored and can certainly not be dismissed. As democratic theorist Giovanni Sartori noted in 1987, democracy has long been held as a universally honorific concept, even if agreement on the specifics of its meaning seem permanently elusive. As will be discussed later, the "specifics" of democracy are of central importance in parsing research in this area. But before exploring those themes it is worth noting that a significant animating force for this work comes from a sense that the health of modern democracies is profoundly threatened by the possibility that core aspects of citizen engagement and participation could become lost in generational turnover, not unlike more pedestrian activities such as hand-written correspondence or landline telephone use.

The second premise in this line of thinking is that in addition to standing at the center of declining trends in democratic engagement, young people possess a number of other relatively unique properties with respect to technology and politics. Throughout history young people have been perennially associated with exciting and often experimental new advances in communications technology, as Carey and many others have noted (Carey 1967; Cassell and Cramer 2008; Sandvig 2008). Indeed, the realization that individuals born from the late 1970s to the late 1990s, and the generation beyond, were and are the first to have known the basic elements of today's broadband infrastructure *their whole lives* has spawned a virtual cottage industry in research on the topic. Whether we refer to them as "millennials," "Generation Y," or the "DotNets," there is certainly no shortage of interest in a generation of "digital natives," who were "born digital" and the oldest of whom are now "grown up digital" (Bennett 2008; Gasser and Palfrey 2008). Possibly most important, by virtue of their youth they are in the process of forming habits and overall orientations toward social and political life that can set them on paths and patterns of political engagement that follow them through their lifetimes (Campbell et al. 1960; Plutzer 2002). With these unique attributes of youth in mind, when we think about the potential implications of broadband technology for civic outcomes, young people are certainly at the center, if not the leading edge of these dynamics.

Combined with a third premise, the obvious and continuing growth in political and civic uses of the internet over the same time period, it is thus unsurprising that many initiatives and policy interventions have blossomed in a climate of relatively sanguine beliefs about potential benefits for the health of modern democracies that may accrue from placing young people, technology, and politics in close proximity. But as the introduction to this volume points out, sound investments in expanding broadband depend on a more comprehensive foundation in careful evaluation of the processes by which digital media may be linked to a variety of outcomes. To be sure, a number of research studies have provided basic support for expectations that internet use is generally beneficial for civic engagement and political participation (e.g., Anduiza, Jensen, and Jorba 2012; Boulianne 2009; Mossberger, Tolbert, and McNeal 2008). However, though typically not generational in focus, a number of studies are also beginning to validate popular concerns about "fake news" and the deterioration of democratic norms online (e.g., Cacciatore et al. 2018; Lee and Xenos 2019; Su et al. 2018). In sum, the complexities of these technologies and the patterns of human behavior surrounding political and civic engagement strongly suggest that continuing efforts in this area will require more complex investigation and evaluation strategies in order for them to be most effective.

In this chapter I hope to facilitate the kind of sophisticated and careful evaluation research for broadband discussed in the introduction and other parts of this volume, within the specific domain of political and civic engagement among young people. In doing so, I review major strands of existing scholarship in this area and identify promising areas for future research into the potential effectiveness of policy interventions designed to use broadband technologies and digital media to stimulate youth citizenship and participation. In the first section I discuss the central dimensions of citizen engagement that existing research has focused on, with an eye toward practical evaluation metrics in the domain of citizenship. In the second section I introduce the archetypical theoretical models of *mobilization* and *differential effects* that characterize scholarship on digital media use and citizenship. In the third section, I discuss two strands of current research that I believe provide the most promising avenues to better and more actionable understandings of how broadband technology may affect political and civic engagement: work on the role played by civic norms, civic education, and other contextual factors in moderating the impacts of digital media on political activity, and research on the effects of social media on a variety of citizen engagement behaviors. Finally, I will conclude with a discussion of challenges and opportunities for future research, both in terms of key substantive questions and particularly useful methodological approaches.

RELEVANT DIMENSIONS OF CITIZEN ENGAGEMENT

The first step toward a better understanding of the potential impacts of broadband technology on civic engagement and political participation is recognizing and appreciating the inherent complexities in the outcomes and dynamics involved. As noted earlier, democratic theory and other research supplies us with an open-ended array of answers as to the meaning of democracy sufficient to support what Sartori characterizes as an unending conversation. In terms of evaluation, this translates to an expansive selection of potential outcomes related to citizenship. In addition, though the basic narrative of additive and positive effects of digital media use on these outcomes enjoys wide appeal, as a whole, scholarship in the area of digital media and politics has also provided an expansive set of possibilities for specifying relationships between broadband technology use and citizenship. Sorting out the most relevant options in each area is an important prerequisite, however, for the discussion of current and promising future trends for the kind of research proposed here.

Two principal factors drive the multiplicity of outcome measures for citizenship available to evaluation research on broadband technologies. The first is a diversity of normative perspectives within democratic theory, which provides distinct and at times competing democratic ideals. These in turn suggest different operationalizations of political participation and civic engagement. Perhaps the most efficient way to parse these operational definitions stems from a simple distinction between "aggregative" or "adversarial" models of democracy and more deliberative strains of democratic theory (see Cohen 1997; Mansbridge 1983). Approaches linked to the former perspective tend to focus on behaviors and attitudes that reflect citizens' ability to discover, as well as promote and defend, their individual interests, typically through formal channels and institutions of government (i.e., voting and electoral participation). Though many of these behaviors and attitudes are consistent with deliberative models of democracy, approaches stemming from these latter models add a focus on vigorous political discussion and debate through which citizens are called upon to act out of an "enlarged mentality" emerging from exposure to, and engagement with, arguments with which they disagree (Benhabib 1996).

The second factor arises from more empirically based research on contemporary political behavior, which draws upon many of the same over-time trends in political participation cited earlier, but cautions us against becoming overly concerned about declines in traditional participatory acts such as voting or membership in political parties. This work suggests that political participation and civic engagement is not so much on the decline, as in a state of transition (e.g., Bennett 2008; Inglehart and Welzel 2005; Norris 2002; Svensson 2011). According to this line of thinking, given the broad social, economic, and political changes witnessed in the early 21st century, it may be not only reasonable but rational for all citizens, but the youngest in particular, to shift their participatory energies toward new ways of discovering, discussing, and expressing their interests in civic and political life (Bennett, Wells, and Freelon 2011). In concrete terms, this is consistent with a shift away from behaviors related to the relatively narrow realm of electoral politics and toward sentiments and activities associated with things like community volunteering, the lighter side of politics as found in political satire or political internet memes, and even consumer behavior in the form of buycotting and boycotting of products for political or moral reasons (Baym 2005; Stolle, Hooghe, and Micheletti 2005; van Deth 2014).

Taken together, these two factors provide a framework for understanding the wide array of outcome measures for evaluation research suggested by contemporary research how digital media use may affect or enhance youth civic and political engagement. By far the most obvious and common set of metrics comes from research inspired by traditional definitions of political participation emerging from political science. Conceiving of political participation largely in terms of formal acts intended to affect government policy directly or indirectly through the selection of those who make government policies (Verba, Schlozman, and Brady 1995), a large body of research has explored relationships between internet use and behaviors or attitudes related to the electoral process. As Boulianne notes in her comprehensive meta-analysis of the literature on internet use and civic and political engagement, measures related to traditional conceptions of political participation of this kind include "voting, donating money to a campaign or political group, working for a political campaign or political group, and attending meetings or a rally for a candidate" as well as traditional avenues of political expression such as wearing political buttons, displaying campaign signs during election season, or writing a letter to the editor of a news outlet (2009, 195–196). In addition to these activities, research in this area has also examined a number of related cognitive or attitudinal outcomes with tangible linkages to the behavioral dimensions of traditional citizenship. Since the early 2000s scholars have examined relationships between internet use and political knowledge, which is a crucial indicator of a citizen's ability to understand their political interests and preferences, as well as political efficacy, or citizen attitudes of confidence and competence toward their ability to meaningfully act on and represent their interests and preferences in the political system (Baumgartner and Morris 2009; Dimitrova et al. 2014; Eveland, Seo, and Marton 2002; Kenski and Stroud 2006; Lariscy, Tinkham, and Sweetser 2011; Scheufele and Nisbet 2002). Work in this vein establishes voting and related campaign activities as well as general attitudes toward these activities, and knowledge of current events, key players, and core processes of government, as the traditional metrics for understanding impacts on political participation and engagement. Some studies may incorporate online versions of these and related behaviors (e.g., Mossberger, Tolbert, and McNeal 2008), but the general focus is often still on these core aspects of democratic citizenship.

Situated between these more traditional indicators and those associated with notions of new or emerging forms of citizenship, one finds other potential outcome measures that are not strictly connected to electoral politics and public policy but are still relatively traditional compared to other available yardsticks of civic and political engagement. These measures emerge from work inspired by deliberative conceptions of democracy, as well as research related to social capital. For example, in response to worries that broadband technologies may usher in a culture of polarized partisan politics characterized by fragmentation and balkanization (e.g., Pariser 2012), a number of scholars have explored conditions under which the internet may be able to foster meaningful political discussion and exposure to political disagreement. As will be discussed later, much of this work focuses on the unique characteristics of social networking media, such as Facebook, and its ability to counteract some of the patterns of partisan selectivity emphasized in early research on the internet and politics (e.g., Kim 2011; Messing and Westwood 2014). Other work along these lines, however, has focused on the potential for different aspects of internet use such as participation in online discussion forums or general digital literacy to have the same kinds of effects in terms of helping people become exposed to political views contrary to their own (Kahne, Lee, and Feezell 2012; Wojcieszak and Mutz 2009). In addition to exposure to disagreement, researchers have also explored the effects of internet use on social capital. Like the scholarship on exposure to disagreement, research focused on these outcomes has also tended to focus on social media (e.g., Ellison, Steinfield, and Lampe 2007; Gil de Zúñiga, Jung, and Valenzuela 2012; Hampton, Lee, and Her 2011; Pasek, More, and Romer 2009; Valenzuela, Park, and Kee 2009). But here too, the basic approach of turning to variables representing networks of reciprocal social relations and trust that "while not explicitly political, have implications for political functioning" has been a common one in political communication research on digital media for some time (Shah, Kwak, and Holbert 2001, 142). Lying outside of the narrow confines of outcomes directly related to campaigns, elections, and the policy process, but still within relatively established terrain, these variables offer a kind of middle-range set of potential measures for evaluating the effects of broadband policies on civic and political life.

Finally, a growing body of literature, largely inspired by assessments of democratic practice as in transition rather than decline, has also suggested additional potential constructs for evaluation research that lie well beyond the realm of traditional approaches to political and civic life. These outcomes reflect a sense that our contemporary political and media environments call for altogether new conceptions of what it means to be an active citizen who is able to effectively engage in civic and political life. A prime example of this is research focusing on the potential for digital media use to facilitate political action that takes place in the market, or the supermarket, as argued by Stolle, Hooghe, and Micheletti (2005), rather than more traditional public or civic spheres. Though certainly overshadowed in terms of volume compared to research focusing on more traditional or middle-range outcomes, a small but growing line of scholarship identifies relationships between internet use and this new form of political action, typically operationalized as choosing to buy (buycotting), or not buy (boycotting) products and services for political, moral, or ethical reasons (Baumgartner and Morris 2009; Ward and de Vreese 2011; Boström, Micheletti, and Oosterveer 2018). Along similar lines, research has also pointed to various forms of online activism and digital production activities as additional possible markers of participation enabled by and associated with digital media use (Earl and Kimport 2010; Gil de Zuniga, Puig-I-Abril, and Rojas 2009). Though sometimes dismissed as mere "slacktivism," based on the sense in which these activities typically take significantly less effort than more traditional forms of participation (Morozov 2011), outcomes in this lie at the outer edge of the envelope in terms of possible metrics for understanding the civic and political potentials of expanded broadband access and use.

Relevant Dynamics in Theorizing the Effects of Digital Media on Citizen Engagement

Using various constructs and indicators from across the spectrum discussed in the preceding section, scholars in political science, communication, and related fields have developed a number of theoretical models for understanding the effects of digital media use on civic and political engagement. Though their principal goals reflect the emphasis of social science on providing explanations for variations in outcomes of interest, rather than evaluation per se, these theories and models are of great value to practical efforts aimed at understanding the effects or likely effects of specific interventions. Evaluation, after all, involves the exploration of specific cause-and-effect relationships that are typically special cases of more general relationships between antecedent and dependent variables. As noted earlier, researchers in the area of digital media and citizen engagement have specified the relationships between these variables in many different ways. It is possible, however, to characterize most of these approaches based on a simple distinction between two archetypical models. The first, and perhaps most familiar in both popular and scholarly discourse, is known as the *mobilization* thesis. The second is what I will refer to as the *differential effects* thesis.

Tracing its roots back to the original wave of exuberance surrounding the rise of the internet and associated technologies, the mobilization thesis straightforwardly posits positive and additive effects of digital media use on civic and political engagement. In doing so, it conjures what Gibson, Lusoli, and Ward describe as "optimistic scenarios of a return to Athenian-style direct democracy and empowered citizens" (2005, 561). Citing classic rational choice models of political behavior and participation, Bimber (2003) characterizes this approach as "instrumental" based on its core assumption that by reducing cost factors associated with citizen engagement (e.g., acquiring political information, expressing and communicating opinions) digital media may facilitate across-the-board increases in participation and engagement. Thus from the perspective of the mobilization thesis, evaluating interventions that expand access to broadband technology becomes a straightforward examination of before-and-after levels of political engagement, again on the assumption that by lowering the costs of virtually all aspects of political engagement the intervention would necessarily make all kinds of political engagement more likely.

The mobilization thesis is typically contrasted with what is called the "normalization" or "reinforcement" thesis, which posits that contrary to optimistic assumptions about universal gains in citizen engagement, expanded access to internet technologies will tend only to produce increases in participation among those already active in civic and political affairs (e.g., Gibson, Lusoli, and Ward 2005; Hirzalla, van Zoonen, and de Ridder 2010). In this chapter and elsewhere, however, I prefer to contrast the normalization perspective with what I call a *differential effects* approach (Xenos and Moy 2007). The reason for this is that analytically, the roots of opposition to the mobilization thesis are most often found in the argument that the central dynamics with respect to digital media use and its effects involve contextual factors and interactions between the technology itself and user predispositions or other characteristics. For this reason, Bimber refers to this as the "psychological approach" to understanding the individual-level effects of broadband technologies, while arguing that effects on political participation will tend toward a "rich-get-richer" dynamic (2003). An added advantage to this approach is that it also leaves room for the possibility that some digital media tools may actually promote an equalizing dynamic in which those less engaged in politics and civic life may reap significantly greater benefits from technology than their more engaged counterparts, as will be discussed later in the case of social media. Overall, whether used to argue that broadband technologies will expand or contract existing inequalities in citizen engagement, the distinctive feature of the *differential effects* approach is an attention to contextual factors and the ways that broadband technology may affect different users in different ways.

Taken together, the outcome indicators and theoretical archetypes reviewed here provide a basic framework for fruitful applications of scholarly research on digital media use and citizen engagement to evaluation efforts involving specific deployments of broadband infrastructure. With such a range of potential measures for citizen engagement, and such a variety of theoretical approaches, it should be clear that it is essential for such projects to attend to the complexities involved in understanding how technology may affect democratic processes. In the next section,

I will discuss two specific strands of research that illustrate the value of attending to such complexities most clearly.

PROMISING TRENDS IN CONTEMPORARY RESEARCH

To be sure, the field of research on digital media use and citizen engagement has matured significantly in the early 21st century and its continued expansion shows no signs of abating. As a result it would be impossible in a chapter of this kind to provide a truly comprehensive review of work in this area that could be of value to broadband evaluation research. Thus in this section I focus on two areas of research that I believe offer particularly valuable insights for evaluation efforts in that they directly engage with the themes discussed in the previous section, and together provide a useful illustration of some of the challenges for future research in this area that I will discuss in the conclusion.

One promising strand of research that directly engages prominent currents in both the conceptualization of citizen engagement by scholars and ongoing theoretical debates about the effects of digital media use on civic and political participation is work exploring the extent to which variations in attitudes and motivations surrounding citizenship may mediate or moderate such effects. This research grows out of scholarship examining the prospect that citizen engagement itself may be in a state of transformation, and that part of this transformation may be the emergence of new civic norms, which may be understood as attitudes and values pertaining to how democracy functions and specifically how "good citizens" relate to the political world. Young people in particular, scholars such as Lance Bennett and Stephen Coleman argue, appear to be moving away from traditional conceptions of "dutiful" citizenship that center on traditional modes of political engagement and loyalties, and toward a more personalized and autonomous politics of self-actualization that tends to facilitate alternative forms of engagement such as digital networking, community volunteering, and consumer activism (Bennett 2008; Coleman 2008). These accounts suggest that rather than viewing citizen engagement as a process of acquiring information about political issues from newspapers and coordinating their engagement through political parties, young people are increasingly coming to see citizenship as making sense of the world through peer-to-peer social networks and taking part in a variety of political activities coordinated by affinity groups and other unconventional political actors. Research into the potential that norms of citizenship may be shifting thus highlights specific individual attitudes and values, as well as contextual factors, such as processes of political socialization in families and schools where such values and attitudes are formed, that can help to better specify and understand potentially differential effects of digital media use.

The implications of this for broadband evaluation are that the effects of particular interventions may take different forms based on variations along the dimension of civic norms either among the recipients of an intervention, or in the interventions themselves. In the former scenario, one might expect different outcomes for different individuals based on the extent to which they continue to adhere to more traditional "dutiful" norms of citizenship, or have adopted some of the newer "actualizing" or "autonomous" norms that are posited to be more consistent with using the internet as a tool and outlet for political activity (Bennett 2008; Coleman 2008; Xenos, Vromen, and Loader 2014). Alternatively, in terms of the latter scenario, scholars pursuing this strand of research have often argued that specific efforts to stimulate greater citizen engagement among youth may fail to realize their potential by not adequately attending to the emerging and evolving political sensibilities of young people (Bennett, Wells, and Freelon 2011; Bennett, Wells, and Rank 2009; Wells 2010; Xenos and Bennett 2007). Though more research into these dynamics is certainly needed, thus far research has suggested that civic norms may provide an important piece of leverage for understanding and evaluating the complexities involved in efforts to facilitate greater political engagement among young people through digital media.

Another line of research that can offer valuable insights to broadband evaluation efforts in the area of civic and political engagement is emerging scholarship on the effects of social media, and the mobile phones through which young people typically access social media platforms. Like the research on youth civic norms, this work is strongly rooted in the ways in which digital media are implicated in evolving patterns of social interaction among young people. Unlike the research on shifting civic norms, however, a significant amount of work in this area attends to some of the more traditional outcome variables discussed earlier. Consider, for example, the research of Bond et al. (2012), which documented tangible increases in voter turnout associated with voter mobilization through Facebook. Another useful example is found in research by Yonghwan Kim and colleagues examining relationships between accessing news via smartphone and political behaviors like political discussion and participation (Kim et al. 2016).

Perhaps one of the most explored outcomes with respect to social media use, however, is social capital. Work in this area has examined and documented that, contrary to concerns that technology use may erode personal relationships (e.g., Turkle 2011), social media use can contribute to increases in the kinds of social connections that researchers have long associated with more active and engaged citizenship (Ellison, Steinfield, and Lampe 2007; Pasek, More, and Romer 2009; Rainie and Wellman 2012; Valenzuela, Park, and Kee 2009). Still other research on the political effects of social media use explores the extent to which the diversity of individuals' online social networks and habitual scrolling through their social media feeds can combine to help users encounter political information and views that they might otherwise avoid, as well as enable individuals less interested in politics to benefit from information circulated by their more politically minded friends (Messing and Westwood 2014; Xenos et al. 2014). While some may question the extent to which social media and associated technologies constitute a fundamentally new "operating system" for social life (as Rainie and Wellman argue), research in this area establishes social media as another important factor for understanding the effects of broadband technology on civic and political outcomes.

The significance of research on the political implications of social and mobile media use for broadband evaluation efforts is that whereas the scholarship on civic norms tends to highlight the ways in which internet use can amplify user predispositions, studies of social media use often identify ways in which digital media can actually stimulate individuals to develop resources and engage in behaviors that they might not otherwise. In this respect, these studies run counter to a significant amount of the broader discussion about internet use and political engagement, which suggests that digital media mainly contribute to the reinforcement of attitudes (cyberbalkanization) and general predispositions toward political engagement (the "rich-get-richer" dynamic discussed earlier). In other words, this work demonstrates a set of contemporary contexts and practices in which expansions in broadband infrastructure could uniquely contribute to qualitatively different patterns of behavior.

CHALLENGES AND OPPORTUNITIES: RECOMMENDATIONS FOR FUTURE RESEARCH

Based on the preceding discussion, it is now possible to reflect more broadly on the principal challenges facing efforts to better understand the potential political implications of broadband as well as the most promising avenues for addressing them. This involves a consideration of both substantive questions arising from the research reviewed earlier, as well as a discussion of analytic and methodological approaches that may provide the most useful means for conducting future research in this area that responds to the fundamental problem of complexity discussed in this volume's introduction. Though it would be foolish to think that one could chart an ideal path toward a perfect understanding of the causal relationships between digital media use and citizen engagement, I believe the basic principles outlined here can move such work in the direction of more effective research on effects in this area.

Given the complex and multidimensional nature of civic and political engagement, which as discussed earlier gives rise to a wide array of possible empirical indicators, as well as the diversity of ways in which digital media use may be linked to such outcomes, I submit that the most pressing substantive puzzles in this area involve the identification of circumstances and contexts in which particular kinds of relationships might be expected. Under what conditions might we expect increases in digital media use to have the strongest positive effects on civic and political engagement? What kinds of contextual factors determine whether the effects of digital media use in these areas will be concentrated within particular sub-populations, or widely experienced among a diverse array of users? What kinds of civic and political engagement might we expect to be affected by specific kinds of policy interventions related to digital media?

To be sure, the review of the scholarly literature provided here helps to identify a variety of conditions and factors that make up the most likely candidates to play various roles in answers to these questions. For example, returning to the discussion that opened this chapter, age and generational identity is certainly a critical factor. Similarly, individual attitudes toward civic and political engagement (civic norms) also appear to be an important fulcrum involved in certain patterns of differential effects. And, the research on social media use (as well as other examples discussed earlier) provides a powerful illustration of how particular kinds of digital media can produce distinct patterns of effects. A significant amount of additional research specifically geared toward exploring and comparing specific contextual scenarios, however, will be necessary in order to produce general principles that can help researchers navigate this complex terrain more effectively.

In pursuit of these substantive questions surrounding various configurations of "treatments" and "outcomes," a number of specific analytic and methodological approaches may be identified as holding the most promise for helping to untangle the complexities involved in understanding the effectiveness of digital media policy interventions in facilitating citizen engagement. The most obvious is experimental research, which enjoys unparalleled capabilities for exploring causal relationships and, more importantly, the mechanisms through which they work. Traditionally, such research designs have been criticized for offering leverage over causal questions at the expense of generalizability and ecological validity. As the familiar critique goes, they often provide us with an exceptional grasp over the inner workings of the mind, but often only the minds of college sophomores. Scholars have also suggested that the logic of random assignment in media experiments may be becoming outdated in a world where the vast choices afforded by digital media limit the extent to which anyone randomly encounters media anymore (Iyengar and Bennett 2008). The increasing availability of tools and infrastructures for conducting web-based experiments on representative samples, as well as methodological innovations in experimental design, however, have both helped to significantly mitigate these concerns (Moy et al. 2012). As an example of the former trend, consider that the Bond et al. study, published in *Nature*, was a classic experimental design administered to over sixty-one million participants through Facebook (Bond et al. 2012).

A second methodological tool that could prove invaluable to exploring the intellectual puzzles outlined earlier is cross-national comparative research. Though such work is rare in the field of political communication research, scholars are increasingly turning to comparative analysis as a source of insights into contextual factors that can condition media effects of the kind considered here (Wojcieszak 2012; Xenos et al. 2014). In particular, research examining the dynamics of broadband adoption and citizen engagement outcomes that enables cross-national comparison can provide valuable leverage over understanding the distinct roles played by many of the factors identified earlier, as well as many others. Indeed, a host of potentially relevant factors such as civic education, telecommunications policies, and political culture all vary significantly across otherwise comparable advanced democracies, which provides numerous opportunities for exploring the ways in which these factors may determine different patterns of effects. Studies that pursue cross-national comparisons are often overlooked due to the costs involved in such work, as well as the difficulties involved in coordinating research teams in distant locations. Thanks to advances in digital media itself, however, one of the factors contributing to increasing cross-national research is the increasing ease with which problems of coordination can be solved through web-based collaboration tools.

In conclusion, the attitudes and behaviors focused on here present distinct challenges for research compared to other kinds of outcomes explored elsewhere in this volume. For this reason, it is difficult if not impossible to identify a clear-cut path for the future of evaluation research in this area. To borrow a phrase brought about by users of online social networking websites involved in unusual personal relationships, one could summarize the preceding review by simply stating that "it's complicated." By drawing attention to the central drivers of complexity involved in understanding relationships between internet use and citizen engagement, and identifying the analytic and methodological approaches that may be best suited to exploring those dynamics, however, it is hoped that this chapter can help foster the kind of sound evaluation research that can inform better directions for future policy interventions in this area.

REFERENCES

Anduiza, E., Perea, E. A., Jensen, M. J., and Jorba, L., eds. 2012. *Digital Media and Political Engagement Worldwide: A Comparative Study*. Cambridge, UK: Cambridge University Press.

Baumgartner, J. C., and Morris, J. S. 2009. "MyFaceTube Politics: Social Networking Web Sites and Political Engagement of Young Adults." *Social Science Computer Review* 28 (1): 24–44. doi:10.1177/0894439309334325

Baym, G. 2005. "The Daily Show: Discursive Integration and the Reinvention of Political Journalism." *Political Communication* 22 (3): 259–276.

Benhabib, S. 1996. "Toward a Deliberative Model of Democratic Legitimacy." In *Democracy and Difference. Contesting the Boundaries of the Political*. Edited by Seyla Benhabib, 34–67. Princeton: Princeton University Press.

Bennett, W. L. 2008. *Civic Life Online. Learning How Digital Media Can Engage Youth*. London and Cambridge: MIT Press.

Bennett, W. L., Wells, C., and Freelon, D. 2011. "Communicating Civic Engagement: Contrasting Models of Citizenship in the Youth Web Sphere." *Journal of Communication* 61 (5): 835–856. doi:10.1111/j.1460-2466.2011.01588.x

Bennett, W. L., Wells, C., and Rank, A. 2009. "Young Citizens and Civic Learning: Two Paradigms of Citizenship in the Digital Age." *Citizenship Studies* 13 (2): 105–120.

Bimber, B. 2003. *Information and American Democracy: Technology in the Evolution of Political Power*. Cambridge University Press.

Bond, R. M., Fariss, C. J., Jones, J. J., Kramer, A. D., Marlow, C., Settle, J. E., and Fowler, J. H. 2012. "A 61-Million-Person Experiment in Social Influence and Political Mobilization." *Nature* 489 (7415): 295–298.

Boström, M., Micheletti, M., and Oosterveer, P., eds. 2019. *The Oxford Handbook of Political Consumerism*. London: Oxford University Press.

Boulianne, S. 2009. "Does Internet Use Affect Engagement? A Meta-Analysis of Research." *Political Communication* 26 (2): 193–211.

Cacciatore, M. A., Yeo, S. K., Scheufele, D. A., Xenos, M. A., Brossard, D., and Corley, E. A. 2018. "Is Facebook Making Us Dumber? Exploring Social Media Use as a Predictor of Knowledge." *Journalism and Mass Communication Quarterly* 95 (2): 404–424.

Campbell, A., Converse, P. E., Miller, W. E., and Stokes, D. E. 1960. *The American Voter.* Chicago: University of Chicago Press.

Carey, J. W. 1967. "Harold Adams Innis and Marshall McLuhan." *The Antioch Review* 27 (1): 5. https://doi.org/10.2307/4610816

Cassell, J., and Cramer, M. 2008. "High Tech or High Risk: Moral Panics about Girls Online." In *Digital Youth, Innovation, and the Unexpected.* Edited by Tara McPherson, 53–76. The John D. and Catherine T. MacArthur Foundation Series on Digital Media and Learning. Cambridge, MA: MIT Press.

Cohen, J. 1997. "Procedure and Substance in Deliberative Democracy." In *Deliberative Democracy: Essays on Reason and Politics.* Edited by James Bohman and William Rehg, 408–437. Cambridge, MA: MIT Press.

Coleman, S. 2008. "Doing IT for Themselves: Management versus Autonomy in Youth E-Citizenship." In *Civic Life Online: Learning How Digital Media Can Engage Youth.* Edited by W. Lance Bennett. The John D. and Catherine T. MacArthur Foundation Series on Digital Media and Learning, 189–206. Cambridge, MA: MIT Press.

Dimitrova, D. V., Shehata, A., Strömbäck, J., and Nord, L. W. 2014. "The Effects of Digital Media on Political Knowledge and Participation in Election Campaigns: Evidence from Panel Data." *Communication Research* 41 (1): 95–118.

Earl, J., and Kimport, K. 2010. "Changing the World One Webpage at a Time: Conceptualizing and Explaining Internet Activism." *Mobilization: An International Quarterly* 15 (4): 425–446. http://mobilization.metapress.com/index/W03123213LH37042.pdf

Ellison, N. B., Steinfield, C., and Lampe, C. 2007. "The Benefits of Facebook 'Friends': Social Capital and College Students' Use of Online Social Network Sites." *Journal of Computer-Mediated Communication* 12 (4): 1143–1168. http://jcmc.indiana.edu/vol12/issue4/ellison.html

Eveland, W. P., Seo, M. S., and Marton, K. 2002. "Learning from the News in Campaign 2000: An Experimental Comparison of TV News, Newspapers, and Online News." *Media Psychology* 4 (4): 353–378.

Gasser, U., and Palfrey, J. 2008. *Born Digital-Connecting with a Global Generation of Digital Natives.* New York: Perseus.

Gibson, R. K., Lusoli, W., and Ward, S. 2005. "Online Participation in the UK: Testing a 'Contextualised' Model of Internet Effects." *British Journal of Political Science and International Relations* 7 (4): 561–583. doi:10.1111/j.1467-856x.2005.00209.x

Gil de Zúñiga, H., Jung, N., and Valenzuela, S. 2012. "Social Media Use for News and Individuals' Social Capital, Civic Engagement and Political Participation." *Journal of Computer-Mediated Communication* 17 (3): 319–336. doi:10.1111/j.1083-6101.2012.01574.x

Gil De Zuniga, H., Puig-I-Abril, E., and Rojas, H. 2009. "Weblogs, Traditional Sources Online and Political Participation: An Assessment of How the Internet Is Changing the Political Environment." *New Media and Society* 11 (4): 553–574. doi:10.1177/1461444809102960

Hampton, K. N., Lee, C.-J., and Her, E. J. 2011. "How New Media Affords Network Diversity: Direct and Mediated Access to Social Capital through Participation in Local Social Settings." *New Media and Society* 13 (7): 1031–1049. doi:10.1177/1461444810390342

Hirzalla, F., Van Zoonen, L., and De Ridder, J. 2010. "Internet Use and Political Participation: Reflections on the Mobilization/Normalization Controversy." *The Information Society* 27 (1): 1–15. doi:10.1080/01972243.2011.534360

Inglehart, R., and Welzel, C. 2005. *Modernization, Cultural Change, and Democracy: The Human Development Sequence.* Cambridge, UK: Cambridge University Press.

Bennett, W. L., and Iyengar, S. 2008. "A New Era of Minimal Effects? The Changing Foundations of Political Communication." *Journal of Communication* 58 (4): 707–731.

Kahne, J., Lee, N., and Feezell, J. T. 2012. "Digital Media Literacy Education and Online Civic and Political Participation." *International Journal of Communication* 6: 1–24.

Kenski, K., and Stroud, N. J. 2006. "Connections between Internet Use and Political Efficacy, Knowledge, and Participation." *Journal of Broadcasting and Electronic Media* 50 (2): 173–192. http://www.tandfonline.com/doi/abs/10.1207/s15506878jobem5002_1

Kim, Y. 2011. "The Contribution of Social Network Sites to Exposure to Political Difference: The Relationships among SNSs, Online Political Messaging, and Exposure to Cross-Cutting Perspectives." *Computers in Human Behavior* 27 (2): 971–977. doi:10.1016/j.chb.2010.12.001

Kim, Y., Chen, H.-T., and Wang, Y. 2016. "Living in the Smartphone Age: Examining the Conditional Indirect Effects of Mobile Phone Use on Political Participation." *Journal of Broadcasting and Electronic Media* 60 (4): 694–713.

Lee, S., and Xenos, M. A. 2019. "Social Distraction? Social Media Use and Political Knowledge in Two U.S. Presidential Elections." *Computers in Human Behavior* 90: 18–25. doi:10.1016/j.chb.2018.08.006

Mansbridge, J. J. 1983. *Beyond Adversary Semocracy.* Chicago, IL: University of Chicago Press.

Martin, Aaron. 2012. *Young People and Politics: Political Engagement in the Anglo-American Democracies.* London: Routledge.

Morozov, E. 2011. *The Net Delusion: How Not to Liberate the World.* United Kingdom: Penguin.

Messing, S., and Westwood, S. J. 2014. "Selective Exposure in the Age of Social Media: Endorsements Trump Partisan Source Affiliation When Selecting News Online." *Communication Research* 41 (8): 1042–1063.

Mossberger, K., Tolbert, C. J., and McNeal, R. S. 2008. *Excerpts from Digital Citizenship: The Internet, Society, and Participation.* Cambridge, MA: MIT Press, 2007. By Karen Mossberger, Caroline J. Tolbert and Ramona S. McNeal, *First Monday* 13 (2–4) (February). https://firstmonday.org/ojs/index.php/fm/article/download/2131/1942

Moy, P., Bimber, B., Rojecki, A., Xenos, M. A., and Iyengar, S. 2012. "Transnational Connections: Shifting Contours in Political Communication Research." *International Journal of Communication* 6: 247–254.

Tolbert, C. J., Mossberger, K., and McNeal, R. 2008. "Institutions, Policy Innovation, and E-Government in the American States." *Public Administration Review* 68 (3): 549–563.

Norris, P. 2001. *Digital Divide: Civic Engagement, Information Poverty, and the Internet Worldwide.* Cambridge, UK: Cambridge University Press.

Norris, P. 2002. *Democratic Phoenix: Reinventing Political Activism.* Cambridge University Press.

Pariser, E. 2012. *The Filter Bubble: How the New Personalized Web Is Changing What We Read and How We Think.* New York: Random House.

Pasek, J., More, E., and Romer, D. 2009. "Realizing the Social Internet? Online Social Networking Meets Offline Civic Engagement." *Journal of Information Technology and Politics* 6 (3–4): 197–215. doi:10.1080/19331680902996403

Plutzer, E. 2002. "Becoming a Habitual Voter: Inertia, Resources, and Growth in Young Adulthood." *American Political Science Review* 96 (1): 41–56.

Putnam, R. D. 2000. *Bowling Alone: The Collapse and Revival of American Community.* New York: Simon and Schuster.

Rainie, L., Anderson, J., and Albright, J. 2017. "The Future of Free Speech, Trolls, Anonymity and Fake News Online." Pew Research Center. http://www.pewinternet.org/2017/03/29/the-future-of-free-speech-trolls-anonymity-and-fake-news-online/

Rainie, H., and Wellman, B. 2012. *Networked: The New Social Operating System.* Cambridge, MA: MIT Press.

Sandvig, C. 2008. "Wireless Play and Unexpected Innovation." In *Digital Youth, Innovation, and the Unexpected.* Edited by Tara McPherson, 77–97. The John D. and Catherine T. MacArthur Foundation Series on Digital Media and Learning. Cambridge, MA: MIT Press. doi: 10.1162/dmal.9780262633598.077

Scheufele, D. A., and Nisbet, M. C. 2002. "Being a Citizen Online: New Opportunities and Dead Ends." *The Harvard International Journal of Press/Politics* 7 (3): 55–75. doi:10.1177/1081180X0200700304

Shah, D. V, Kwak, N., and Holbert, R. L. 2001. "'Connecting' and 'Disconnecting' with Civic Life: Patterns of Internet Use and the Production of Social Capital." *Political Communication* 18 (2): 141–162.

Stolle, D., Hooghe, M., and Micheletti, M. 2005. "Politics in the Supermarket: Political Consumerism as a Form of Political Participation." *International Political Science Review* 26 (3): 245–269.

Su, L. Y.-F., Xenos, M. A., Rose, K. M., Wirz, C. D., Scheufele, D. A., and Brossard, D. 2018. "Uncivil and Personal? Comparing Patterns of Incivility in Comments on the Facebook Pages of News Outlets." *New Media and Society* 20 (10): 3678–3699. doi:10.1177/1461444818757205

Svensson, J. 2011. "The Expressive Turn of Citizenship in Digital Late Modernity." *JeDEM-eJournal of eDemocracy and Open Government* 3 (1): 42–56.

Tedesco, J. C. 2011. "Political Information Efficacy and Internet Effects in the 2008 U.S. Presidential Election." *American Behavioral Scientist* 55 (6): 696–713. doi:10.1177/0002764211398089

Tolbert, C. J., and Mcneal, R. S. 2003. "Unraveling the Effects of the Internet on Political Participation?" *Political Research Quarterly* 56 (2): 175–185. doi:10.1177/106591290305600206

Turkle, S. 2011. *Life on the Screen*. New York: Simon and Schuster.

Valenzuela, S., Park, N., and Kee, K. F. 2009. "Is There Social Capital in a Social Network Site?: Facebook Use and College Students' Life Satisfaction, Trust, and Participation." *Journal of Computer-Mediated Communication* 14 (4): 875–901. doi:10.1111/j.1083-6101.2009.01474.x

van Deth, J. 2014. "A Conceptual Map of Political Participation." *Acta Politica* 49 (3): 349–367. doi:10.1057/ap.2014.6

Verba, S., Schlozman, K. L., and Brady, H. E. 1995. *Voice and Equality: Civic Voluntarism in American Politics*. Cambridge, MA: Harvard University Press.

Vitak, J., Zube, P., Smock, A., Carr, C. T., Ellison, N., and Lampe, C. 2011. "It's Complicated: Facebook Users' Political Participation in the 2008 Election." *Cyberpsychology, Behavior and Social Networking* 14 (3): 107–114. doi:10.1089/cyber.2009.0226

Ward, J., and de Vreese, C. 2011. "Political Consumerism, Young Citizens, and the Internet." *Media Culture and Society* 33 (3): 399–413.

Weaver Lariscy, R., Tinkham, S. F., and Sweetser, K. D. 2011. "Kids These Days: Examining Differences in Political Uses and Gratifications, Internet Political Participation, Political Information Efficacy, and Cynicism on the Basis of Age." *American Behavioral Scientist* 55 (6): 749–764. doi:10.1177/0002764211398091

Wells, C. 2010. "Citizenship and Communication in Online Youth Civic Engagement Projects." *Information, Communication and Society* 13 (3): 419–441.

Wojcieszak, M. E. 2012. "Transational Connections Symposium: Challenges and Opportunities for Political Communication Research." *International Journal of Communication* 6: 255–264.

Wojcieszak, M. E., and Mutz, D. C. 2009. "Online Groups and Political Discourse: Do Online Discussion Spaces Facilitate Exposure to Political Disagreement?" *Journal of Communication* 59 (1): 40–56. doi:10.1111/j.1460-2466.2008.01403.x

Xenos, M., and Lance Bennett, W. 2007. "The Disconnection in Online Politics: The Youth Political Web Sphere and US Election Sites, 2002–2004." *Information, Community and Society* 10 (4): 443–464.

Xenos, M. A., and Kyoung, K. 2008. "Rocking the Vote and More: An Experimental Study of the Impact of Youth Political Portals." *Journal of Information Technology and Politics* 5 (2): 175–189. doi:10.1080/19331680802291400

Xenos, M., and Moy, P. 2007. "Direct and Differential Effects of the Internet on Political and Civic Engagement. *Journal of Communication* 57 (4): 704–718.

Xenos, M. A., Vromen, A., and Loader, B. L. 2014. "The Great Equalizer? Patterns of Social Media Use and Youth Political Engagement in Three Advanced Democracies." *Information, Communication, and Society* 17 (2): 151–167.

Conclusion

Evaluation for the Broadband Future

ERIC W. WELCH

INTRODUCTION

Broadband technology, as presented in this book, is a national infrastructure investment that will continue to alter many aspects of modern life. Similar to many other policy interventions and major technological advances, there exist significant gaps between intentions and expectations on the one hand and actual outcomes and impacts on the other. Efficient deployment and ubiquitous use of broadband are challenged by technical, economic, social, and political complexities inherent to implementing large technological systems. As a result, online service quality is not equivalent across localities, and popularized stories documenting the technology's benefits for some serve only as tantalizing half-truths for others. Yet these discrepancies and contradictions are not unique or random, nor are they necessarily permanent fissures to be accepted or endured. Rather, as this book points out, it is the job of evaluation to investigate the patterns of deployment, use, and impacts through use of robust methods to understand,

Eric W. Welch, *Conclusion* In: *Transforming Everything?*. Edited by: Karen Mossberger, Eric W. Welch, and Yonghong Wu, Oxford University Press. © Oxford University Press 2022. DOI: 10.1093/oso/9780190082871.003.0010 learn, and recommend improvements that maximize benefits and minimize inequities.

This book comes at an opportune moment as the White House has raised the bar for evaluation at the national level. Federal agencies are currently developing capacities and approaches to respond to the *Foundations for Evidence-Based Policymaking Act of 2018* (P.L. 115-435, The Evidence Act), which designates the US Office of Management and Budget (OMB) as the lead agency for building a new evaluation infrastructure to "strengthen the role of program evaluation and better understand how we are investing in evaluation across the government" (Office of Management and Budget 2018). Agencies must designate an evaluation officer and develop a multiyear learning agenda designed to use evidence for improving the effectiveness of agency programs. Importantly, the White House also comments on methodology: "The questions of interest should serve as the starting point for building evidence; once questions are identified, then the appropriate methods should be selected to answer those questions. Once methods are identified, a study should then be designed to answer the questions of interest in the most rigorous manner possible that is both appropriate for those questions and feasible within budget and other constraints" (Office of Management and Budget 2019).

We agree. At a time when the social, economic, and political divides are arguably as great or greater than ever in US history, it is important to highlight evidentiary bases for policy and program learning and decision-making. But it is equally essential to note that evaluation is socially constructed. Evaluators of broadband technology at different levels of government and from different sectors will have different experiences and perspectives, identify different purposes, focus on different issues, recognize different intended and unintended consequences, and ask different questions. Yet there needs to be some common understanding of the value of different methodologies. The aim of this book is to establish methodological choices for broadband evaluators of all stripes such that their questions, assumptions, approaches, metrics, data, and methods are clear, transparent, and professionally rigorous. The impacts of broadband technology in a complex national setting will be varied and possibly contradictory, but evidence-based decision-making must use a commonly recognized toolkit with which evidence is gathered and upon which recommendations are debated. The remainder of this chapter discusses the highlights from this volume and key issues for the future of broadband evaluation.

HIGHLIGHTS OF THIS VOLUME

Broadband is not one specific technology, it is the basic technological infrastructure on which modern information and communication systems operate and through which individuals, groups, networks, and organizations interact, exchange resources, and develop. William Lehr notes in the second chapter that as an infrastructure, broadband can be characterized and measured in terms of coverage, speed, latency, and integration. However, the impacts of broadband depend on many contingent factors, such as complementary technologies and services, customizability, embeddedness of *Smart* functionality and, perhaps most importantly, human behavior and preferences. Determining how to best invest to encourage positive outcomes while also limiting the potential downsides requires a sophisticated approach to evaluation that recognizes diverse intentions, modalities, and usage contexts. Moreover, in an era of big data analytics, evaluators must actively identify outcomes of greatest importance, select metrics, collect and integrate novel datasets, and undertake robust interdisciplinary studies to assess an accelerating and dynamic process. This is a tall order, but one that the three methods-focused chapters (Chapters 3–5) of the book seek to address.

Evaluating the impacts of broadband requires the effective matching of the research method with the evaluation question. Evaluation based on questions about the type and quality of connectivity, frequency of access, types of use, and user perceptions provides insight into understanding the range of services, attitudes, and behaviors. Evaluation questions may focus on differences in outcomes and impacts across regions, levels of education, and demographic characteristics. Other evaluation questions seek to understand before-after differences or changes over time in levels of connectivity and use, for example. While these questions may seem relatively straightforward, the evaluation devil is in the details of measurement, method selection, unit of analysis, and many other critical research design factors. As John B. Horrigan's chapter points out, surveys are important research tools that can help answer some of these basic questions, but they are only as good as the measures used, the representativeness of the sample frame, and the willingness of individuals to respond. Robert Fairlie's chapter discusses some of these methodological challenges in more detail. Issues of selection bias often make it necessary to use methods such as fixed effects models, regression discontinuity, or the well-regarded, randomized experiments, to evaluate impacts. Nevertheless, as he carefully points out, these methods also have inherent limitations that require careful specification and interpretation.

Evaluation of the complex sociotechnical system of broadband, in which behaviors and perceptions are not well understood, also calls for the use of qualitative research. Often the evaluation questions posed are not answerable with existing metrics or existing metrics only explain a small proportion of the variability in outcomes. When causal relationships—for example between the availability of broadband and its use—are poorly understood qualitative methods help fill in the gaps in understanding. As noted in the chapter by Jessica Crowell, ethnographic research collects observation and interview-based data to provide a rich description of the interplay of context and behavior with the aim of explaining why or how some outcomes occur while others do not. This kind of deep exploration into a particular community also informs quantitative metric design, method selection, model development, and, perhaps most importantly, confirms causal linkages between otherwise crudely specified inputs, activities, and outcomes and rejects alternative explanations. Failure to understand the causal connections risks misinterpreting results and recommending inappropriate, unworkable, or counterproductive solutions.

Evaluation must specify the unit-of-analysis. Is it focused at the level of individual citizen, work unit, community, or region? As the chapter by Caroline J. Tolbert and colleagues demonstrates, the unit-of-analysis determines the type of question, data, and method. This chapter makes the case for evaluation at the community level, recognizing the importance of social relationships and structures in the neighborhood that accelerate or decelerate use and impact. Moreover, there is an opportunity to examine long-term outcomes at the community level, tracking whether increases in broadband use are sustained following an initiative and whether that in turn is related to other impacts for the community. Longitudinal studies and other quasi-experimental approaches can strengthen confidence in the causal role that the intervention played in community outcomes.

The remaining three chapters of this book examine broadband dependent domains—healthcare, public management, and youth civic engagement—where there exist significant gaps in understanding about outcomes and impacts. Sharon Strover's chapter lays out the opportunities that broadband offers for improving access to telehealth services, particularly for rural populations that often do not have sufficient access to quality healthcare. Alfred Ho looks at the role of broadband for management and governance including public service provision and citizen engagement with government, and Michael Xenos investigates the potential impact of broadband on youth civic and political engagement. Each of these chapters raises similar types of questions about the many contingent factors that might intervene to affect broadband outcomes. Strover identifies the importance of defining and measuring "meaningful use"; Ho raises the importance of false claims, broken promises, institutional fragmentation, and poor communication as factors that limit potential; and Xenos recognizes political knowledge and social network connectivity as potentially important determinants of youth civic activity.

Beyond these similarities, the three chapters also identify theoretical challenges to broadband evaluation. Strover highlights the need for better theory for evaluating broadband impacts on healthcare, particularly given the dynamic nature of the technology. Ho recognizes the need for better conceptualization of the demand environment, pointing out that different stakeholders have different expectations and use intentions. His logic model framework shows, for example, that broadband expectations and evaluation questions vary by stakeholder. While Xenos posits literature-based mobilization and differential effects as rationales for explaining civic engagement outcomes, he also moves the conversation forward by recognizing that youth may be responding to technology through social networks in ways that produce new and qualitatively different forms of civic engagement.

Despite their different disciplinary backgrounds, all authors raise similar challenges of research design, theory, measurement, and data availability that limit understanding of one of the most significant national investments in technological infrastructure in history. Yet it is equally true that because the chapters take different approaches and have different perspectives, it is possible to now explore a structured way forward for broadband evaluation.

A WAY FORWARD

Because broadband is a basic infrastructure, it encompasses numerous technological, economic, and social goals that form the basis from which evaluation is framed and conducted. As shown in the chapters that make up most of this book, broadband could affect education, health, civic engagement, employment, and numerous other categories of outcomes. Evaluation could address multiple different, potentially competing goals at different levels of analysis, and evaluation results may result in recommendations for future investment that prioritize one set of stakeholders or types of activity over another. The complexity of the context of evaluation is discussed in several chapters, but it is important to appreciate the consequences of a robust and multifaceted understanding of broadband's impacts and the usefulness of evaluation. The remainder of this chapter reflects on some of these complexities and sets out a way forward for a fully operational evaluation of broadband technology.

Considering a Systems Approach

Given the multilayered nature of broadband investments, activities, and impacts, as well as the strong potential for feedback effects across different layers, it is useful to explore a systems approach to framing broadband evaluation. A systems approach acknowledges the interactions, for example, between individual-level use and community-level initiatives, or between state-level investments and firm-level innovations. Systems approaches are used broadly in fields such as ecology (Hartvigsen and Levin 1997), education (Bronfenbrenner 1979, 2005), and innovation studies (Edquist 1997) to show the nesting of different subsystems and to articulate the dynamic relationships among them.

For the evaluation of broadband, it is important to recognize that individual habits, cognitions, and behaviors are nested within communities, neighborhoods, or organizations. In turn, these groupings lie within administrative jurisdictions such as cities, counties, or states, and within even more macro social systems of established culture and accepted institutions that guide behavior. The macro social level provides the norms and expectations within which cities or counties create services and opportunities and neighborhoods devise ways for individuals to take advantage of the technology. The relationships across subsystems are dynamic, changing over time as individual capacities increase, technology changes, or new rules or incentives are established. Moreover, there are feedback effects such that individual outcomes both effect and are affected by features of the community, for example. *For evaluation of a technological infrastructure such as broadband, the systems approach both highlights the social embeddedness of the individuals and cautions against unconditionally elevating micro-level evaluation findings to macro-level insights.*

Theorizing

While a systems approach helps to organize complexity, evaluations are typically framed around a set of specific policy or program goals articulated as specific research questions. The chapters in this volume all raise important research questions about access, equity, use, and impact of broadband and all propose different methods to investigate them. While they vary in approach each seeks to explain, for example, why some outcomes are more or less likely than others, why some subpopulations show impacts from broadband access or the conditions under which positive attitudes toward technology use increase. Each author theorizes in slightly different ways. Alfred Ho uses a logic model, Michael Xenos turns to literature to build mobilization and differential effects theses, and Jessica Crowell uses ethnographic methods to develop a better causal explanation. The use of theory to predict and explain outcomes and impacts is a critical but often under-emphasized component of evaluation. Without theoretical rationales linking outcomes to antecedent causes, recommendations for changes to implementation or investment may be ineffective or worse, damaging.

Evaluators tend use two main types of theory building: implicit and explicit. Implicit theorizing is most evident in logic models or theories of change, which provides an "understood" or "anticipated" causal story for how investments and inputs result in outcomes and impacts that fulfill policy or program goals. Theories of change typically include inputs, activities, outputs, and outcomes (see Figure 9.1). Inputs are the resources applied to enable activities that result in outputs, which are the immediate effects of a policy or program. Outcomes comprise the near and longer-term changes that represent the attainment of intended goals of a policy or program. Theories of change help explain *what* outputs would occur given certain activities, for example. Although a theory of change provides a powerful conceptual core around which evaluators can identify possible

Figure 9.1 General Theory of Change
NOTE: Research design, measurement, data collection, analysis, findings and recommendations, and policy and program goals.

metrics or indicators and build an evaluation design, they are often highly complex (e.g., multiple activities, outputs, and outcomes over long periods of time) and make it difficult to generate richly argued causal mechanisms.

By contrast, explicit theorizing, more common in social science research, either uses causal explanation found in the academic literature to guide hypothesis development for formal testing, or conducts exploratory research with the aim of establishing causal relationships that informs the literature. Explicit theorizing aims to "generalize" such that the predictive value holds over multiple contexts. For evaluation of broadband technology, both types of implicit and explicit theorizing are important. Theories of change provide a conceptual mechanism to identify multiple relationships, even though they often do not generate detailed causal rationales. The theoretical literature in social science supports more carefully reasoned arguments about "how," "why," and "the conditions under which" outcomes and impacts occur. Explicit theorizing may lead to stronger and more reliable bases for attribution and recommendations for adjustment. *For future evaluation of broadband, researchers should continue to use both types of theory building, paying particular attention to increasing explicit theorizing.*

Measuring

Strong research designs articulate the linkage between concepts, constructs, and measures (CCM). For example, the concept of "meaningful use" may be defined as individual citizen use of broadband for activities and information that enhance or sustain livelihoods. As a construct, meaningful use would be more narrowly defined and measurable, such that it could be used to develop a theoretically informed statement (e.g., hypothesis) about cause and effect, which can then be tested. Good measures provide a valid and reliable means of quantitatively or qualitatively representing the construct, such that it is possible to ascertain whether, for example, some type of training actually increased meaningful broadband use for health.

CCM can be tightly or loosely coupled, depending upon the evaluator and the evaluation design. CCM coupling is also influenced by the availability of data and the cost of data collection. Tight coupling implies a strong research design in which specific measures are developed, collected, and tested over time to demonstrate measurement reliability and construct validity. Data, which may include transactions, survey responses, or qualitative data (e.g., coded observation), may be costly to collect. In cases where data are collected for other purposes or through institutionalized processes, such as through regular surveys or transactions, tight coupling can be challenging.

The rise of big data and the development of new tools of data scraping and machine learning enable the evaluator to collect different types of extant data. Such big data are increasingly available and potentially more conveniently collected. The rise of data informatics creates a significant opportunity for advancing broadband evaluation. For example, efforts to examine broadband-enabled civic engagement through Facebook or Twitter likely requires a big data or data informatics approach. While such data collection activities may be cost effective, there may be limitations for tight CCM coupling. Hence, while data-driven evaluation likely provides significant advantages for evaluation, there are measurement risks. Measures collected through scraping or machine learning may not actually be representative of the intended population, and measurement validity and linkage to theory may be weak. *As big data and informatics approaches to evaluation advance, researchers should work toward ensuring tighter coupling of concepts, constructs, and measures for measurement. Additionally, the importance of tight CCM coupling requires the investment in new, theoretically informed data sources.*

Learning

As noted in the introduction to this volume, evaluation places a premium on learning. Although the 2019 Evidence Act rarely discusses the value of evaluation for learning, the subsequent Federal Data Strategy 2020 Action Plan (Government Services Administration and Office of Management and Budget 2020, 22) does identify learning as a goal for evaluation and other data-driven processes.

> The Evidence Act now requires the development of learning agendas . . . using the process to generate and organize priority agency questions that can be pursued through activities that include statistics, program evaluation, research, performance management, and policy analysis. Adopting this approach of identifying priority agency questions at the outset helps to establish a process through which an agency can allocate its statistical, performance management, research and evaluation efforts, and funding to the most critical questions that face the agency.

The research design as well as other elements of the evaluation process determine the production of evidence for learning and the opportunity for adjustment and revision. Key learning questions include: Does the evaluation design enable learning while doing or is the evaluation focused on demonstrating accomplishment of outcomes that will be linked to longer-term policy and investment decision cycles? How rigid or adaptable is the evaluation research design? What is the evaluation timeline? How are evaluations and evaluators built into implementation and decision-making processes? These and other questions highlight the potential that research designs provide different types of information and are embedded in different learning contexts and processes.

Some methods, such as random control designs provide a more structured experimental approach with intervention at the outset of a project and assessment conducted at a specific future post-implementation stage. Qualitative designs that collect interview or observational data are often more exploratory and aim to understand contextual complexities, or in the case of Crowell's chapter, why certain behaviors occur or how poorly understood processes operate. Quasi-experimental research designs sit somewhere in between.

The research design will likely affect learning. While random control designs have the potential to isolate pre-post impacts, the relevance of findings might be challenged in situations where technological change creates significant levels of complexity. As a result, what is learned may be valuable and definitive, but only for a technological context that no longer exists. Qualitative research provides rich contextual data that, done well, helps clarify the complex human-technology interface over time. Nevertheless, what is learned may be highly situation specific and difficult to transfer. Research designs that use mixed methods and allow some adaptation over time may enable a broader base of evidence for learning. *In general, future evaluation of broadband should aim to enhance learning for purposive action. It is the responsibility of researchers and evaluators to tailor research designs to learning needs, and to communicate both the advantages and limitations of the research designs for the evidentiary basis for decision-making.*

Research in Evaluation and Evaluation as Research

Academic research and the field of professional evaluation are in some ways two overlapping institutionalized circles in a Venn diagram. Numerous companies and non-profit organizations conduct contracted program evaluation activities for government, including those that assess broadband impacts. The profession of program evaluation "circle" has its own culture, norms, approaches, and expectations. Not all professional evaluators are trained in the advanced research methods explored in this volume, though some are. The tools of the profession typically include theorizing through the joint development of logic models with program stakeholders, recognizing the importance on both formative and summative approaches to evaluation, and aligning evaluation reports and recommendations with program decision cycles. Broadly construed, program evaluation professionals build evidence to increase program learning and improve operations and activities that produce intended outcomes.

While the academic policy analysis and program evaluation "circle" prioritizes the application of advanced research methods and theoretically informed designs to understand program outcomes and impacts, it is less committed to guiding and advising ongoing program implementation.

Evaluation as research incentivizes the production of publishable journal articles in policy and evaluation journals. It also focuses on the training of policy and program analysts, including at the doctoral level. Because academic researchers often are not engaged at the project design stage, much evaluation as research is based on quasi-experimental designs that occur well after a program has started (or even finished). *For future evaluation of broadband it is important to balance evaluation as research and research in evaluation—to increase the overlap in the Venn diagram. Emphasis on theoretical reasoning, strong research design, and tight CCM coupling will increase the research in evaluation. Emphasis on learning and client engagement will increase the value of evaluation as research.*

CONCLUSION

Broadband infrastructure and complementary technologies will continue to affect the socio-technical system within which key actors—individuals, firms, public agencies, non-profit organizations—interact and communicate, seek information and assistance, provide services, and generate opportunities. The complex and continuously evolving nature of the system makes it difficult to identify, assess, and attribute the effects of broadband—positive and negative, intentional and unintentional—across groups, geographies, or potential uses. As a result, the role of evaluation is critical to maximize investment outcomes in the most efficient, effective, and equitable ways possible. The chapters presented in this book begin to orient broadband evaluation toward a more rigorous agenda using advanced research design as a foundation for inquiry.

Evaluation of broadband is both a science and an art. As researchers, evaluators have the responsibility to develop robust evaluation designs based on rigorous research methods. Methods should integrate a systems approach, increase explicit theorizing of cause-effect relationships, and engineer tight coupling of concepts, constructs, and measures. As trained professionals, evaluators must engage stakeholders on an iterative basis to develop and revise evaluation approaches that maximize learning for decision-making for purposive adjustments that improve outcomes. Broadband evaluation requires innovative research designs that produce actionable evidence in a highly dynamic environment.

Although the principles, approaches, and methods presented in this volume provide a strong basis for broadband evaluation, the profession also requires commitment by policymakers and program implementers. In particular, evaluation requires ongoing investment such that evaluation has sufficient financial support to develop effective designs and collect high-quality data. Investment also requires access to and commitment from decision makers, such that evaluation has influence on program and policy direction. Given the national level of cross-sectoral investment in broadband, effective evaluation has the potential to reduce waste, minimize disparities, and maximize positive system-wide impacts.

REFERENCES

Bronfenbrenner, U. 1979. *The Ecology of Human Development: Experiments in Nature and Design*. Cambridge, MA: Harvard University Press.

Bronfenbrenner, U. 2005. *Making Human Beings Human: Bioecological Perspectives on Human Development*. Thousand Oaks, CA: Sage.

Edquist, C., ed. 1997. *Systems of Innovation: Technologies, Institutions, and Organizations*. London: Psychology Press.

Office of Management and Budget. 2020. *Federal Data Strategy 2020 Action Plan,* The White House, Washington DC. https://strategy.data.gov/assets/docs/2020-federal-data-strategy-action-plan.pdf

Hartvigsen, G., and Levin, S. A. 1997. "Evolution and Spatial Structure Interact to Influence Plant-Herbivore Population and Community Dynamics." *Proceedings of the Royal Society of London. Series B: Biological Sciences,* 264 (1388): 1677–1685.

Office of Management and Budget. 2018. *Delivering Government Solutions in the 21st Century Reform Plan and Reorganization Recommendations,* Pg. 119, The White House, Washington DC. https://www.whitehouse.gov/wp-content/uploads/2018/06/Government-Reform-and-Reorg-Plan.pdf

Office of Management and Budget. 2019. *Building and Using Evidence to Improve Government Effectiveness—FY 2020 Budget Analytical Perspectives Chapter 6,* The White House, Washington DC, pg. 59. https://www.whitehouse.gov/wp-content/uploads/2019/03/ap_6_evidence-fy2020.pdf

For the benefit of digital users, indexed terms that span two pages (e.g., 52–53) may, on occasion, appear on only one of those pages.

Figures and tables are indicated by an italic *f* and *t* following the page number.